# *Selections from the Monthly Journal Anarchy 1961-1970*

# FREEDOM PRESS CENTENARY SERIES
## 1886-1986

TO COMMEMORATE the Centenary of FREEDOM and the
FREEDOM PRESS in 1986 the editors have produced a special issue of
FREEDOM which is available as a FREEDOM PRESS title:

*FREEDOM A HUNDRED YEARS October 1886 to October 1986*
88 pages (A4 11¾" x 8¼") 2 colour cover ISBN 0 900384 35 2

This volume is one of six FREEDOM PRESS are producing to cover a
century of Periodical publishing:

Volume 1    Selections from FREEDOM 1886-1936
Volume 2    Selections from SPAIN & THE WORLD 1936-1939
Volume 3    Selections from WAR COMMENTARY 1939-1945
Volume 4    Selections from FREEDOM 1945-1964
Volume 5    Selections from ANARCHY 1961-1970
Volume 6    Selections from FREEDOM 1965-1986

This ambitious project has been made financially possible firstly by a
major contribution from the FRIENDS OF FREEDOM PRESS Ltd for
FREEDOM's Centenary issue, and for the six volumes by the
generosity of a long-standing friend of FREEDOM PRESS: Hans
Deichmann.

# A DECADE OF ANARCHY 1961-1970

*Selections from the Monthly Journal* Anarchy

Compiled
&
Introduced
by
**COLIN WARD**

FREEDOM PRESS
London
1987

*Published by*
FREEDOM PRESS
84B Whitechapel High St
London E1 7QX

**1987**

*ISBN 0 900384 37 9*

PRINTED IN Gt. BRITAIN BY ALDGATE PRESS LONDON E.1.

# CONTENTS

# Foreword

THIS BOOK is a selection of articles from *Anarchy*, a monthly journal published by FREEDOM PRESS from 1961 to 1970. In a very long history, FREEDOM PRESS has published or distributed journals with a variety of formats and titles, reflecting people's convictions on where the market was to be found for effective anarchist propaganda. Early in this century FREEDOM PRESS published *The Voice of Labour*, a valiant attempt to inject an anarcho-syndicalist message into the syndicalist propaganda of the years before the First World War. The FREEDOM PRESS publication *Spain and the World*, published between 1936 and 1939, was an equally brave effort to link real and current events with what remained of an anarchist movement, and in fact it led to a continuing revival of anarchist publishing.

During and after the Second World War, FREEDOM PRESS distributed George Woodcock's magazine *Now*, and after the war it published Philip Sansom's *The Syndicalist*, which sought to breathe a little life into the tradition of workers' control as a focus for industrial struggle. Ever so many years later an Institute for Workers' Control was founded in Nottingham, and I have never seen in all its useful publications any acknowledgement that a tiny handful of people kept this particular torch burning in the unfashionable years.

All publishing ventures with a long life have good and bad periods. This is inevitable and is partly to do with the climate outside – the existence of a receptive audience – and partly to do with the people involved and the way in which they approach the task. I have more than once raised a smile by saying that one of the great periods of *Freedom* was the time just before I was invited to join the editorial group in 1947. But I meant it. Here was a group of like-minded people who trusted each other and brought to the spare-time task of editing an anarchist paper a wide variety of personal experiences. They didn't need to vet each other's articles for ideological rectitude, and they knew that each member would write from a *Freedom* standpoint rather than pursue personal idiosyncrasies. I can only once remember anything I wrote being censored. John Hewetson as a doctor objected to my calling Sir Will Lawther, the miners' leader 'a dyspeptic clown' on the grounds that my diagnosis was not accurate.

The file, or at least the microfilm, exists to show what an excellent journal *Freedom* was in those days. But circumstances were working against it. There was a kind of wartime coalition among the non-Communist press in the tiny world of opposition in the war years. They read and supported each other's journals. This solidarity was bound to be broken by the end of the war. At the same time, the overwhelming electoral victory of the Labour Party in 1945, after which it conscientiously implemented its Clause 4 programme of nationalising the commanding heights of the economy meant that left-wing socialist support for an anarchist journal was dwindling too. FREEDOM PRESS's wartime paper *War Commentary* had already committed itself to a position on the post-war welfare legislation with the headline, 'Scavengers of Misery – Our view of the Beveridge Report'.

This was not the view of the British public, but just as the Bolshevik Revolution generations earlier profoundly affected the future of left-wing opposition movements throughout the world, so the reception of the minority press after the Second World War was inevitably changed by external events, even after the end of the post-war Labour goverment. Electoral propaganda apart, the essentially bi-partisan nature of British politics in those days, known as Butskellism, led many to believe that there weren't 'any good brave causes any more'. Osborne's *Look Back in Anger* (1956), now a period piece, did symbolise a change in the climate brought about by Suez, Hungary and the birth of the anti-bomb movement.

By the end of the 1950s, a new potential readership for anarchist propaganda had emerged, not least because of the enormous expansion of higher education where, it seemed to me, political activity was dominated by automatic Marxism. By the late 1950s I was advocating that, rather than use up all our energy in producing a weekly, with no time left either to propagate the journal effectively or to give ourselves the chance to stop to think, we should produce a monthly, in what we would in those days call a quarto format. (I find it interesting that in fact, in the 1980s, *Freedom* has settled down to an A4 monthly form.) At the end of the 1950s I wrote several articles in *Freedom* setting out the reasons why I thought that a change 'would enable us to make more comprehensive and clearer statements of anarchist attitudes to the social facts of the contemporary world', that 'it would also give them greater permanence and greater propaganda effect' (*Freedom* 10 December 1960). I urged that 'if we are ever to effect the transition from a sect to a social force we needed a revitalised *Freedom*, and that it was 'because we have had to formulate anarchist alternatives in the most prosaic as well as the most important fields of life, that the very people who could bring life to our own activities cannot bring themselves to take us seriously' (*Freedom* 3 December 1960).

I thought these were important matters and I produced mock-ups to show what I thought such a journal would look like. My colleagues in the FREEDOM PRESS group responded with a quite reckless open-mindedness and said, in effect, let those who want to produce a weekly do so, and let those who want to produce a monthly do so too. It was decided that in the first week of every month the monthly journal should appear instead of the weekly, and that it should have, not the quarto format that I envisaged for a monthly *Freedom*, but an octavo (A5) page. (I now think this was a good idea, simply because even today I visit people and they pull copies out of their bookshelves, preserved just because they were easy to keep).

Faced with the need to find a title, I selected *Autonomy*, with the subtitle 'a journal of anarchist ideas'. This had been the title of one of the first anarchist journals published in Britain. Pressure was put on me to change the title to *Anarchy*, which made the subtitle rather superfluous, though it was retained until the 27th issue, after which it seems to have been dropped by the cover designer, Rufus Segar, who describes *his* autonomy and the constraints on it in the last item in this volume.

I had envisaged a monthly *Freedom*. I found myself producing an entirely different journal of which I was the sole editor. And once the original decisions had been made, *I* was given an absolute autonomy. Nobody questioned what went in to *Anarchy*. Other people in the group undertook the now additionally complicated tasks of coping with *Freedom*-only subscriptions, *Anarchy*-only subscriptions, and the joint subscriptions we all hoped the newly-tapped readership would opt for, as well as the bulk orders, stamping and dispatching.

Rather than write with hindsight about where *Anarchy* had succeeded and where it had failed, I include as the penultimate item in this book an article I was asked to write for *Freedom* at the time of the hundredth issue in 1969. In the following year I gave my colleagues six months' notice of my intention to give up the editorship. Ten years is long enough for any but the most exceptional of editors to bring out any journal. Routine and ready-made formulas begin to intrude. And even though people often say to me that *Anarchy* discussed in the 1960s topics which were perceived to be important in the 1970s, we were moving into a very different decade.

It is extraordinarily difficult to make an adequate selection from

*Anarchy*, partly because there was so much good material and partly because the typical article was very long. Quite often an issue was
virtually devoted to a single long article. Some of these later took on
a life of their own, like the *Spies for Peace Story*, or Nicolas Walter's
*About Anarchism*, which like many other *Anarchy* items has been
translated and reprinted all over the world. Others, like the essays
'Ecology and Revolutionary Thought' and 'Towards a Liberatory
Technology' by Murray Bookchin ('Lewis Herber') have found a
permanent home in his book *Post-Scarcity Anarchism* (1970).
Others among these issue-long articles, like the late Martin Small's
'De-revolutionisation' or the late Kate Vandegrift's 'trying it on –
an experiment in anarchy', are cherished by their friends as memen-
tos.

Twenty years later, may I thank everyone who contributed to a
decade of *Anarchy*? It was, to use the ponderous jargon of education, a 'learning process' for readers and writers alike. To take just
one of the themes of this book, crime and punishment. All the
bright young criminologists of what was seen as the 'new' sociology
of deviance, David Downes, Ian Taylor, Laurie Taylor, Jock
Young and Stan Cohen, wrote for *Anarchy*, and were thus linked
with an older tradition of anarchist criticism. They have gone their
different ways, but I for one was cheered to read in Professor
Cohen's most recent book, *Visions of Social Control* (1985), that
'mutual aid, fraternity and good-neighbourliness still sound better
than dependence on bureaucracies and professions' and that 'this
means coming back to the political philosophy most consistent with
sociology, namely anarchism'. (Sad to say, his contribution to this
present volume is still so apposite that it could have been written
yesterday.)

Every one of the books I have written myself since ceasing to be
an anarchist editor carries the same message.

*June 1986*                                    COLIN WARD

# I. RESTATEMENTS

## 1. Conversations about anarchism

### Richard Boston

RICHARD BOSTON went round with a tape-recorder interviewing anarchists, and reduced eight or nine hours of tape to a forty-minute radio programme, produced by Tony Gould for BBC Radio 3, and broadcast on January 10th and 30th 1968. The voices heard, apart from that of Richard Boston, were those of Bill Christopher, Paul Goodman, George Melly, Jack Robinson, Donald and Irene Rooum, Peter Turner, Nicolas Walter and Colin Ward. The following is the text of the programme.

*Announcer:* Who are the anarchists? What do they believe? What sort of society do they want, and what actions do they take to realise it?

*CW*: I consider myself to be an anarchist-communist, in the Kropotkin tradition.

*NW*: I think that if I had to label myself very quickly I would say I was an anarchist-socialist, or libertarian socialist even, if the word anarchist gave rise to misunderstanding.

*BC*: I would describe myself as an anarcho-syndicalist, anarchism being my philosophy and syndicalism the method of struggle.

*JR*: I don't call myself an anarcho-syndicalist. I could be called an anarcho-pacifist-individualist with slight communist tendencies, which is a long title, but this is a way of defining a compass point.

*PT*: First of all I'm an anarchist because I don't believe in governments, and also I think that syndicalism is the anarchist application to organising industry.

*DR*:I describe myself as a Stirnerite, a conscious egoist.

*JR*: We even have a strange aberration known as Catholic anarchists, which seems to be a contradiction in terms, but nevertheless they seem to get along with it.

11

*RB*: There are so many sorts of anarchist that one sometimes wonders whether such a thing as a plain and simple anarchist even exists, but the differences are mainly differences of emphasis. Anarchists are agreed on the basic principle: anarchy – the absence of rule, which is not the same thing as chaos, although the words anarchy and chaos are popularly confused. As the anarchist sees it, chaos is what we've got now. Anarchy is the alternative he offers. In the 11th edition of the *Encyclopaedia Britannica*, Kropotkin defined anarchism as, 'The name given to a principle or theory of life and conduct under which society is conceived without government, harmony in such a society being obtained not by submission to law or by obedience to any authority, but by free agreements concluded between the various groups, territorial and professional, freely constituted for the sake of production and consumption.' I think most anarchists today of whatever label would agree with this. Where do they differ then? Well, one important difference is between those who, like the anarchist-communists and anarcho-syndicalists, emphasise collective organisation and those like the Stirnerites whose chief concern is with the individual. But in fact an anarchist-communist like Colin Ward and an individualist anarchist like Donald Rooum still have a great deal in common.

*CW*: For me anarchism is a social philosophy based on the absence of authority. Anarchism can be an individual outlook or a social one. I'm concerned with anarchism as a social point of view – the idea that we could have a society and that it's desirable that we should have a society, in which the principle of authority is superseded by that of voluntary co-operation. You could say that anarchism is the ultimate decentralisation. I believe in a decentralised society. What I want to do is to change a mass society into a mass of societies.

*DR*: The anarchist thinks that society is there for the benefit of the individual. The individual doesn't owe anything to society at all. Society is the creation of individuals, it is there for their benefit. And from that the rest of it follows. Eventually, as the ultimate aim of anarchism, which may or may not be achieved, the idea is to have a society of sovereign individuals.

*RB*: But how do you set about achieving an anarchist society? Well, there are two traditional anarchist methods, propaganda of the deed – at one time this meant assassinating royalty and statesmen, but nowadays is almost invariably non-violent – and propaganda of the word. Propaganda of the word is partly the spoken word. In London, for example, Speakers' Corner, and the meeting every Sunday night at the Lamb and Flag in Covent Garden, where there are usually about fifty people, but mostly the word means the printed word, and, apart from the Syndicalist Workers' Federation's monthly paper *Direct Action*, this mostly centres round the publications of the FREEDOM PRESS.

*CW*: *Anarchy* was started in 1961. It's an offshoot of the anarchist weekly *Freedom* which is the oldest newspaper of the Left in this country I think. It was founded by Kropotkin in 1886. In *Anarchy* what I try to do is to find ways of relating a way-out ideology like anarchism to contemporary life and to find those positive applications which people are looking for. There are problems you see. If you have a revolutionary ideology in a non-revolutionary situation, what exactly do you do? If you've got a point of view which everybody considers to be way out, do you act up to it, or do you lean over backwards to show how normal and practical your ideas are? What I would like anarchism to have is intellectual respectability.

*RB*: What sort of subjects are discussed in *Anarchy*?

*CW*: There do seem to be recurring themes, principally because they are what people will write about. They are topics like education, like this question of a technology in which people would have a certain degree of personal freedom and personal choice in work, instead of none at all, as the vast majority of people have today.. *Anarchy* discusses topics like housing, *Anarchy* tries to take the problems which face people in our society, the society we're living in, and to see if there are anarchist solutions.

*RB*: *Anarchy* is a monthly. *Freedom*, on the other hand, as a weekly paper, is more concerned with commenting on day-to-day political events and reporting on anarchist activities. It is itself run on anarchist lines. Jack Robinson of the Freedom Group.

*JR*: The whole of *Freedom* is produced with voluntary labour. I myself have a slight grant of £3 a week, and thus we exploit labour. Lilian Wolfe, who is working with us, is now 91 years of age, which I think is a record in the exploitation of old people's labour, but nevertheless she still comes in cheerfully three days a week. There is a carpenter, a print-worker, a furniture remover, who do the editorial work, and there is a type-designer who actually does the layout for us. Every member of the editorial committee has the power of veto but we do try to argue things out until a unanimous decision is arrived at.

*RB*: Propaganda of the deed nowadays mostly means what anarchists call Direct Action, that is to say, doing something yourself about your own problems rather than waiting for someone else to come along and do it for you. Sometimes this may take the form of illegal action.

*CW*: It does seem to me amazing that in the last few years, for instance, there hasn't been mass squatting in office blocks, when you get the situation of local authorities having huge housing waiting lists while you can see dozens of new speculative office blocks with TO LET plastered all over them. The very interesting instance in the last few years, of course, was the King Hill Hostel affair. King Hill Hostel was a reception centre for homeless families in Kent where all sorts of restrictions were placed on the homeless, the most striking of which, of course, was the separation of husbands from wives. People were treated in a punitive way as though their homelessness were somehow the result of their own moral turpitude. A handful of people adopted Direct Action methods to embarrass the authorities, and they embarrassed them so much that they achieved much more for improving the conditions of reception centres for the homeless than had ever been done by legislative action for years. Direct Action is an anarchist method because it is a method which expands. People are pushed on by success. They are given more confidence in their own ability to shape their own destiny by being successful in some small way. The person who takes Direct Action is a different kind of person from the person who just lets things happen to him.

*RB*: Colin Ward gives another example of Direct Action in the mass squatting campaign that took place after the war when the homeless seized derelict army camps.

*CW*: The Minister of Health at the time, the Labour Minister of Health who was in charge of housing, Aneurin Bevan, said that these people were somehow jumping their place in the housing queue, they were part of a Communist plot, and all sorts of rubbish of that kind. But local authorities were very soon empowered to take over army camps for themselves. People who went round noticed that the people who had seized the places for themselves had done a great deal to make them habitable – the usual temporary, makeshift improvisations to make life, family life, possible in such places. Those who were installed there by local councils did nothing. They waited for things to happen to them. This is an example, it seems to me, of the social psychology of Direct Action. The direct-actionist is someone who shapes his own destiny while other people are the victims of circumstances, of the whims of authority: things happen to them.

*RB*:Direct Action has also been the anarchists' preferred method in their opposition to war and the state's preparations for war, and their most conspicuous contributions to the peace movement have been when the peace movement has turned to Direct Action. One anarchist who has been active in the peace movement is Nicolas Walter.

*NW*: As soon as the Committee of 100 was formed I knew that I agreed with what it was trying to do. So I joined. And I've been active in that sort of thing more or less ever since, and I did all the normal things, I went on sit-downs, I got arrested, got fined and so on. But, more than that, there are things which I have done in the general anti-war movement, which I suppose one could say are the sort of things which I've done as an anarchist. One thing was being involved in the Spies for Peace, which, I think, is a perfect example of anarchist activity although not all the people involved in it were anarchists, in that here was a situation in which the Government had done something, for the sake of the people officially, which the people didn't know about.

*RB*: What was this?

*NW*: Setting up a regional organisation to rule the country in the event of nuclear war demolishing the State apparatus, so that if for example, South-West England was cut off from the rest of England, there would be a ready-made government to take it over and rule it. And this was all set up, it was set up secretly behind the scenes. No one knew about it. And, just by chance, this information fell into the hands of people in the Committee of 100, of whom I was one. And we published it, secretly, we didn't want to get caught. Then another, in a sense much smaller, thing, though it had more effect on me, was going along to a church where the Prime Minister was going to read the lesson, before the Labour Party Conference, and interrupting to say that I thought this was hypocrisy. This isn't a very serious thing, it was just propaganda by deed. It was to try and say, at the time and place where a lot of people would take notice, what I thought about the sort of thing the Labour Government does. And this got us landed in prison, a couple of us.

*RB*: For the anarchist, in Randolph Bourne's phrase, 'War is the health of the State.' This sounds like a paradox, but, as Jack Robinson says, 'to speak of a healthy state is like talking about a healthy cancer'. The anarchist doesn't want a healthy state, he wants a healthy society. for this reason alone, many anarchists are also pacifists, even if they don't always rule out violence altogether. Here is the American writer Paul Goodman.

*PG*: My background is psycho-analytic, and psycho-analytically, we feel that face-to-face violence, like a fist fight, is natural, and it does damage to try to repress it; that it's better to have the fight out. Therefore on that level I have no opposition to violence. Naturally I don't like to see people punching each other, but anger is a rather beautiful thing, and anger will lead to a blow, and there you are. When people are under a terrible oppression, as say Negroes in the United States or the Parisians, let's say, during Hitler's occupation of Paris, it seems inevitable that at a certain point they are going to blow up and fight back. And that seems to me like a force of nature. You can do nothing about that, and therefore I don't disapprove. That kind of warfare, guerilla warfare, partisan warfare, brutalises people, of course it does, but it's human and I would make no moral judgement.

As soon as warfare, violence, becomes organised, however, and you are told by somebody else, 'Kill him', where it's not your own hatred and anger which are pouring out, but some abstract policy or party line or a complicated strategic campaign, then to exert violence turns you into a thing, because violence involves too much of you to be able to do it at somebody else's direction. Therefore I am entirely opposed to any kind of warfare, standing armies as opposed to guerilla armies and so forth. Therefore all war is entirely unacceptable because it mechanises human beings and inevitably leads to more harm than good. Therefore I am a pacifist.

*IR*: I'm a pacifist. I call myself a pacifist anarchist and I think that is basic really. I disapprove of governments because they wage war. I don't want to die, I don't want my children to die, and I don't want to have to watch other people dying for government, and killing people they don't know and have never met and have got nothing to do with.

*RB*: That was Irene Rooum. A frequent criticism of anarchists is that their ideas are utopian. How can they answer this?

*CW*: It's perfectly possible to say that anarchism is utopian, but of course so is socialism or any other political 'ism'. All the 'isms' are what the sociologists call 'ideal types' and you can make fun of the ideal type of an anarchist society, but you can also do it to that of a socialist society, which is very different from anything Harold Wilson has in mind. It seems to me that all societies are mixed societies, and while, if it cheers us up, we can dream about an anarchist society, the sort of society that we or our descendants are going to get is a society where these two principles of authority and voluntarism are struggling. But because no road leads to utopia it doesn't mean that no road leads anywhere.

*NW*: I want to work towards anarchy. I don't want to establish it overnight, so I would take the – almost a slogan – view that means are ends, that what happens now is an end. To say that you are working towards an end strikes me as meaningless. What you are working towards is what you are actually doing. If you overthrow a government overnight you could say that this is establishing anarchy. I would say that you are much more likely to establish an extreme dictatorship.

*GM*: There are in the world thousands of people who haven't enough to eat, there are wars going on, there are far too many people over the earth's surface, there are diseases yet unchecked. There is an enormous amount of money being spent in flinging expensive toys up into outer space, when there are people rotting from disease and lack of food down here. And it seems to me that the argument against anarchism that it is an impractical, lovable idea which could never be realised, is unproven in the face of the inefficiency of the forms of government that have existed and exist on the earth's surface.

*PG*: The important crisis at present has to do with authority and militarism. That's the real danger, and if we could get rid of the militarism and if we could get rid of this principle of authority by which people don't run their own lives, then society could become decent, and that's all you want of society. It is not up to governments or states to make anybody happy. They can't do it. What they can do is maintain a minimum level of decency and freedom.

*NW*: Yes, in general I want a government that governs less, but I want the lessening process to be continuous, so that government always governs less and less, and the people always look after themselves more and more until in the end there is a government that does not govern at all – is simply a clearing-house, a post box, a way for people to collect their health benefits.

*BC*:Probably now, more than any other time, ordinary people have got more than a slightly cynical approach to parliament and politicians. People are beginning to say that they're all alike and we're just not going to bother to vote at all. But going on from there and saying, 'What are we going to do?', this is the crunch, this is the problem. We have had illustrations in recent by-elections of people abstaining. But I think we can get over the idea now that the parliamentary system is a big laugh, a big giggle. Once you start getting people thinking in terms of really querying the parliamentary system and exposing it for what it's worth – a gasworks – then I think we're making progress.

*CW*: Well, anarchists in elections usually indulge in anti-election propaganda, that is to say, they say 'Don't vote for anybody!' And they're very often criticised for this. This is pointed out to be somehow negative or irresponsible and so on. Obviously, being opposed to the principle of authority, anarchists don't see the point in deciding which group of authoritarians are going to rule us.

*RB*: Authoritarians, centralisation, coercion, capitalism, these are
the sort of things anarchists are against. George Melly:
*GM*: With a thing like the motor car, which is one of the great killers
of our time, you have a whole society geared to sell people motor
cars, to impress them with the idea that without one they are failures, it will give them sexual potency, and a thousand other ideas;
entirely linked to an economic situation in which people have to
make motor cars and people have to sell motor cars and therefore
motor cars have to be used. But why do they have to make them?
Because if they didn't make them the whole economic machine
would break down. But this machine is artificial in itself. There's no
need for everybody to be employed all the time. The more unpleasant jobs are always produced as an excuse against anarchism.
Who would sweep roads, who would mine coal? But a lot of these
things would be solved so that nobody need do them at all. There
could be automatic street washers and the use of atomic energy
instead of coal, but we daren't use atomic energy instead of coal
because this would shut the mines and this would create an economic crisis. Economics is an artificial deformation, or seems to me to
be it, and if one scrapped it all and started from human needs, and if
one scrapped the whole of the thousands of law books in every
country and started from good sense and good will, one might be
moving towards a freer society.
*PG*: You see it isn't industrialisation which makes for centralisation, it's an error to think that. It's the way we do the industrialisation. Now in Yugoslavia at present, they're trying to extend workers' management to considerable control over the actual designing
and engineering process, and they have found, of course it's obvious, that in order to do that, they'll have to bring the university
right into the factory. Now the worker can get technical training –
great. So now Yugoslavia is the one country in the world, it seems to
me, that at present is taking, is trying to tend towards anarcho-
syndicalism. Now if you talk to Yugoslavs – and I have recently been
talking to a lot of them – I like their attitude. They're extremely
sceptical about the whole thing. It's extremely inefficient and there
are all kinds of error, etc. – and they're fantastically proud of it, and
I love that attitude. You see they don't try to sell you a bill of goods,
but they know they're right – and that I like. Now they wouldn't call
it anarchism, but I don't care about the word.
*CW*: I think it started merely as a political gimmick to differentiate
Yugoslav socialism from Stalinist communism, but that it has been
taken seriously. I'm quite sure that some of the Yugoslav communists are determined to develop a system of workers' control. As

things stand, of course, it is workers' control within those limits set by the Party, just as these experiments here are workers' control within the limits set by a capitalist market economy.

*RB*: But how do anarchists see such principles of organisation working on a larger scale, nationally or even internationally?

*CW*: I think the most complex industrial organisation could be broken down on the federative principle, that is to say, a federation of autonomous groups. This is not so far-fetched, because you see it in operation today in different international organisations. You can post a letter from here to Valparaiso or Chungking and know it will get there because of the federal arrangements of a dozen different national post offices. Now there is no world post office capital. There are no directives. There is an International Postal Union, which is not a mandatory body. It is all done by free arrangement between separate national post offices. Or you can buy a ticket in London from here to Osaka and you travel on the railway lines of a dozen different countries, communist, capitalist, state-owned and privately owned, and you get there with no bother. But there is no international railway authority.

*RB*: The anarchist's opposition to the state obviously involves opposition to the state's coercive institutions such as the police and prisons. One anarchist whose dealings with the police hit the headlines is Donald Rooum.

*DR*: I suppose that my arrest by Detective-Sergeant Challenor had nothing to do with my being an anarchist. As you know, three or four perfectly innocent boys who were coming back from a game of tennis were arrested too, but I think it had something to do with my being an anarchist that I was able to spot an error made by this policeman in planting his evidence and that the general suspicion of policemen which for instance prevented me from complaining against the behaviour of one policeman to another policeman, that suspicion made me keep quiet in the police station and hold my story and my evidence and my defence until we came to the magistrate's court. I think it takes either an anarchist or a lawyer to realise that this is a sensible thing to do. Before the Challenor case I mainly thought of the police as a repressive agency and something that one ought to fight against. Since then I've had it rammed down my throat through watching it, what the policeman's job was. It's a very difficult job and instead of saying now we ought to be rid of the police force I would rather say that the society which needs a police force is a sick society. It's not the same thing at all as saying that you could cure society by getting rid of the police force. The police force is rather like crutches. With all its faults I suppose at the present day it's necessary. And that's an opinion that I didn't have before I was arrested.

*NW*: The one emotion I have after being inside Brixton prison is that I'd like to see Brixton prison blown up. But apart from that it hasn't changed my conviction at all, which is that in order to try and prevent people from hurting other people, to put them into a room and lock them up is the worst thing one can do. I can't think of anybody who was in Brixton whom I met who should have been locked up. I can't think of anyone in Brixton who would be any danger if let out, any more than he is going to be as soon as he comes out anyway. I would say with Kropotkin (this is the sort of thing anarchists do: they quote other anarchists), I would say that prisons are universities of crime, and that the state and society ought to consider whether the enormous expense and effort put into keeping people in prison wouldn't be much better used in trying to help people in some other way.

*RB*: On the political scene anarchists don't seem to have made much visible impact, but they feel that their ideas have made headway in the increasingly libertarian attitudes apparent in the social field, in attitudes to the mentally ill, for example, in education, in the whole permissive climate of modern society. Of course they don't take all the credit for it, though they have made a contribution and on the whole they welcome it.

*CW*: Years ago, shortly after the war, Alex Comfort gave a series of lectures to the London Anarchist Group and they were published by Freedom Press under the title *Barbarism and Sexual Freedom*. Comfort's ideas on sex have reached the stage of course of being published many years later as a Penguin book, and what appeared revolutionary to people or somehow *outré* in one way or another in 1948, is almost *passé* by 1966. The revolution in sexual attitudes has happened. Take anarchist ideas about education – you've only got to see how every child today looks like the progressive school children of twenty years ago.

*IR*: Of course I haven't married, and I've had my own children. This wasn't very important at the time, we didn't think it was very important, and I still don't think it's important. I like to think that society is in fact getting more and more towards anarchism because now there are more and more people in fact living together and having children without being married and without asking the State if they may or may not.

*DR*: We thought that agreement to have a home and a family was a matter for two people and that in a marriage you don't have two parties, whatever the pundits are always saying, you don't have two parties to a marriage, you have three parties, a man, a woman and the State.

*RB*: In this sort of area, in personal morality, in society's considerable advance towards permissiveness in the past few years, the anarchists are probably in substantial agreement with a great many people who wouldn't call themselves anarchists. What about what is called the underground, the hippies, the drop-outs, flower people and so on? Is this a form of anarchism?

*CW*: My kind of anarchism wants to change the structure of society and the anarchist hippies simply walk out on authoritarian society. But it does seem to me that the wildly individual anarchism of the young is a good thing. I think we should be wildly individualistic when we are eighteen and twenty. Personally I'm not interested in individualism because I'm twice that age.

*GM*: The thing about hippies is that they are over-excited by certain aspects of freedom, I think. They're over-excited by the idea of drugs because drugs are something which older people disapprove of. They're a useful form of revolt. It used to be sex, when I was eighteen or seventeen because older people apparently in those days disapproved more of sex, so one went round having as many people as possible, as noisily as possible and telling everyone about it. On the other hand, since the *Lady Chatterley* trial, sex has become respectable. Even bishops admit an orgasm is a marvellous thing to have and so on, nobody condemns masturbation, and so on, so that sex is out and drugs are in, and I think that the whole emphasis on drugs in the hippy thing is hysterical and not altogether sympathetic. But I think that the hippy *feeling* for the idea of love instead of hate, of openness, of people doing what they want, of freedom, is on the contrary, very sympathetic, and the interview recently between Mick Jagger and various members of the establishment – bishops, the Editor of *The Times* and so on – seemed to me to indicate that although Jagger is rather naïve in certain of his ideas, he also is on a track which they were unable to answer.

*NW*: I don't mean it as a criticism, but I do feel that a lot of the modern bohemian anarchists, or whatever particular label they have for that year, are to some extent a commercial phenomenon, rather than a political one, that they are people who are either trying to drop out of a commercial life or are trying to make money out of pretending to drop out of commercial life. I wouldn't see them in fact as part of the anarchist movement, though they are certainly relevant to the anarchist movement.

*RB*: As the anarchists don't have any form of membership it's hard to say how many of them there are, or even with any certainty whether or not someone is an anarchist, but certainly there must be quite a few people who like George Melly would go along with them most of the way.

*GM*: I think to say to me that I am an anarchist is overstating it because I would call myself more an anarchist sympathiser in that I feel that to be an anarchist completely it's necessary to rid oneself of practically everything that one holds except one's own body and a few clothes. And as someone who has a house, a car, pays insurance, and so on, I wouldn't consider myself an anarchist but someone who would hope that society would move towards anarchism, and who is occasionally provoked by the monstrosities in this society to an act of anarchist revolt or at least to an anarchist statement. Anarchism for me equals freedom. I mean the two words are interchangeable. But freedom in the absolute sense, not freedom shouted by one politician against another, freedom of each individual to exist entirely within his desires.

*RB*: The anarchists have had an erratic and lively history and have been particularly strong in the Latin countries. There are still many Spanish anarchists in exile after the Civil War, particularly in France, and there are small anarchist groups in most countries throughout the world. But in this country about how many anarchists are there, and what sort of people are they?

*CW*: I think that social attitudes have changed. People no longer equate anarchism with bomb-throwing. Anarchism perhaps is becoming almost modish. I think that there is a certain anarchy in the air today, yes.

*JR*: One of our disreputable comrades said that the membership of the anarchist movement is between one and two million and this actually meant that it was between the figure one and the figure two million.

*RB*: The size of the readership of Freedom gives some indication of their numbers.

*JR*: Roughly our circulation is round about the 2,000 or 3,000 mark.

*CW*: Anarchists tend not to be industrial workers and I think that the reason for this is that they won't stick the discipline of factory life. Anarchists tend to be self-employed people or people employed in some of the apparen᷄ ⸲ ᷄efu᷄ ᷄r s᷄᷄ᴧal service type activities. They tend to be people who have a l᷄.ge amount of freedom in their work, simply because, I suppose, ᴦhey have opted for that sort of life, being the kind of people that they are.

*RB*: Though they are very much a minority group the anarchists do include some well-known names, Sir Herbert Read ᷄nd Alex Comfort, for example, but as Jack Robinson says, there are anarchists who are prominent but there are no prominent anarchists.

*JR*: No, we have never had any leaders because one thing about anarchists is that, if people do set themselves up to be leaders, they have the unfortunate experience that nobody ever follows them, which is the best thing that could happen to any leader.

*RB*: We've heard a little about who the anarchists are in this country and what they think, what sort of society they want and what sort of action they take to work towards such a society. One thing we haven't heard is how they, or at least how some of them, became anarchists.

*CW*: Well I became an anarchist when I was a soldier in the army. I think that's enough to make anyone an anarchist. The anarchists then, just as I am now, were hanging out their little rags of propaganda and I was one of the people that nibbled.

*JR*: I always say that I became an anarchist when I was in Wormwood Scrubs, which is probably true because I had been on the verge of anarchism and during the war I was imprisoned as a conscientious objector and I was meditating on what actually the State did contribute and I discovered that really the only contribution of the State as distinct from society was the contribution of the army and the police and the prisons whose guest I was and the army I had declined to go into.

*BC*: First of all I was in the Labour Party. I came out of that over German rearmament and the hydrogen bomb, I went to the ILP and I felt that I didn't seem to fit in there either. The party machine, not so much in the ILP of course, but in the Labour Party. I felt a rejection, a complete rejection of the parliamentary system. To my mind the parliamentary system is completely outdated and useless and therefore I reject the whole parliamentary system.

*NW*: Well in a sense I was an anarchist before I was born in that I had an anarchist grandfather, but I was in fact brought up more or less as a Labour Party supporter – an extreme left-wing Labour Party supporter and it gradually occurred to me that in fact I was an anarchist as well as being a socialist.

*DR*: Actually I was on some kind of Government potato-picking scheme, in 1944 I think it was, and I bought a copy of *War Commentary*, as it was then, one of the forerunners of FREEDOM, at Marble Arch. I read it and I thought, 'Well, this is the gen. I agree with it'.

# 2. Conflicting strains in anarchist thought

## George Molnar

# I.

ON A liberal-democratic view the State is a harmonizer of social conflicts. Supposedly disinterested, it stands above classes and meliorates their struggles in the interest of the common good. Anarchists have often criticised the view that the State is a disinterested arbiter, that it represents, in some sense, the common good. It is not possible for the State to serve the common good, even if there were such a thing.

'If you see the State as it was in history and as it is in essence today', wrote Kropotkin, 'and if you consider moreover that a social institution cannot serve *all* aims indiscriminately...you will understand why we desire the abolition of the State.'[1]

The same point is made by Bakunin, according to whom:

'There is no intellect that can devise a social organisation capable of satisfying each and all',[2] because 'the State is government from above downwards of an immense number of men, very different from the point of view of...the interests and the aspirations directing them – the State is government of all these by some or other minority...it is impossible that (this minority) could know and foresee the needs, or satisfy with an even justice the most legitimate and pressing interests in the world. There will always be discontented people because there will always be some who are sacrificed.'[3]

Malatesta held that

The government – or the State if you will – as judge, moderator of social strife, impartial administrator of the public interests is a lie, an illusion, a Utopia, never realised and never realisable.[4]

and he went on the indicate the role of this illusion in the following words:

A government cannot rule for any length of time without hiding its true nature behind the pretence of general utility. It cannot respect the lives of the privileged without assuming the air of wishing to repect the lives of all. It cannot cause the privileges of some to be tolerated without appearing as the custodian of the right of everybody.[5]

24

Anarchists argue that in a society characterized by economic, cultural and other inequalities there is no common good; that as long as, for instance, the *economic* powers of various classes are disparate, no *political* arrangement can be equitable, despite any liberality it may seem to have.

> Whatever may be the form of government, whilst human society remains divided into different classes because of the hereditary inequality of occupations, wealth, education and privileges, there will always be a minority government and the exploitation of the majority by that minority.[6]

Political rule is always rule by minorities. The system of parliamentary electoral representation does not change this.

> The people have neither the leisure nor the necessary education to occupy themselves with the matters of government. The bourgeoisie, possessing both, has in fact if not by right, the exclusive privilege of governing.[7]

Anarchists endorse Proudhon's description of elected government as oligarchical ('Universal suffrage is counter-revolution'). The concept of self-government through elective representation is unreal because elections vest actual control, *i.e.* the power to make decisions and see them enforced, in the hands of a minority. A ruler, a member of this minority, unless he

> 'is frequently reinvigorated by contacts with the life of the people; unless he is compelled to act openly under conditions of full publicity; unless he is subjected to a salutary and uninterrupted regime of popular control and criticism, which is to remind him constantly that he is not the master nor even the guardian of the masses but only their proxy or their elected functionary who is always subject to recall – unless he is placed under those conditions', be he ' the most liberal and popular man', will nevertheless 'undergo a complete change in outlook and attitude.'[8]

These essential popular controls are lacking in any democracy. Politicians meet the people only at election time, for a 'brief interlude of unpleasantness'.

> On the day after the elections everyone goes back to his daily business: the people to their work, and the bourgeoisie to their lucrative affairs and political intrigues. They do not meet and they do not know each other any more.[9]

Large masses of people are frequently indifferent to their political fate, and have no interest in controlling their rulers, even if this were possible. The germ of power, wrote Bakunin, will develop

> if only it finds in its environment favourable conditions. These conditions in human society are the stupidity, ignorance, apathetic indifference, and servile habits of the masses... When the masses are deeply sunk in their sleep, patiently resigned to their degradation and slavery the best men in their midst...necessarily become despots. Often they

become such by entertaining the illusion that they are working for the good of those whom they oppress.[10]

It is for reasons such as these that the State cannot be regarded as the guardian of the 'common good', nor indeed as the guardian of the interests of the majority.

> The very existence of the State demands that there be some privileged class vitally interested in maintaining that existence. And it is precisely the group interests of this privileged class that are called patriotism.[11]

The State exists, say anarchists, in an inequalitarian society; and in such an environment it cannot be impartial: its intervention in social conflicts will be conservative, it will always tend to maintain an unequal distribution of wealth, privilege, and power. In the Marxist tradition the State is viewed as fundamentally the upholder of economic inequalities; the other differential distributions which it upholds (of privilege, power, etc) are treated as subordinate and incidental to its main task. Anarchists escape this reductionism by recognising that the State, apart from upholding the interests of the economically dominant classes, has interests of its own which are not derived from the interests of the classes surrounding it, interests which the State will continue to have irrespective both of the legal *forms* of the government and of the *platforms* of the ruling parties. Anarchists base their criticism of parliamentary action by socialists on this fact.

> The modern radical is a centraliser, a State partisan, a Jacobin to the core, and the Socialist walks in his footsteps.[12]

When they are elected to parliament,

> those very workers who are now staunch democrats and socialists, will become determined aristocrats, bold or timid worshippers of the principle of authority, and will also become oppressors and exploiters.[13]

On attaining to parliamentary power Socialists inevitably become conservative. This is not due to the personal weakness of individual socialists.

> Usually these backslidings are attributed to treason (says Bakunin). That however, is an erroneous idea: they have for their main cause the change of position and perspective.[14]

The results of the exercise of political power do not depend on the good intentions or sound policies of the parties, groups or classes which rule, but on the inescapable demands imposed by institutions and organisations on those who hold power within them. Speaking of sincere republicans who wanted to utilise the institution that already existed, Kropotkin remarked:

> And for not having understood that you cannot make an historical

institution go in any direction you would have it, that it must go its own way, they were swallowed up by the institution.[15]
The State is not merely an instrument in the hands of the powerful, it has its own way which cannot be circumvented by labour politicians, or by anyone else. This point is central to anarchist theory. It enables anarchists to explain some important features of modern political life which other social theories of radical orientation can, at best, only explain away. Contemporary States are not simply the upholders of the interests of an economically privileged minority against the rest of society; put in the language of class-struggle, modern States are, to varying extents, at war with all classes. They are internally expansionist, and far from always securing the gains of capitalists against the demands of others, the Welfare State often promotes an exchange whereby it increases the supply of goods to the underprivileged while in turn depriving them of enacted or *de facto* rights. (The operating of compulsory arbitration in Australia is an instance of this.) In general, State control is never relinquished voluntarily or in good grace, but always only under pressure and as a result of struggle. Since any State's power depends on its ability to restrain as many interest groups as possible from acting outside the confines of legality and of politics, organs of the contemporary State have developed concealed police functions along with their other functions: they have become watchdogs of society. Proudhon already foreshadowed this development: 'The government must have laws,' he wrote:

> It must make as many laws as it finds interests; and, as interests are innumerable, relations arising from one another multiply to infinity, and antagonism is endless, law-making must go on without stopping. Laws, decrees, ordinances, resolutions will fall like hail upon the unfortunate people. After a time the political ground will be covered with a layer of paper, which the geologists will put down among the vicissitudes of the earth as the *papyraceous formation*.[16]

This domestic imperialism of the State frequently compels all parties, despite any allegiance they may have to specific classes or groups, to frame and execute policies, which, irrespective of the *intentions* behind them, have the *effect* of extending state tutelage over wide areas of society formerly not under central control. All parties, socialist, communist or conservative, thus attack self-reliance and intitiative among all classes, and foster dependence and servility. A signal feature of anarchism is precisely its early recognition and forceful exposure of the bureaucratisation of social life which, from its slender start in the days of Proudhon and Bakunin, has grown to univers і proportions in our days.

This point, that social institutions cannot be made the vehicle for any policy whatever but have their own ways, underlies also the criticism anarchists have made of the Marxist doctrine that 'Political power, properly so called, is merely the organised power of one class for oppressing another'.[17] On the basis of this theory Lenin adduced that the emancipation of the toilers must take the political form of the dictatorship of the proletariat.[18] Organisationally this requires a party of professional revolutionaries who would bring social-democratic consciousness to the workers 'from without'.[19] The aim of such a movement is 'the seizure of power – the political purpose will become clear after the seizure'.[20] Against Lenin's theory of a revolutionary seizure of power by a vanguard, anarchists argue that this will not result in the dictatorship of the whole class.

> 'If the proletariat is to be the new ruling class, over whom will it rule?' asked Bakunin.[21]

To the contention that the dictatorship will be temporary and will come to an end when the former ruling classes, the enemies of the workers, are crushed, anarchists reply:

> No dictatorship can have any other aim but that of self-perpetuation...freedom can only be created by freedom.[22]

The eventual outcome of the Bolshevik revolution, in terms of the authoritarianism of the emergent régime, was indicated by the organisational precepts on which Leninists had based themselves: because Bolshevism saw the working class as not spontaneously socialist in aspirations, it commenced by bringing socialism to the proletariat 'from without' and ended up, after the seizure of power, by imposing socialism as the policy of the State. This imposition of socialism was unavoidable because in Russia socialists were hopelessly outnumbered; the majority of the nation was non-proletarian, and among urban workers Bolsheviks commanded on overwhelming or lasting majorities. The barrack-room socialism imposed by the State was no longer the socialism which members of the vanguard had envisaged and in the name of which they had seized power: it lacked precisely those liberating, emancipating and ennobling features which gained it support in its struggle against Tsarist oppression.[23] The dictatorship of the proletariat turned out to be the government of

> ex-workers, who once they become rulers or representatives of the people, cease to be workers and begin to look down upon the toiling masses. From that time on they represent not the people but themselves and their own claims to govern the people.[24]

Anarchists see in the Russian revolution a verification of their own views: the institution of the State engulfed those who tried to use it, the State asserted its own way. Even Lenin, in one of the last speeches of his life, gave belated recognition to the fact that the autonomy of political institutions can foil the revolutionaries:

> Here we have lived a year, with the state in our hands, and under the New Economic Policy. Has it operated our way? No. We don't like to acknowledge this, but it hasn't. And how has it operated? The machine isn't going where we guide it... A machine doesn't travel exactly the way, and often travels just exactly not the way, that the man imagines who sits at the wheel.[25]


# II.

Anarchists believe that

> It would be impossible to make the State change its nature, for it is such only because of this nature, and in foregoing the latter it would cease to be a State[26]

Consequently, when they came to frame their own, anarchist, policies for the emancipation of the exploited majority and for the abolition of economic classes and of political domination, they were committed to a programme of attacking existing political institutions without, in the process, substituting new ones. Their success, or failure, to work out adequately the theoretical problems arising out of this requirement, gives the answer to the celebrated question 'Is anarchism practicable?'

All anarchists are revolutionaries, but not all have revolutionary programmes. Thinkers such as Proudhon or Kropotkin give no instructions as to what should be done and how and by whom in order to bring about an anarchist revolution. In the absence of such instructions, in the absence of an organisational and tactical plan, the vision of anarchist society must remain chimerical. Social changes cannot take place without the action of social agencies, that is, of institutions and of people; a plan for a new society which gives no answer to the question 'What social procedures will actually move us from the one situation in the direction of the other?'[27] is, perforce, utopian.

Not all anarchists, however, are utopian in this sense. Two types of anarchism, in particular, stand out as having a practical programme. The first is anarcho-syndicalism, to which the overwhelming majority of contemporary anarchists subscribe; the second, little known to modern anarchists and not acknowledged by them, is the revolutionary organisational doctrine of Michael Bakunin.

Anarcho-syndicalism is revolutionary trade-unionism. In agreement with Lenin, syndicalists hold that trade-union meliorism is not a proper method of social emancipation, and that conventional political parties are authoritarian in structure and achievement. According to syndicalists the way to bring about a free society is by the organisation of workers in autonomous, federated syndicates, whose aim is socialism and whose revolutionary method is the general strike. The syndicates are in principle completely independent of all political parties, having recognised 'in a clear and penetrating manner... the dangers of bourgeois democracy'.[28] Internally, they aim at a non-authoritarian organisation as an 'antidote to oligarchy'. In the words of a contemporary anarchist:

> Syndicalists... adopt a federal organisation, in which local units are autonomous... In this way greater elasticity and speed of action are gained and there is no chance of the betrayal of the workers by a governing bureaucracy. Affairs concerning the syndicate as a whole are conducted by delegates who are only allowed to voice the will of the workers who elected them, and there is a minimum of officials elected for short periods, after which they return to the bench or field, and subject to recall if their actions dissatisfy the workers. In this way the rise of a bureacracy divorced from the workers is avoided and the revolutionary nature of the syndicate preserved.[29]

In practice syndicalism has failed to live up to these hopes. The French CGT, at one time the most important of European syndicalist organisations, was never completely revolutionary; and everywhere, including in Catalonia where it became very influential, syndicalism remained a minority movement in two senses: the industrial proletariat was a minority among 'the people', and the syndicalist workers were a minority among the industrial proletariat. This fact immediately assigned syndicalists to the role of a revolutionary vanguard which had to intitiate, and, if need be, to enforce revolutionary action since this was not occurring spontaneously among the rest of the exploited. This necessity to extend their influence forced syndicalists into making political alliances. Syndicalism managed to abstain from politics only on paper, in practice, especially in times of pressure, such as the Spanish Civil War, anarcho-syndicalists were obliged to resort to those methods which their own theory had shown them to be anti-revolutionary,[30] and which they had on that account rejected. Similarly, safeguards on internal freedom and self-government failed to insure against the rise of an oligarchical leadership which 'represented' the masses at decisive moments,[31] edited the press, acted as spokesmen, and negotiated with outsiders. The principles of autonomy and recall fell into disuse,[32] and leaders who rose, from among the syndicates, had as a rule no difficulty in consolidating their position. A number of these, in France, Italy and Spain, have used the prominence they have gained in the syndicalist movement as a stepping stone to a political career, sometimes a very brilliant one... *'Usually these back-slidings are attributed to treason. That, however, is an erroneous idea: they have for their main cause the change in position and perspective.'*

The theory of mass action professed by syndicalists rests largely on fiction, for nowhere have syndicalists attained to influence over more than a fraction of the people.

'Among organised workers,' wrote Robert Michels in 1915, 'it is once more only a minority which plays an active part in trade-union life. The syndicalists at once lament this fact and rejoice at it... They rejoice to rid of the dead weight of those who are still indifferent and immature... If they were logical the syndicalists would draw the conclusion that the general movement of the modern proletariat must necessarily be the work of a minority of enlightened proletarians'[33]

This is the actual conclusion that Lenin came to in 1902. In this however he had been anticipated by none other than Michael Bakunin. The anarcho-syndicalist prescription to revolutionize the trade-unions does not, in practice, have the required consequences of the movement, and the emancipation of the whole of society from oppression. Bakunin clearly recognised the second of these points, for he believed that

only a sweeping revolution, embracing both the city workers and the peasants would be sufficiently strong to overthrow and break the organised power of the state.[34]

The general strike can never be general enough, even if it embraced the whole of the urban proletariat. Other discontented elements, such as the peasants or the *declasse* intellectuals, whom Bakunin saw as also part of a revolutionary force, could not by definition take part in a general strike. Besides, mass action, such as was envisaged by the syndicalists, need not necessarily have revolutionary consequences.

Instinct, left to itself, and inasmuch as it has not been transformed into consciously reflected, clearly determined thought, lends itself easily to falsification, distortion and deceit. Yet it is impossible for it to rise to this state of self-awareness without the aid of education, of science; and science, knowledge of affairs and people, and political experience – these are things which the proletariat completely lacks.[35]

Here Bakunin, in phrases strikingly similar to Lenin's, is denying the theory of popular spontaneity:

An elemental force lacking organisation is not a real power... the question is not whether the people have the capacity to rebel, but whether they are capable of building up an organisation enabling them

to bring the rebellion to a victorious end – not just to a casual victory but
to a prolonged and ultimate triumph... The first condition of victory is...
*organisation* of the people's forces.[36]

As a condition of organising the people's forces, Bakunin, like
Lenin afterwards, envisaged a group of professional revolutionaries, who would

bring to the people the essential knowledge, the ability to generalise
facts, the skill needed to organise, to create association. This produces
the conscious fighting force without which victory is unthinkable.[37]

This 'conscious fighting force' is the organisation of the professional revolutionaries which would be secret, few in numbers, but
consisting of 'devoted, energetic and talented' persons, who

must devote their whole existence to the service of the international
revolutionary association. [38]

The association would function as the 'general staff', 'the invisible pilot'[39] of the revolution.

The internal organisation of Bakunin's association reveals further similarities to the Bolshevik model. Membership was selective, a
new member,

must have proven himself not by words, but by deeds.[40]

Bakunin was as anxious as Lenin to exclude those, in the words of
Eastman, 'to whom ideas do not mean action'. Unconditional
acceptance of the association's theoretical premises; obliteration of
all personal interests: submission to strict discipline sanctioned by
expulsion and vengeance; the duty to divulge all secrets to the association including the duty to spy on other members; unquestioning
acceptance of actual majority decisions of the Council of Derectorium – these are among other features of Bakunin's plan.[41] Within
the association rigid centralisation was to reign, ideationally and
tactically. Moreover the association was not to disband on the
morning after the successful revolution.

After the revolution the members will retain and consolidate their
organisation, so that in their solidarity their combined action may replace an official dictatorship.[42]

Although he would allow no 'official dictatorship', Bakunin
planned an invisible dictatorship. He described it as

a power free in direction and spirit, but without freedom of the
press; surrounded by the unamimous people, hallowed by their *soviets*,
strengthened by their free activity, but unlimited by anything or
anybody.[43]

It needs hardly to be argued that this scheme is Leninist not only
in principle, but even in fine detail. Therefore it is subject to the
same criticism which anarchists levelled at the doctrine of the dictatorship of the proletariat, namely, 'No dictatorship can have any
other aim but that of self perpetuation... freedom can only be cre-

ated by freedom'. These words are Bakunin's own, and we can now see that while in expressing his anarchism he trenchantly criticised centralist, oligarchical and other authoritarian conceptions found among revolutionaries, in order to produce a realistic revolutionary programme of his own he had to uphold these very principles. This not only shows that Bakunin's political thought consisted of two incompatible parts, but it finally forces on us the suggestion that anarchist theory as a whole is subject to a fundamental, unresolved contradiction.

# III.

The central inconsistency of anarchism can be summed up, in the light of previous discussion, as follows.

On the one hand anarchism presents a critique of social conditions which takes up, in a realistic manner, some questions of the nature of political domination. Fully worked out, this critique leads to the most pessimistic conclusions, for implicit in anarchism is the contention that all political action is by nature conservative, and no effective safeguards can be devised which would combine the possession of social influence with the absence of political authoritarianism.

On the other hand anarchists, although freely prepared to apply their theories to the analysis of all other movements, stopped short of applying their conclusions to anarchism itself. Instead they treated anarchism as a potential mass movement with the aim of abolishing all obstacles in the way of a free and classless society. Relative to this aim, some anarchists remain utopian (Kropotkin, etc). Others (anarcho-syndicalists) attempt to pursue a course of action outside accepted political forms, in the belief that they will thus escape the odious effects of politics, while still enjoying the power of being organised. This belief, based on the false distinction between 'free' and 'authoritarian' forms of mass organisation, has no substance: where anarcho-syndicalists have gained sufficient strength to operate as a mass movement, there they have exhibited unanarchist, political tendencies. Yet other anarchists, now no longer influential, have subscribed to practicable revolutionary schemes, which, however, if successful, would have produced not anarchy but its exact opposite. Anarchism as a plan for the liberation of society does not work: in practice such plans always yield either wishful thinking, or eventual regimentation.

This conclusion implies that the conflicting strains in anarchism cannot be resolved until anarchism is altogether purged of its association with a programme of secular salvation. In order to consistently uphold the libertarian and anti-authoritarian aspects of anarchism it will have to be understood that these aspects cannot be secured by converting society to them; that universal liberation is an illusion; that revolutions *always* involve seizing and exercising power; that 'the abolition of the State', in the sense extolled by classic anarchism, is a myth. If, as anarchists have always argued, many little reforms will not eliminate authoritarianism, neither will One Big Reform. The muck of ages, as Marx called it, clings to revolutionaries as fast as it does to the orthodox, and anarchist revolutionaries are not exempt from this mournful generalisation. It is only too evident, in any case, that the critical aspects of anarchism will not attract large numbers of people, that anarchism is not something which can assert itself over the whole of society. Anarchism, consistently interpreted, is permanent opposition.

# Footnotes

1 Peter Kropotkin: *The State: Its Historic Role*, London, 1946, p.41.
2 *The Political Philosophy of Bakunin: Scientific Anarchism*, ed. and trans. by G P Maximoff, Glencoe, Ill., 1953, p.299.
3 Michael Bakunin: *Marxism, Freedom and the State*, ed. and trans. K J Kenafick, London, 1950, p.31.
4 Errico Malatesta: *Anarchy*, London, 1958
5 *ibid*.p.15. Anarchists share this criticism of the liberal notion of the 'common good' with conservatives *e.g.*; 'The doctrine of the harmony of interests...is the natural assumption of a prosperous and privileged class, whose members have a dominant voice in the community and are therefore naturally prone to identify its interests with their own. In virtue of this identification, any assailant of the interests of the dominant group is made to incur the odium of assailing the alleged common interest of the whole community, and is told that in making this assault he is attacking his own higher interests. The doctrine of the harmony of interests thus serves as an ingenious moral device invoked, in perfect sincerity, by privileged groups in order to justify and maintain their dominant position'. E H Carr: *The Twenty Years' Crisis. 1919–1939*, London, 1946 (2nd ed.), p.80.
6 Kenafick: *op. cit.* p.36.
7 Maximoff: *op. cit.* p.218.
8 *ibid*. pp.212–13.
9 *ibid*. p.219.
10 *ibid*. pp.248–49.

11 *ibid.* p.232.

12 Kropotkin: *op. cit.* p.41.

13 Maximoff: *op. cit.* p.218.

14 *ibid.* p.218.

15 Kropotkin: *op. cit.* p.42.

16 P J Proudhon: *The General Idea of the Revolution in the Nineteenth Century*, London, 1923, p.132.

17 K Marx and F Engels: *Manifesto of the Communist Party*, Marx and Engels Selected Works, Moscow, 1915. Vol. 1, p.51

18 *cf.* V I Lenin: *State and Revolution.*

19 V I Lenin: *What is To Be Done?*, Moscow, 1952, p.52.

20 V I Lenin: *A Letter to the Members of the Central Committee*, Selected Works, Moscow, 1951, Vol. 1, Part 1, p.197.

21 Maximoff: *op. cit.* p.286.

22 *ibid.* p.288.

23 *cf.* the remarks of a recent historian of the Bolshevik party: 'All governments are concerned to retain power, though they may differ in the means which they adopt to this end, and the government of the communist party is no exception...there are many, many actions of the party in the course of my story which would be quite unintelligible unless they were seen in the light of the fact that over long periods the party's hold over the country was precarious and a false move would have meant its downfall. To ignore this factor, which runs like a thread of scarlet through Soviet history, is to write about phantoms and not about what really happened... I have discovered many instances in which it seemed to me that the theoretical considerations had to be sacrificed to the realities of the situation, I have as yet discovered no single instance in which the party was prepared to risk its own survival in power for considerations of doctrine'. L Schapiro: *The Communist Party of the Soviet Union*, London, 1960. Preface, p.xi.

24 Maximoff: *op. cit.* p.286.

25 quoted by Leon Trotsky in *The Real Situation in Russia*, New York, 1928, p.23.

26 Maximoff: *op. cit.* p.224.

27 Max Eastman: *Marx, Lenin and the Science of Revolution*, London, 1926, p.133. Eastman makes some sound criticisms of Kropotkin, but identifies all anarchist programmes with Kropotkin's utopianism.

28 Robert Michels: *Political Parties*, London, 1915, p.362.

29 George Woodcock: *Anarchy or Chaos*, London, 1944, p.58.

30 *cf.* V Richards: *Lessons of the Spanish Revolution*, London, 1953, esp. Ch. 7, for a description of the 'united front' practices of the C.N.T.-F.A.I. and the results of these practices.

31 Michels: *op. cit.* pp.364 *et seq.*

34 Eugene Pyziur: *The Doctrine of Anarchism of Michael Bakunin*, Milwaukee, 1955, p.66.

35 Maximoff: *op. cit.* p.215.

36 *ibid.* p.367, emphasis in original.

37 Pyziur: *op. cit.* p.82. The sinister phrase 'to create association' is worthy
  of note here, especially in contrast to the other anarchist notion, emphasised by Kropotkin, that association (co-operation, mutual aid) occurs
  spontaneously in social life. Practical revolutionaries cannot base their
  plans on the romantic conclusions Kropotkin drew from his observations: if , as the practicalists see, associations of the kind they require do
  not form spontaneously, then they will have to be created by the revolutionaries. In the course of creating associations however, revolutionaries
  forsake all pretence that what they are doing fits in with the *manifest*
  interests of the masses in whose name they speak.
38 *ibid.* p.87.
39 *ibid.* p.86.
40 *ibid.* p.87.
41 *ibid.* pp.87–89
42 *ibid.* p.95.
43 *ibid.* pp.97–98. *cf.* Max Nomad: *Apostles of Revolution*, London, 1939,
  pp.158–210, 224–234.

*Anarchy 4*                                                    *June 1961*


# 3.  Reflections on anarchism

## I.  Contracting other relationships
### Geoffrey Ostergaard

SINCE THE days of Marx and largely owing to the influence of
Marx, socialism has been conceived in terms of ownership. Until
recently at least, a socialist has been defined as one who believes in
common, usually State, ownership as opposed to private ownership. However, with the experience of Russia and even this country to guide us, it is becoming increasingly evident, as it has been
evident to anarchists all along, that a mere change of ownership

effects no radical change in social relations. When common own-ership takes the form of State ownership, all that happens is that the State becomes the universal employer and the possibilities of tyran-ny are multiplied by the union of economic and political power. The values underlying capitalism are not changed; the worker remains essentially a thing, a commodity, a unit of labour: he has only changed one set of masters, the capitalists, for another set of mas-ters, the political and managerial bureaucrats.

A change of ownership in the means of production may be a *necessary* condition for the transformation of a capitalist into a co-operative social order but it is not, as most socialists have assumed, a *sufficient* condition. What matters to the worker is not who owns the enterprise he works in but 'the actual and realistic conditions of his work, the relation of the worker to his work, to his fellow-workers and to those directing the enterprise'. It is for this reason that anarchists remain today the advocates of workers' con-trol of industry – a condition in which all would participate on equal terms in determining the organisation of their working lives; where work would become meaningful and attractive; and where capital would not employ labour but labour, capital.

Anarchism, it may be objected, is all very well in theory but tails, or would fail, in practice. Anarchists, however, would not accept the implied opposition between theory and practice: good theory leads to good practice and good practice is based on good theory. I do not say that it is easy to act anarchistically: the temptation to act in an authoritarian manner – to impose solutions rather than to resolve difficulties – is always very great; and it may be that in the short run at least, authoritarian organisations are more efficient in their results. But efficiency, exalted by capitalist and modern social-ist alike, is only one value and too high a price can be paid for it. More important than efficiency is the dignity of the responsible individual and solutions to what used to be called 'the social prob-lem' are not worth applying unless they are consonant with indi-vidual dignity and responsibility.

The task of the anarchist is not, however, to dream about the future society; rather it is to act as anarchistically as he can within the present society; to avoid as far as possible situations in which he is commanded or is impelled to command; and to endeavour to foster relations of mutual and voluntary co-operation between his fellow-men. In the modern world, the State is the most important manifestation of the principle of coercion. To achieve anarchy, therefore, the State must be dispensed with; and it will be dispensed with to the extent that men become capable of living without it. As the German anarchist, Gustav Landauer, puts it: 'The State is a condition, a certain relationship between human beings, a mode of behaviour; we destroy it by contracting other relationships, by behaving differently'.

In the last analysis, an anarchist is not a person who subscribes to a certain body of doctrine or set of beliefs: he is a person who behaves, or strives to behave, *differently* – in a way consistent with respect for the individuality inherent in all men.

*Anarchy 20*                                                    *October 1962*

## II.   The anarchist principle
## Paul Goodman

ANARCHISM is grounded in a rather definite proposition: that valuable behaviour occurs only by the free and direct response of individuals or voluntary groups to the conditions presented by the historical environment. It claims that in most human affairs, whether political, economic, military, religious, moral, pedagogic, or cultural, more harm than good results from coercion, top-down direction, central authority, bureaucracy, jails, conscription, states, pre-ordained standardisation, excessive planning, etc. Anarchists want to increase intrinsic functioning and diminish extrinsic power. This is a social-psychological hypothesis with obvious political implications.

Depending on varying historical conditions that present various threats to the anarchist principle, anarchists have laid their emphasis in varying places: sometimes agrarian, sometimes free-city and guild-oriented; sometimes technological, sometimes anti-technological; sometimes Communist, sometimes affirming property; sometimes individualist, sometimes collective; sometimes speaking of Liberty as almost an absolute good, sometimes relying on custom and 'nature'. Nevertheless, despite these differences, anarchists seldom fail to recognize one another, and they do not consider the differences to be incompatibilities. Consider a crucial modern problem, violence. Guerilla fighting has been a classic anarchist technique; yet where, especially in modern conditions, *any* violent means tends to reinforce centralism and authoritarianism, anarchists have tended to see the beauty of non-violence.

Now the anarchist principle is by and large true.* And far from being 'utopian' or a 'glorious failure', it has proved itself and won out in many spectacular historical crises. In the period of mercantilism and patents royal, free enterprise by joint stock companies was anarchist. The Jeffersonian bill of rights and independent judiciary were anarchist. Congregational churches were anarchist. Progressive education was anarchist. The free cities and corporate law in the feudal system were anarchist. At present, the civil rights movement in the United States has been almost classically decentralist and anarchist. And so forth, down to details like free access in public libraries. Of course, to later historians these things do not seem to be anarchist, but in their own time they were all regarded as such and often literally called such, with the usual dire threats of chaos. But this relativity of the anarchist principle to the actual situation is of the essence of anarchism. There *cannot* be a history of anarchism in the sense of establishing a permanent state of things called 'anarchist'. It is always a continual coping with the next situation, and a vigilance to make sure that past freedoms are not lost and do not turn into the opposite, as free enterprise turned into wage-slavery and monopoly capitalism, or the independent judiciary turned into a monopoly of courts, cops, and lawyers, or free education turned into School Systems.

*Anarchy 62*                                               *April 1966*

---

* I, and other anarchists, would except certain states of temporary emergency, if we can be confident that the emergency is *temporary*. We might except certain simple logistic arrangements, like ticketing or metric standards or tax-collection, if we can be confident that the administration, the "secretariat", will not begin to run the show. And we might except certain "natural monopolies", like epidemic-control, water-supply, etc.

# III. On authority
## Jeremy Westall

SOMEONE who is regarded as *an* authority is a person who is competent and well versed in a specific subject. Sir Ivor Jennings is an authority on the Constitution. Sir Herbert Read is an authority on modern art. By this we acknowledge that these men are expert in their chosen fields, their views are considered even if they are not accepted. Doubt about some matter concerning the Constitution occasions one to consult Jennings due to his being an authority on the subject. Anarchists, in argument, may well refer to anarchist authorities: Rocker, Malatesta, Comfort – men with established reputations.

To *have* authority is *an* ability usually inherent in the make-up of certain individuals; this characteristic involves many small actions portraying a self-assured bearing and manner. A teacher can be said to have authority if his pupils are interested and co-operative without the use or threat of force. Chaos in a class-room is indicative of a lack of authority in the teacher. To have authority does not involve conceit or arrogance, it involves a firm, determined, self-assured manner which generates itself in the group involved.

To be *in* authority is to have powers of coercion; to be in a position where the wielding of power is a necessary part of one's life. The administrator is a man in authority and he attains such a position in one of three ways. He may seize power and assert his authority by compelling obedience in one way or another. He may be appointed by an authority already established, as with the Civil Service. Or he may be elected and is thus in authority by the consent of a voting populace. One who does not consent to the system of voting, or who does not recognise the authority which is established by any of the three means cited above, is still subject in the eyes of the law to a person *in* authority.

Anarchists, in speaking of a society without authority, must make the above distinctions clear. The anarchist can be *an* authority or he can *have* authority, but he can never be *in* authority.

The rôle assigned to authority for the anarchist is therefore one who represents a group of others without imposition and who respects the autonomy and opinions of others in that group. Only in small groups is such delegated authority possible, for in a larger group one will find at some stage that the will of a minority or a majority will have to be imposed in order to achieve a 'unity'.

Thus anarchism envisages the development of small fluid groupings, with delegated authority only in the hands of a single person or a group for a certain specified time, no privilege being attached to such responsibility other than the natural goodwill that will be attached to the delegate. Our groupings will be co-ordinated by personal links forged by the groups' delegates.

Authority of this kind, recognised as essential by anarchists who none the less keep themselves thoroughly alive to the danger of its abuse, involves a certain amount of power. But it is a power that must coax and not coerce, educate not compel. We must all recognise the paradox that people *in* authority lack authority, in that they recognise their own weakness by having to lean on coercive power when their will is flouted.

*Anarchy 21* *November 1962*

# IV.  The habit of direct action
## David Wieck

ALL ACTION, we can see upon reflection, realizes *some* belief. Indirect action is often criticized on the ground that the means employed are unreliable; a strong point, but perhaps applied too sweepingly, and I think less fundamental than another. I want to distinguish (as direct action) that action which, in respect to a situation, *realizes the end desired*, so far as this lies in one's power or the power of one's group; from action (indirect action) which realizes *an irrelevant or even contradictory end*, presumably as a means to the 'good' end. The most significant – but not the only – distinction lies in the kind of fact thereby created for other persons. It is direct action, to present a person with the kind of attitude towards 'race' which one advocates; it is indirect action to rely on legal enforcement because in this is realized the concept that these people must obey the law simply because it is the law, and this may hopelessly obscure the aim.

Persons with no patience often make a bad distinction between 'talk' and 'action'. It can be seen that the important distinction is between talk that is mere moral assertion or propositional argument, and talk (in fact: direct action) which conveys a feeling, an attitude relevant to the desired end.

To take a homely example. If the butcher weighs one's meat with his thumb on the scale, one may complain about it and tell him he is a bandit who robs the poor, and if he persists and one does nothing else, this is *mere talk*; one may call the Department of Weights and Measures, and this is *indirect action*; or one may, talk failing, insist on weighing one's own meat, bring along a scale to check the butcher's weight, take one's business somewhere else, help open a co-operative store, etc., and these are *direct actions*.

Proceeding with the belief that in every situation, every individual and group has the possibility of *some* direct action on *some* level of generality, we may discover much that has been unrecognized, and the importance of much that has been under-rated. So politicalized is our thinking, so focussed to the motions of governmental institutions, that the effects of direct efforts to modify one's environment are unexplored.

The habit of direct action is, perhaps, identical with the habit of being a free man, prepared to live responsibly in a free society. Saying this, one recognizes that just this moment, just this issue, is not likely to be the occasion when we all come of age. All true. The question is, when will we begin?

*Anarchy 13*                                              *March 1962*


# 4. Anarchism and the cybernetics of self-organising systems
## John D. McEwan

THE INTENTION of this article is to suggest that some of the concepts used by cyberneticians studying evolving self-organising systems may be relevant to anarchist theory, and that some of the conclusions drawn from this study tend to favour libertarian models of social organisation. Much of the specifically cybernetic material is drawn from lectures given by Gordon Pask and Stafford Beer at Salford College of Advanced Technology. They are not, of course, responsible for any conclusions drawn, except where explicitly stated.

Firstly, what do we mean by a self-organising system? One definition is simply "a system in which the *order* increases as time passes", that is, in which the ratio of the *variety* exhibited to the maximum possible variety decreases; variety being a measure of the complexity of the system as it appears to an observer, the uncertainty for the observer regarding its behaviour. A system with large variety will have a larger number of possible states than one with smaller variety. Thus such a system may start by exhibiting very varied behaviour, e.g. a large number of different responses to a given stimulus may appear equally likely, but over a period of time the behaviour becomes less erratic, more predictable – fewer and fewer distinct responses to a given stimulus are possible (or, better, have a significantly high probability.)

This definition is, however, in some ways restrictive. The best such a system can do is to reach some sort of optimum state and stay there. Also, if we regard the system as a control system attempting to maintain stability in a fluctuating environment, the types of disturbance with which it can deal are limited by the fixed maximum variety of the system. This point will be dealt with later. The essential thing is that unpredictable disturbances are liable to prove too much for the system.

Such considerations suggest that it would be more fruitful to incorporate in the definition the idea that the maximum possible variety might also differ at different times. Thus Pask restricts the term to situations where the history of "the system" can best be represented as a series $S_0 S_{...} S_n$ each term a system with fixed maximum variety, and each self-organising in the first sense. With this definition we are able to deal with control systems of the type found in living organisms. Indeed, with a few limited exceptions, biological and social organisation are, up to now, the only fields in which such control systems can be found. Some of the exceptions, in the shape of artificially constructed systems, despite their crude and elementary nature in comparison with living organisms, do however exhibit remarkably advanced behaviour, at least in comparison with conventional controllers.

For an example of self-organising behaviour in this sense, we may consider a human being learning to solve certain types of problem, as his behaviour appears to an observer. Over an interval the behaviour may appear self-organising in the first sense. When, however, the learner adopts a new concept or method, there will be a discontinuity in the development of the behaviour, after which it will again be self-organising in the first sense, for a time, but now incorporating new possiblities, and so on.

In many discussions of control situations the concept of "Hierarchy" appears very quickly. This may tend to make the anarchist recoil, but should not do so, since the usage is a technical one and does not coincide with the use of the term in anarchist criticisms of political organisation.

Firstly, the cybernetician makes a very important distinction between two types of hierarchy, the *anatomical* and the *functional*, to use the terminology adopted by Pask. The former is the type exemplified in part by hierarchical social organisation in the normal sense (*e.g.* "tree of command" structure in industry), that is: there are two (if two levels) actual distinguishable concrete entities involved. The latter refers to the case where there may be only one entity, but there are two or more levels of information structure operating in the system – as for example in some types of neuron networks. A comparable concept is Melman's "disalienated decision procedure".[1] This idea might, I think, be suggestive to anarchists.

Secondly, even in the case of "anatomical hierarchy", the term only means that parts of the system can be distinguished dealing with different levels of decision making and learning. *e.g.* some parts may deal directly with the environment, while other parts relate to activity of these first parts, or some parts learn about individual occurrences, while others learn about sequences of individual occurrences, while others again about classes of sequences.

Even in the anatomical sense, then, the term need have none of the connotations of coercive sanctions in a ruler-ruled relationship which are common in other usages.

An important phenomenon in self-organising systems is interaction between the information flowing in the system and the structure of the system. In a complex system this leads to *Redundancy of Potential Command* – it is *impossible to pick out the critical decision-making element,* since this will change from one time to another, and depend on the information in the system. It will be evident that this implies that the idea of a hierarchy can have only limited application in such a system.

I will now attempt to give a brief sketch of a partly artificial self-organising system, involving the interaction beween human beings and a machine. This provides examples of the concepts introduced, and also, I feel, suggests important general conclusions about the characteristics of self-organising groups – characteristics which may sound familiar to libertarians. The machine in question is a group teaching machine developed by Gordon Pask.[2]

Prior to this Pask had developed individual teaching machines which were important advances in the growth of applied cybernetics.[3] However, on considering the problem of group teaching (for skills where some calculable measure of the pupils' performance, the rate of change of which will serve as a suitable indication of learning, exists), he did not simply combine individual machines.

The important insight he had was that a group of human beings, in a learning situation, is itself an evolutionary system, which suggested the idea of the machine as a catalyst, *modifying the communication channels in the group*, and thus producing different group structures.

In the development of the individual teaching machines, the possibility of the pupil dominating the machine had already arisen. This Pask now extended by introducing the idea of a quality "money" allocated to each member of the group, and used by each of them to "buy" for himself control over the communication structure of the group and over the partial specification of the solution provided by the machine. Now, in the individual machine, the degree to which the pupil was helped was coupled to change of his degree of success. If he was becoming more successful then the help given was decreased. In the group machine, the allocation of "money" is couple to *two* conditions – increasing success *and* increasing variety in the group structure. This second condition is the key to the novelty of the system.

This system, then, has changing dominance and exhibits redundancy of potential command.

In practice, each pupil sits in a little cubicle provided with buttons and indicators for communication, and a computor is used for control, calculating the various measures, etc. The operator is provided with some way of seeing what is going on, and can deliberately make things difficult for the group, by introducing false information into the channels, etc., seeing how the group copes with it.

The problems which Pask, at the time, had used in these group experiments had been formulated as conveying information about the position of a point in some space, with noise in the communication channels. The group had been asked to imagine that they are air traffic controllers, given co-ordinates specifying the position of an aircraft at a certain time, for example.

He suggests, however, that problems of agreeing on a choice of policy on a basis of agreed facts is not, in principle, very different from this case in which 'the facts' are in dispute, and there is no question of adopting any future policy – except of course the policy to adopt in order to ascertain the true facts and communicate them; this being the problem which the group solves for itself. It is in this sense that the group may be regarded as a decision maker.

It will be noted that the state of the system when in equilibrium *is* the solution to the problem. Also that this solution changes with time. This is also the case in the first example from purely human organisation which occurred to me – a jazz band (an example also suggested by Pask).

Pask emphasised that he had not then had the opportunity to obtain sufficient data to make any far-reaching well substantiated generalisations from these experiments. The results he had obtained, however, were very interesting and, I think, give considerable insight into the characteristics of self-organising systems, and their advantages over other types of decision-makers.

Some groups, after an initial stage while they were gaining familiarity with the machine, began assigning specific roles to their members and introducing standard procedures. This led to a drop in efficiency and inability to handle new factors introduced by spurious information, etc. The learning curve rises, flattens, then drops sharply whenever some new element is introduced. The system is now no longer self-organising.

Necessary characteristics for a group to constituted self-organising system, Pask suggests, are avoidance of fixed role-assignments and stereotyped procedures. This is of course tied up with redundancy of potential command.

I think we might sum up 'fixed role assignment and stereotyped procedures' in one word – institutionalisation.

Note that these characteristics are *necessary*, not *sufficient* – at the very least the group must first of all constitute a system in a meaningful sense; there must be communication between the members, a sufficient structure of information channels and feedback loops.

The role of the computer in Pask's system may be worrying some. Is this not an analogue of an authoritarian 'guiding hand'? The answer is, I think, no. It must be remembered that this is an artificial exercise the group is performing. A problem is set up by the operator. There is therefore no real situation in actuality for the group to affect and observe the result of their efforts. It is in this function of determining and feeding back the success/failure information which the machine fulfils.

The other important aspect of the machine as a catalyst in the learning process, we have already mentioned. There is a rough analogy here with the role of 'influence leader' in the Hausers' sense,[4] rather than any authoritarian 'overseer'. I will return to this question of the role of the machine shortly.

Regarding the group as a decision maker, Pask suggests that this is perhaps the only sense in which 'two heads are better than one' is true – if the 'two heads' constitute a self-organising system. The clue as to why a number of heads, *e.g.*, notoriously, in committees, often turn out to be much worse than one, is, he suggests, this business of role assignment and stereotyped procedure. He has not, however, suggested why this should arise.

Drawing on knowledge of behaviour of a self-organising nature exhibited in other groups, *e.g.* informal shop-floor organisation, the adaptability and efficiency exhibited in instances of collective contract working, and similar phenomena,[5] we may perhaps offer some suggestions as to how institutionalisation may arise in certain types of circumstances.

Imagine a workshop of reasonable size, in which a number of connected processes are going on, and where there is some variation in the factors affecting the work to be taken into account. There is considerable evidence that the workers in such a shop, working as a co-operating group, are able to organise themselves without outside interference, in such a way as to cope efficiently with the job, and show remarkable facility in coping with unforseeable difficulties and disruptions of normal procedure.

There are two levels of task here:
1. The complex of actual production tasks.
2. The task of solving the problem of how the group should be organised to perform these first level tasks, and how information about them should be dealt with by the group.

In situations of the kind I am imagining, the organisation of the group is largely determined by the needs of the job, which are fairly obvious to all concerned. There is continual feed-back of information from the job to the group. Any unusual occurrence will force itself on their notice and will be dealt with according to their resources at that time.

Purely for the purpose of illustration, let us now consider the situation of the same type of shop, only this time assuming that it is organised by a committee from outside the shop. The situation in which the committee finds itself is completely different from that of the work group. There are now three levels of problem:

1. The problems solved by the individual workers, *i.e.* their jobs.
2. The problem of the organisation of the work group.
3. The problem of the organisation of the committee itself.

The determining success/failure information for all these has still to come from (or at least is supposed to come from), the net result of the solution of the first level problems, *i.e.* the state of production in the shop.

The committee is denied the continuous feed-back which the group had. While working on its solution to the second level problem, it will have no information about the success of its alternatives, only previous findings, coded, in practice, in an inadequate way. The degree of success will only be observable after a trial period after they have decided on a solution. (Also unusual circumstances can only be dealt with as *types* of occurrence, since they cannot enumerate all possibilities. This is important in determining the relative efficiency of the two methods of organisation, but is of less importance in our immediate problem.)

It follows that the committee cannot solve the third problem by a method analogous to that used by the original work group in solving the second level problem; while working on the second level problem the committee has no comparable information available to determine the solution of the third level problem. But they must adopt some procedure, some organisation at a given time. How then is it to be determined?

In theory, such a controller could still remain an adoptive self-organising system, learning the structure to adopt in particular circumstances over a longer period of time, though it would still suffer from imperfect information.

In practice, however, the committee promptly convene a meeting, assign specific functions and decide on standard procedures. The actual determining information is probably a mixture of personality factors (including externally deprived status) and the existing ideas on organisation theory (including local precedent) possessed by the members. Once decided they will shelve the third level problem unless disaster, or a new superior, strikes, when a similar, but more cumbersome, procedure will be necessary to re-organise the committee along the same general lines.

In other words, within the closed system of the committee and work group, there is no, or virtually no, coupling between the success of the actual undertaking, *i.e.* the production job, and the decision procedure solving the third level problem. Worse, the factors influencing the solution of this problem, far from increasing the possible variety of the committee, lead to rigidity and low variety. Owing to this structure it will generally prove less efficient than a single imaginative person.

We might suggest, then, that it is this isolation from the process in terms of which the success of their own activity is defined, which is generally typical of the committee situation, which leads to their common failure to exhibit self-organising characteristics, and frequent inadequacy as decision makers.

Consider the first case of the self-organising work group again. Here it is the *job itself* which provides the analogue of Pask's machine, as far as feedback of success/failure information is concerned. Also, it has frequently been pointed out that in a 'face-to-face' group in this kind of situation (*i.e.* where the need for the situation demanding collective action are fairly obvious, and where some common criteria of success exist), that group leadership tends to be granted to the member or members best suited to the particular circumstances obtaining,* and to change as these circumstances change. In other words, changing dominance, determined by the needs of the situation. Here again, the job, acting through the group psychology of the face-to-face group performs a function analogous to Pask's machine, allocating temporary dominance in accordance with success.

I now wish to turn from this question of small group organisation to that of larger systems, and consider some criticisms of conventional industrial organisation developed, in particular, by Stafford Beer. He maintains that conventional ideas of control in complex situations, such as an industrial company, or the economy of a country, are crude and inadequate. "The fact is," he says, "that our whole concept of control is naive, primitive, and ridden with an almost retributive idea of causality. Control to most people (and what a reflection this is upon a sophisticated society!) is a crude process of coercion".[6]

In the lecture referred to earlier, his main thesis was the impossibility of truly efficient control of a complex undertaking by the type of rigid hierarchic organisation with which we are at present familiar. That such systems manage to survive, and work in some sort of

---

*"best suited" that is from the point of view of the group.

manner, as they obviously do, is, he suggested, due to the fact that they are not entirely what they are supposed to be – that there are unofficial self-organising systems and tendencies in the organisation which are essential to its survival.

Beer is usually perceptive, and frank, in emphasising the prevalence and importance of unofficial initiatives at all levels, *e.g.* (of shop-floor workers). "They arrange things which would horrify management, if they ever found out", (of charge-hands, etc.) "If *they* did not talk things over and come to mutual agreements, the whole business would collapse".

The main keystones in Beer's argument are Ashby's "Principle Requisite Variety" from the theory of homeostats, and information-theoretic requirements for adequate channel capacity in a multi-level system.

The principle of requisite variety states that, if stability is to be attained, the variety of the controlling system must be at least as great as the variety of the system to be controlled. We have already had an instance of this, for this was really the trouble with our hypothetical committee: due to its rigid structure and the need to issue instructions in terms of standard procedures to be adopted, it could not possibly be efficient in a situation of any complexity. If we made the further assumption that there was no organisation of the work group other than that imposed by the committee, chaos would be unavoidable. Approximations to this occur in 'working to rule'. In normal working, the initiatives of the shop-floor workers would serve as an additional source of variety, this enabling the principle of requisite variety to be satisfied, at least as far as normal variations in the factors affecting the production situation were concerned.

The relevance of the requirements of channel capacity is to the inadequate, attenuated information available at the top of the hierarchy – this is inevitable, for, in practice, the channel capacity could never be made adequate in the sort of pyramidical structures we have – and also to the inadequacy of the formal channels between subsystems (*e.g.* departments) which require to co-ordinate their activities.

To emphasise how far conventional managerial ideas of organisation are from satisfying the principle of requisite variety, Beer used an amusing parable concerning a Martian visitor to Earth, who examines the activities at the lower levels of some large undertaking, the brains of the workers concerned, and the organisational chart purporting to show how the undertaking is controlled. The visitor is most impressed, and deduces that the creatures at the top of the hierarchy must have heads yards wide.

In discussing the attempts of an inadequate control system to control a system of greater variety, Beer pointed to the accumulation of unassimilable information likely to occur as the control vainly struggles to keep track of the situation.

A comparable converse phenomenon was pointed out by Proudhon in 1851, in what must rank as one of the most prophetic statements about the development of social organisation ever written: "(The government) must make as many laws as it finds interests, and, as interests are innumerable, *relations arising from one another multiply to infinity*, and antagonism is endless, lawmaking must go on without stopping. Laws, decrees, ordinances, resolutions, will fall like hail upon the unfortunate people. After a time the political ground will be covered with a layer of paper, which the geologists will put down among the vicissitudes of the earth as the *papyraceous formation*"[7] (The first italics are mine.)

This is also an early, and lucid, statement of the complexity of the control situation in social organisation.

Beer has some suggestive ideas on the question of centralisation *vs.* decentralisation in industry. (That is, centralisation of control. The question of centralisation of *plant* is a different, if related, problem.) He puts the dilemma thus:

Centralise: insufficient channel capacity, etc. – cannot work efficiently.
Decentralise: completely autonomous units – no cohesion, probably ceases to be a system at all.

The point, he suggests, is that neither alternative corresponds to what we find in really efficient systems, *i.e.* complex living organisms. What we do find are a number of different, interlocking control systems. Beer also draws attention to the prevalence, and importance, of redundancy of potential command in self-organising systems, and points out that it is completely alien to the sort of theory of organisation found in industry and in similar undertakings.

The type of organisation at which we should aim is, he suggests, an organic one, involving interlocking control systems, intermeshing at all levels, utilising the principle of evolving self-organising systems, with the channel capacity and flow of information kept as high as possible.[8]

He mentioned in this connection an American businessman who claimed that his business was, in part, organised along somewhat similar lines and seemed to work very well. The idea was that anybody at all, no matter how 'junior' (I do not know whether this was actually restricted to what are termed 'staff' or not'), could call a conference at short notice, to discuss anything they wanted, whether connected with their work or not. Such a meeting could call in the president of the company himself, or anyone they thought they needed.

In context of interlocking control structures, we may note, as a fairly crude example, the syndicalist attempt to co-ordinate the activity of their basic units, the factory unions, through an interlocking two-fold structure of industrial and territorial federation.

Let us now contrast two models of decision making and control. First we have the model current among management theorists in industry, with its counterpart in conventional thinking about government in society as a whole. This is the model of a rigid pyramidal hierarchy, with lines of 'communication and command' running from the top to the bottom of the pyramid. There is fixed delineation of responsibility, each element has a specified role, and the procedures to be followed at any level are determined within fairly narrow limits, and may only be changed by decisions of elements higher in the hierarchy. The role of the top group of the hierarchy is sometimes supposed to be comparable to the 'brain' of the system.

The other model is from the cybernetics of evolving self-organising systems. Here we have a system of large variety, sufficient to cope with a complex unpredictable environment. Its characteristics are changing structure, modifying itself under continual feedback from the environment, exhibiting redundancy of potential command, and involving complex interlocking control structures. Learning and decision-making are distributed throughout the system, denser perhaps in some areas than in others.

Has any social thinker thought of social organisation, actual or possible, in terms comparable with this model? I think so. Compare Kropotkin on that society which "seeks the fullest development of free association in all its aspects, in all possible degrees, for all conceivable purposes: an ever-changing association bearing in itself the elements of its own duration, and taking on the forms which at any moment best correspond to the manifold endeavours of all".[9]

Further, "A society to which pre-established forms crystallised by law, are repugnant, which looks for harmony in an ever-changing and fugitive equilibrium between a multitude of varied forces and influences of every kind, following their own course".

The language is perhaps somewhat vague and ambiguous, but for a brief description in non-technical terms, of a society conceived as a complex evolving self-organising system, it could hardly be bettered. Certainly not in 1896.

The tragedy is not that so-called progressive thinkers today think that anarchist ideas of society and social organisation are inadequate. (This is excusable, and indicates failure on the part of anarchist propagandists to develop and spread their ideas.) It is that they think the other model *is* adequate. Also that they are incapable of thinking in any other terms.

Hence such thinkers are surprised when they cannot find the great efficient decision makers they expect in control of our institutions. The 'solutions' they propose to the muddle they do find, would require super-men-gods to work – even if the supermen could obtain adequate information to determine their decisions. This, from the nature of the structure, they can never do.

Again, when existing systems break down, as in industrial disputes, the tendency for the leaders on both sides is to attempt to remedy the situation by measures which increase the inadequacy of the system. That is, they attempt, by reorganisation and contractual measures, to increase the rigidity of the system by defining roles and responsibilities more closely, and try to confine the activities of human beings, who are themselves evolving self-organising systems, within a predetermined contractual framework. An interesting example of this will be found in *Wildcat Strike* by A.W. Gouldner.

To return to the conventional picture of government and the supposed control by the governed in democratic theory:

Firstly, does what I have said about the inefficiency and crudity of the governmental model as a control mechanism conflict with Grey Walter's analysis in his article "The Development and Significance of Cybernetics" in ANARCHY 25, in which he claimed that Western democratic systems were remarkably sophisticated from the cybernetic point of view?

I do not think so. The point is that what I am claiming is that they are inadequate for controlling the economy, say, or providing the greatest compatible satisfactions for the governed, as Proudhon pointed out. I would also claim that they are inadequate as mechanisms for maintaining order in society, unless society is conceived as largely self-regulating without the governmental institutions. Given this, I do not deny that the government-electorate system has proved an efficient *machine for maintaining itself*, although I might be inclined to give a little more importance to unofficial, informal elements in the system in this context than Grey Walter does in his article.

I agree that the system is well adapted to this task. Also, various psychological factors outside the scope of cybernetics help in the self-perpetuation of a system of this nature.

If the model of effective control by the government is inadequate, the naive democratic theory of control of the government by the people is much more so. This theory puts great stress on the importance of elections as the means by which the governed control their rulers and on the results of the elections, and hence, derivatively, on the constitution and behaviour of the government, as expressions of 'the will of the people'.

If we consider the individual, in a two party system, he is allowed one binary choice every five years or so, in which to reflect all the complex, dimly understood effects of governmental actions, intended and unintended. The model seems to allow of no structured subsystem to be identified as 'the people' – there is only an aggregate of individual choices.

It seems to me significant that this theory of self-government of the people, by the people, through universal, or at least wide, suffrage, developed in the 18th and 19th centuries along with the growth of the 'rabble hypothesis' of society (*i.e.* society as an unstructured aggregate of individual social atoms, pursuing their own egocentric interests, held together only by authority and coercion). Sociologists and social psychologists now find this picture of society completely inadequate.[10]

This is not to deny the genius of some of the thinkers who worked within the limitations of this model of democracy, for they were able to see the difficulties in practice, and devised most complicated systems of checks and balances to render their systems practicable, (*e.g.* the architects of the American constitution, as Grey Walter points out). However, they could not be expected to overcome the fundamental inadequacies of their model of government of the people, by the people, for the people, no matter how successful they were in developing the skeletons of viable self-perpetuating systems.

In contrast to the 'rabble hypothesis', we find that libertarian socialist thought, especially in Kropotkin and Landauer, showed an early grasp of the complex group structure of society; society as a complex network of changing relationships, involving many structures of correlated activity and mutual aid, independent of authoritarian coercion. It was against this background that they developed their theories of social organisation.

Neither am I convinced by the more sophisticated pressure group theory of democracy, introduced in an attempt to avoid the obvious inadequacy of the naive theory. As a descriptive theory of the actual situation it does seem reasonably adequate, but as a means by which the individual obtains a voice in decisions affecting him, it is just as inadequate as the naive theory. This in fact is generally admitted by its adherents, who have largely dropped the idea of democracy as self-government.[11]

In the case where a group, of a self-organising type, freely organises itself to tackle some situation, the resulting structure adopted by the group might be taken to exhibit 'the will of the group'. More generally, groups of this nature are capable of genuine group decisions. Such expressions as 'the will of the group (people)' are, I suggest, acceptable, and only as a rather dangerous shorthand, solely in cases of this sort.

In direct application, this is, of course, limited to fairly small groups, since, beyond a certain size, an unstructured aggregate of human beings is unable to act as a group, because there is too much information to be handled. The channel capacity is probably inadequate, and, even if the individual member could be presented with sufficient information, he would be unable to deal with it.

In certain work situations where the job effectively constrains the system, and only part of the behaviour needs to be correlated, we might expect larger aggregates to be capable of behaviour as a group. This is borne out by experience. In a situation where complex activity has to be correlated and there are few prior constraints, e.g. collective improvisation in a jazz band, most research groups, discussion groups, a maximum of the order of ten seems to be imposed; in manual jobs of certain types, and in the groups of the gang system at Coventry, much larger aggregates are found capable of coherent behaviour – groups of the order of a hundred or even a thousand members. Some of the very large groups, e.g. in the motor industry, may, however, be examples of more complex organisation.

We have said that only small aggregates of human beings, if regarded initially as unstructured, can exhibit genuine group behaviour. There is no reason, however, why large aggregates, if *sufficiently structured*, should not maintain coherent behaviour, while retaining genuine self-organising characteristics enabling them to deal with unpredictable disturbances in their environment (including in 'environment' their own 'substance', i.e. the human being constituting the aggregate) without developing a hierarchic structure in the authoritarian sense.

This is not to say that there will be no hierarchy in the *logical* sense. There will certainly be functional hierarchy in the sense of multi-level information flow, *i.e.* problem solving at the level of group environment, internal activity of subgroup, relations between sub-groups, and so on. We have seen that this need not *necessarily* mean different isolatable physical parts handling the different levels. In a situation of great complexity, however, we would expect to find anatomical hierarchies, in a far as there would be identifiable subgroups, of varying degrees of permanence of form and constitution, dealing with different levels of activity.

The essential points are that the existence of redundancy of potential command, with changing dominance, means that any analysis of part of the system at any time in terms of a hierarchical model must be regarded with caution, and that, where such anatomical hierarchy is distinguishable, it need not be a question of the higher levels controlling the lower by coercive sanctions, but rather of feeding back information to bias the autonomous activity of the other subgroup. In short, a very different sort of hierarchy from that of managerial theory.

There certainly need not be any isolatable 'control unit' controlling the rest.

I am using 'structured' here in a sense comparable to Buber, *i.e.* possessing a structure of connected subgroups, groupings or subgroups, etc., of a functional nature, but I would place relatively less emphasis on formal federation of subgroups, even in multiple federation, than Buber,[12] and more on more complex forms of connection. Also I am counting as subgroups both localised and more diffuse structures, formal and informal. One form of connection which seems to be of importance, is the case of diffuse substructures 'penetrating' into more localised ones, *e.g.* certain members of a particular subgrouping being members of some more widespread grouping, some sort of interest association, say, and thus serving as a means by which information about special forms of activity, passing in the more widespread structures, can pass into the localised structure, and play a part in determining its subsequent behaviour.

I hope I have shown that ideas derived from cybernetics and information theory are suggestive of fruitful lines of approach in considering social organisation, especially to the libertarian. I would not, however, expect too much in the way of rigorous direct application of cybernetic technique to social situations, for two reasons. Firstly there is the difficulty of specifying adequate and generally acceptable models of complex social situations, where the bias of the observer is notoriously effective in determining the picture he adopts. Secondly, the information theoretic concept of 'information' is an abstract one which emphasises only the selective characteristic on information. There are situations in which this is not entirely adequate.

This, however, is no excuse for remaining bound by a primitive and inadequate model of decision-making and control procedures. The basic premise of the governmentalist – namely, that any society must incorporate some mechanism for overall control – is certainly true, if we use 'control' in the sense of "maintain a large number of critical variables within limits of toleration". Indeed, the statement is virtually a tautology, since if such a situation did not exist, the aggregate would not possess sufficient stability to merit the designation 'a society'.

The error of the governmentalist is to think that 'incorporate some mechanism for control' is always equivalent to 'include a fixed isolatable control unit to which the rest, *i.e.* the majority, of the system of subservient'. This may be an adequate interpretation in the case of a model railway system, but not for a human society.

The alternative model is complex, and changing in its search for stability in the face of unpredictable disturbances – and much less easy to describe. Indeed, we are perhaps just beginning to develop an adequate language to describe such situations, despite the prophetic insights of a few men in the past.

A quotation from Proudhon makes a fitting conclusion – and starting point – "People like simple ideas and are right to like them. Unfortunately, the simplicity they seek is only to be found in elementary things; and the world, society, and man are made up of insoluble problems, contrary principles, and conflicting forces. Organism means complication, and multiplicity means contradiction, opposition, independence".[13]

# Footnotes

1 See Seymour Melman:*Decision-Making and Productivity* (Blackwell, 1958).

2 Gordon Pask: "Interaction between a Group of Subjects and an Adaptive Automaton to produce a Self-Organising System for Decision-Making" in the symposium *Self-Organising Systems, 1962*, ed. Jovits, Jacobi and Goldstein (Spartan Books).

3 See Stafford Beer: *Cybernetics and Management* (English Universities Press, 1959) pp.123–127, and Gordon Pask: *An Approach to Cybernetics* (Hutchinson 1961).

4 See Richard and Hephzibah Hauser: *The Fraternal Society* (Bodley Head, 1962).

5 See, for example, the paper by Trist on collective contract working in the Durham coalfield quoted by H. Clegg in *A New Approach to Industrial Democracy* (Blackwell 1960) and the discussion of this book by Geoffrey Ostergaard in ANARCHY 2. Note the appearance of new elements of job rotation.

Despite his emphasis on the formal aspects of worker organisation, Melman's analysis (see Note 1) of the worker decision process at Standard's brings out many of the characteristics of a self-organising system: the evolving nature of the process; the difficulty of determining where a particular decision was made; changing dominance; the way in which the cumulative experience of the group changes the frame of reference against which subsequent problems are set for solution. A better idea of the gang system from which this derives can, however, be obtained from Reg Wright's articles in ANARCHY 2 & 8.

6 Beer, *op.cit.* p.21.

7 P.-J. Proudhon: *The General Idea of the Revolution in the Nineteenth Century* (Freedom Press, 1923)

8 Compare also the concluding section of Pask's *An Approach to Cybernetics*, in particular the discussion of a 'biologically organised' factory.

9 Peter Kropotkin: *Anarchism, its Philosophy and Ideal* (Freedom Press, 1895)

0 See, for example J A C Brown: *The Social Psychology of Industry* (Penguin 1954), Ch.2.

1 See Clegg: *A New Approach to Industrial Democracy* and G Ostergaard's discussion in ANARCHY 2

2 See Martin Buber: *Paths in Utopia* (Routledge, 1949).

3 P-J Proudhon: The Theory of Taxation (1861) quoted in Buber *op. cit.*.

*Anarchy 31*                                        *September 1963*

# 5. Primitive societies and social myths

## Kenneth Maddock

IN THIS paper I wish to discuss the relation between the future societies visualized by anarchist and communist writers, and the nature of social existence in primitive societies. In doing so I will hold up to scrutiny those aspects of life in primitive society which anthropologists and utopian thinkers have referred to by such terms as "ordered anarchy" and "primitive communism". My premise is that a social existence which is either anarchic or communistic has been realized only in such societies. As an American anthropologist, Leslie White, stresses, it is only here that liberty, equality and fraternity have been realized. In stepping toward civilization we have stepped away from liberty, equality and fraternity.

In speaking, therefore, of the "withering away of the state" and the ushering of a society based on the principle "to each according to his need, from each according to his ability", anarchist and communist writers are projecting into the future a form of social existence, the like of which has been approximated to only in the past. (By the past, I mean the social or cultural, rather than the chronological past, for in historical times primitive societies have functioned despite the rise of civilization, and some still exist today.)

I am further going to suggest to you that talk of the withering away of the state and the ushering in of a society based on the principle "to each according to his need, from each according to his ability", can be regarded as a social mythology, a mythology for radicals and revolutionaries. The social myths are not a set of propositions predicting what life will be like in some future time, but can more fruitfully be regarded as a critique of present society. They are a spur to action in the present.

I now propose to take a look at those aspects of primitive society which are anarchic or communistic. In what ways are they anarchic? In what ways are they communistic? And what do I mean by a primitive society?

When classifying certain societies as primitive, anthropologists have in mind such characteristics as non-literacy, simple technology, small size, lack of specialization and importance of kinship in determining social relations. Why is it that some societies have not reduced their language to writing? Why do they lack specialization? One useful way of explaining these characteristics is to introduce the concept of energy. Societies are primitive when they harness only a small quantity of energy *per capita*. One thinks of the Eskimos and Australian aborigines, who are virtually dependent on human energy alone. The domestication of animals and cultivation of plants lays the foundation for the transition from primitive society to civilization, through greatly increasing quantities of energy *per capita*. The social consequences include surplus production, specialization, growth of population, dominant and subordinate classes and ultimately cities, nations and empires. This is the Agricultural Revolution.

The transition from primitive to civilized life is also a transition from a social existence in which liberty, equality and fraternity are realized, or approximated to, to one in which these values are absent or attenuated. Because the quantities of energy harnessed are low in the primitive societies their life is necessarily characterized by many features which are anarchic or communistic.

In delineating primitive anarchy I can do no better than to begin with the wonderfully anarchic Nuer, a pastoral people living in the southern Sudan, who were studied by the Oxford anthropologist, E.E. Evans-Pritchard. He described them as living in "ordered anarchy" (Evans-Pritchard 1940: 181), without law in any strict sense of the word, and without government.

How does their social system, lacking law and government, work? The Nuer are divided into tribes, each of which segments according to circumstance into smaller and still smaller sections. Thus the Lou tribe segments into the Mor and Gun primary sections. Gun segments into Rumjok and Gaathal secondary sections. Gaathal segments into Leng and Nyarkwas tertiary sections. The tertiary sections, in turn, segment into village communities, the smallest political units of Nuerland. And every tribe segments in the way I have described for Lou. Each tribal section has many of the characteristics of the tribe itself: thus a segment, any segment, compares to the tribe in that it has a name, is infused with a common sentiment, is associated with a territory and is aware of its position in the segmentary system.

Branching through the segmentary political system is a kinship system of clans and lineages, which also operate on the segmentary system. For each order of political segmentation there is a matching order of kinship segmentation. In fact, the two systems are inseparable. The clan, and the segmentary lineages thereof, resemble the tribe and the segmentary sections thereof, in possessing a name, a common sentiment, an association with a territory and an awareness of position in the system as a whole. There is more than one clan in a tribe, and therefore more than one set of lineages, but the Nuer regard one clan and its lineages as dominant. It is this dominant clan, and the lineages thereof, which is associated with the tribe, and the sections thereof. "Dominance", I might add, does not imply for the Nuer any ruler-subject relationship.

The Nuer tribe is defined not only by its distinctive name and so on, but by two other features. One is that it is the largest unit within which feuds are fought and compensation paid for homicide and other torts. The other is that it is the smallest unit to engage in war. In short, disputes within the tribe are settled by the exacting of vengeance or the payment of bloodwealth; disputes outside the tribe can be settled only by war.

I have sketched out some of the structural principles on which this anarchic social system is based. How does it cohere?

Because the system is segmentary it involves a balance of alliances and oppositions between the parts, one of the effects of which is to maintain the whole. Thus, within a tribe, two village communities of the same tertiary section may be in opposition, but, if either is threatened by a village of another tertiary section, they will both join in alliance against the new danger. An endless process of fission and fusion takes place at all levels of segmentation. The tribal segments combine, split away and recombine in pursuit of their various ends. The fact that parts aligned against one another on one occasion are aligned with one another on other occasions has an overall unifying effect on the whole.

The tribe is also unified by the cross-cutting kinship bonds between the tribal segments. Because the clans are exogamous a man must take his wife from some other clan. This gives him kin in clans other than his own, and the presence of such kin in other villages, other tertiary sections, other secondary and primary sections, inhibits too great a development of hostility between segments within the tribe. Moreover, not all the members of the dominant clan or lineage live in the political section associated with it; they live perhaps in adjacent areas and this, too, inhibits hostility. Indeed, Evans-Pritchard likens these cross-cutting kinship ties to elastic bands which stretch apart in time of injury by one man to another, but eventually pull the opposed segments together.

Ritual beliefs are another mechanism of integration. Members of groups between which there is a blood feud cannot eat or drink together. Social relations are severed. This is a further incentive to heal the breach by pressing the injured party to accept compensation, instead of seeking vengeance.

Finally, we must note the ecology of the Nuer. They are a pastoral people and migrate each dry season from their villages inland to rivers and other watering places. Because they must cross the territory of other Nuer groups, whether of the same tribe or not, there is an incentive imposed by ecological conditions to keep the peace, at least to some degree.

No account of the Nuer social system would be complete without a glimpse of the people themselves:

> The lack of governmental organs among the Nuer, the absence of legal institutions, of developed leadership, and, generally, of organized political life is remarkable. The ordered anarchy in which they live accords well with their character, for it is impossible to live among Nuer and conceive of rulers ruling over them.
>
> The Nuer is a product of a hard and egalitarian upbringing, is deeply democratic, and is easily roused to violence. His turbulent spirit finds any restraint irksome and no man recognizes a superior. Wealth makes no difference... Birth makes no difference...
>
> That every Nuer considers himself as good as his neighbour is evident in their every movement. They strut about like lords of the earth, which, indeed, they consider themselves to be. There is no master and no servant in their society, but only equals who regard themselves as God's noblest creation. Among themselves even the suspicion of an order riles a man, and he either does not carry it out or he carries it out in a casual and dilatory manner that is more insulting than a refusal. (Evans-Pritchard, 1940: 181–2).

The Nuer are aware of the difference in spirit between themselves and neighbouring peoples whose social systems are governmental. Thus, in speaking of the Shilluk, one Nuer told Evans-Pritchard:

> They have one big chief, but we have not. This chief can send for a man and demand a cow or he can cut a man's throat. Whoever saw a Nuer do such a thing? What Nuer ever came when some one sent for him or paid any one a cow? (Evans-Pritchard, 1940:182)

In passing from the Nuer to the Shilluk we are passing from primitive anarchy to the servile state.

I wish now to describe the social system of a quite different, though still anarchic, people – the Land Dayaks of Sarawak in Borneo. Like the Nuer, the Land Dayaks live in villages. But, unlike the Nuer, they lack a segmentary system to unite the villages in larger and still larger units. Instead, each village is economically, politically and ritually autonomous, though there may be ties with one or two neighbouring villages which were once parts of the same settlement.

Each village has a headman, chosen for his possession of qualities of the kind valued by the Land Dayaks. His powers are very limited, and, indeed, he may not have existed at all in pre-colonial times. He certainly does not dominate the village:

> It must be remembered that we are dealing with a society of democrats, if not anarchists. The small boy scarcely hesitates to tell a headman if he thinks he has made a mistake, and criticism by his adult equals at village meetings is often forthright. He must labour on his own behalf like the poorest man in the village. Any attempts to maintain a superior dignity would be laughed down. (Geddes 1954: 51)

In reading this passage I am reminded of the relation between pupils and staff, including headmaster, at A S Neill's famous school, Summerhill. The non-coercive and non-authoritarian character of social life is striking:

> Every man is to some extent a chief, and instructs others, even including the headman, what to do, but no notice other than a retort is taken of such commands unless they express what the person is going to do in any case, or show him a more pleasing way of doing it. (Geddes 1954: 51)

The Nuer are fierce individualists. The Land Dayaks are gentle individualists, timid and peaceful folk among whom violence is so rare as to be practically non-existent. How, then, do they settle disputes? There are three means for this.

In the first place, the offended party may himself assess a fine and impose it on the wrongdoer. Such fines are usually paid. If this delightfully simple and harmonious means fails to work, then the matter may be referred to the headman. He arranges a time for a hearing, at which he sits with some elders and anyone else who cares to participate. The proceedings are quite informal, and resemble a public debate rather than a law suit. The headman is guided to his verdict by the tenor of opinion expressed, and only in fixing the penalty does he exercise much personal initiative, though even here the views of other people count. The third means of settling a dispute is to refer it to authorities at a level higher than the village headman. This, however, seldom occurs.

A Nuer relies for what is his due not on force, or the threat of it. With the Land Dayaks force is not a sanction, Instead, there is the fear of punishment by demons. And there is shame, resulting from loss of public esteem, which a person experiences when he knows that others are aware of his act and regard it as unworthy. This is the strongest sanction of all, and may even drive a wrongdoer out of the community altogether. Finally, there is a belief that demons will punish those who do not receive what is their due. Thus, if a wrongdoer is fined but fails to pay, the offended party is in danger of injury from demons. The wrongdoer now faces even stronger public disapproval, for the demonic injury has been added to the original one.

From my description of the Nuer and Land Dayaks it can be seen that, if not actually living in anarchy, they are as close to it as social existence could be. And this anarchic way of life is widespread in the primitive world, wherever the quantity of energy harnessed is too low to produce large societies, centralized and stratified.

The term "ordered anarchy", initiated, I think, by Evans-Pritchard, has now become quite commonplace among students of the stateless societies, but "primitive communism" can be used only at some peril. Why it should be held in such odium can be briefly explained. The standard objections are that it is ambiguous, for communism means all things to all people, has emotional undertones and is misleading, for it blurs the network of clan, family, individual and other rights which are found in all primitive societies.

What these critics overlook, however, are the qualitative differences between primitive and civilized societies. In contrast to the latter, the former are characterized by a high development of co-operation and mutual aid in social and economic life. Members of the group enjoy free access to the resources of nature, and society is not divided into antagonistic classes. It is to qualities of this kind that the proponents of primitive communism were drawing attention. The best of them never denied the existence of group and individual rights; indeed, it is hard to see what these have to do with the issue. One of the principles underlying social and economic life in the primitive societies is *reciprocity* , according to which a person who receives some benefit now is obligated to return an equivalent at a later date. In what way is this inconsistent with communism'? I would say that it is inseparable from any system of mutual aid. *Mutual Aid* was, of course, the title of Kropotkin's most famous book, and it is interesting to note how frequently this term crops up in anthropological monographs, though Kropotkin is never mentioned.

At least some of the opposition to the concept of primitive communism arises on other grounds. Engels borrowed the term from Lewis Henry Morgan for his *The Origin of the Family, Private Property and the State*, and the concept entered the armoury of communist thinkers. This, together with the dogmatic and vituperative spirit in which Marxists defend certain otherwise useful ideas, is probably an incentive to non-Marxists to drop it themselves. Nor, though, should we forget White's apt comment on opponents of the concept: "It would appear that an attempt was being made to 'make the world safe for private property'". (White 1959: 256)

I would now like to look quickly at some aspects of Nuer and Land Dayak economy. Each Nuer tribe and section thereof has its own pastures and water supplies, freely available to its members. The cattle, which are the pride of every Nuer, are owned in family herds over which the head of the household has rights of disposal while still alive. But his wives enjoy rights of use, and each son is entitled to cattle from the herd for his marriage payment. When a daughter marries, the cattle received for her are distributed among a wide number of kin. The small local groups pasture their cattle in common, for individual households are too small to protect and graze their herd alone. The Nuer also grow millet, but questions of land tenue never arise because there is land for everyone. A man may cultivate the ground behind his homestead, unless someone else is already using it, and unused land outside the village is freely available to all.

Each Nuer household owns its own food, but Nuer eat in one another's homes to so great an extent that, in effect, the community is sharing in a common supply. Hospitality and the rules for distribution of meat and fish ensure that available supplies are widely distributed. The Nuer do tend to suffer from food shortages, but this does not result in satiation and hunger existing side by side, as in more civilized communities. Instead, it gives rise to "share and share alike...since everybody is thereby insured against hunger. He who is in need today receives help from him who may be in need tomorrow" (Evans-Pritchard 1940: 85).

With the Land Dayaks, also, there is no shortage of land and anyone may clear jungle to establish a paddy field. While the person who cleared the field is still alive, he enjoys individual tenure but after death his rights pass to all his descendants. Fortunately, people tend to forget many of their claims; if they did not the system would become very cumbersome. How does a man go about using a field cleared by one of his ancestors? If none of those who share rights in it object, he is free to use it. If someone does object, then there are two simple rules to determine who has the best claim. First, the rule of least use, by which the claimant who has made least use of the land recently has the right. Secondly, superior right of the older claimant where both are descended from the person who last used the field. This rule can be interpreted as an extension of the first, since the older a person is, relative to other claimants, the less his opportunity of farming the land before death.

The Land Dayaks work their land in groups recruited according to a complex labour exchange system based on the reciprocity to which I referred earlier. A man seeks the aid of friends, kinsmen and neighbours in working his fields, and owes each a day's labour for each day each of them puts in on his field. Usually the labour groups so recruited are larger than efficiency dictates, but this is more than offset by the value the people place on working in company with others.

When a party goes hunting or fishing, an equal distribution is made among its members, whatever their roles. Geddes interprets equal distribution as a manifestation of extreme individualism, not of primitive communism, for each is reluctant to give more than he himself receives (Geddes 1954: 90). Be that as it may, the Land Dayaks do have marked uncommunistic features, manifested, for instance, in their practice of usury. Shortages of food are remedied among the Nuer by mutual aid, among the Land Dayaks by usury.

From my description of the Nuer and Land Dayaks it can be seen that, whether or not living in primitive communism, their life is characterized to a high degree by co-operation and mutual aid, reciprocity and free access to nature. And these qualities are true also of other primitive societies. In summing up the anarchic and communistic features of primitive societies I can do no better than quote Leslie White:

> The type of social system developed during the human-energy era was unquestionably the most satisfying kind of social environment that man has ever lived in. By this we mean that the institutions of primitive society were the most compatible with the needs and desires of the human primate, the most congenial to his nature and temperament. In primitive society all men were brothers, or kinsmen. All were free. Everyone had free access to the resources of nature. And all were equal; no one held another in servitude or bondage. Mutual aid characterized these primitive societies. Production was carried on for use, and human rights and welfare were placed above property rights and institutions. (White 1959: 367)

Now what is interesting about this passage is that it could almost be drawn from a description by an anarchist or communist writer of life in the future utopia, when the state has been abolished or has withered away. I wish therefore to look at the kind of society envisaged by these writers.

William Godwin, perhaps the earliest of systematic anarchist thinkers, drew a distinction between society and government. The former is produced by our wants, men associating for the sake of mutual assistance. The latter is the product of our wickedness and is, at best, a necessary evil. When men apply the supreme law of human existence, which is the general welfare, there will be no state. Instead, matters affecting the general good will be the subject of deliberations in which all will be free to participate. Property is to be abolished, and goods distributed according to need. Godwin is one of those thinkers whom it is fashionable to dismiss as utopian. Certainly, he laid down no convincing strategy for realizing the goals he proclaimed. Let us turn, therefore, to anarchists who thought they understood the paths to the future.

Bakunin and Kropotkin were both evolutionists, which is not surprising considering the climate of progressive opinion in their day. For Bakunin, mankind is evolving from a less perfect to a more perfect existence; from bestial to human existence. For Kropotkin, there is a process of transformation from a less happy to a more happy form of existence. Both conveniently regard those aspects of society of which they disapprove as products of an early stage of evolution. Thus the state and enacted law will pass, for both are now retarding the evolutionary process. Bakunin sees private property in capital goods as also belonging to a low evolutionary stage, but private property in consumer goods will remain. For Kropotkin, however, future society will be communistic, with the joint property freely available for use by all. Men will live in free association without the state, says Kropotkin. Men will achieve complete humanity only when living together in a society without the state, says Bakunin. This is the direction in which human society is growing, but both advocate revolution to supplement the slower evolutionary process. Indeed, as Kropotkin rather nicely says, revolution is accelerated evolution (see Eltzbacher 1960 for the anarchists referred to).

Now for the communists. Marx and Engels share an evolutionary perspective with the contemporary anarchists, and both are also in favour of revolution to remove obstacles in the path of mankind's progress onward. The state has not always existed, for there have been societies without it. Instead, economic development, producing a cleavage of society into classes, necessitated the state form. The continuation of economic development will, one day, make these classes a hindrance to production, just as once it had called them into being. When this happens the state will wither, giving way to "an association, in which the free development of each is the condition for the free development of all" (Marx and Engels 1958: Vol i, 54). In this new form of social existence, "the government of persons is replaced by the administration of things"(Engels. 1958: Vol. ii, 151).

Future utopian society bears a close resemblance to past primitive society. The evolutionary process will return man to a form of social existence like that from which it has taken him, though technology and scientific knowledge will have been greatly advanced in the intervening ages. The simple technology of primitive peoples necessitated a way of life which was anarchic and communistic in many aspects; the tremendously powerful technology of the future will also necessitate such a life. I am not suggesting that the utopias are simply mirror images of primitive social existence; they *are* different, but only in degree, not in kind:

> Democracy in government, brotherhood in society, equality in rights and privileges, and universal education, foreshadow the next higher plane of society to which experience, intelligence and knowledge are steadily tending. It will be a revival, in a higher form, of the liberty, equality and fraternity of the ancient gentes.

Engels approvingly quotes this passage from Morgan's *Ancient Society* at the end of his *The Origin of the Family, Private Property and the State*. It is an attractive vision, and one which has intoxicated the imagination of radicals and revolutionaries.

The kind of historical perspective held by Bakunin and Kropotkin and Marx and Engels is still officially adhered to in Russia. In the latest textbook the withering away of the state and the ushering in of a society based on the principle "to each according to his need, from each according to his ability" is affirmed. Moreover, "Communism is the most just social system. It will fully realise the principles of equality and freedom, ensure the development of the human personality and turn society into a harmonious association, a commonwealth of men of labour" (Kuusinen: 866).

At the beginning of this paper I suggested that the utopian predictions of anarchist and communist writers are social myths, whose usefulness depends on their capacity to spur men to action in the here and now. Far from foreshadowing the future, these myths reflect the past of mankind. The Left "sucks its life from utopia", says Nicolas Walter. Fair enough, but the utopias suck whatever reality they have from the primitive world. How do the social myths stimulate action? They hold up an attractive prospect toward which history can be steered, though it would arrive there in any case. Man has fallen from liberty, equality and fraternity, but he can be redeemed. The social myths, as we have seen, are accompanied by schemes of action, some more practicable than others. The prospect of redemption inspires the believers to get these schemes under way. Revolutions and general strikes and awakening the working class to a consciousness of its historic mission, may be viewed, according to taste, as the birthpangs of a new society or as essential steps towards it.

Whatever Bakunin and Kropotkin, Marx and Engels may have thought, whatever utopian socialists and scientific socialists may suppose, the social myths are not scientific hypotheses. But implicit in my chain of argument is the notion that at one point the social myths do run parallel to scientific hypotheses. But implicit in my chain of argument is the notion that at one point the social myths do run parallel to scientific hypotheses: just as one test of the usefulness of a scientific hypothesis is the fruitfulness of the research it stimulates, so, too, I am arguing, one test of the usefulness of a social myth is the fruitfulness of the action it stimulates. We need no reminding of the many beneficent changes brought about in our society through the striving of reformers and revolutionaries, whether proletarian or bourgeois.

The social myths are not merely reflections of the primitive past. They are also reverse reflections of the present. We can appreciate this better by considering the nature of myth. Since Malinowski, anthropologists, to use Firth's words, have ceased to regard myths as "descriptive embryonic records of the past, or as simple intellectual products" (Firth 1961: 5). The interpretation of myths is a sociological one. The myths of a society are ideologies which can be related point by point to the existing political system, as Nadel has demonstrated for the Kede of Nigeria and Firth for the Tikopia. Variations in ideology within the one society can, as Firth has shown, be related to the variations in power and influence of different factions.

Accepting this interpretation, we can regard the social myths, not as descriptive embryonic records of the future, or as simple intellectual products, but as reverse reflections of present sociological reality. Not straight reflections, mark you, but reverse reflections which mirror the qualities absent or attenuated in our society. In a primitive society liberty, equality and fraternity are real; with us they are aspirations. Just as utopian constructs may be interpreted as a turning back toward the primitive past, so, too, may they be interpreted as a turning away from the civilised present. Indeed, the words Marx applied to religious myths can appositely be applied to utopian myths, including his own:

> Religious distress is at the same time the expression of real distress and the protest against real distress. Religion is the sigh of the oppressed creature, the heart of a heartless world, just as it is the spirit of a spiritless situation. It is the opium of the people. (Marx and Engels 1957: 42).

There is only one point at which we must disagree with Marx's formulation. Utopian myths are not opium-like, though I suppose they could begin to play that function when the utopians win power in a country, as in Russia, for instance. Instead, as Lasswell and Kaplan put it, in their *Power and Society*, "The *ideology* is the political myth functioning to preserve the social structure; the *utopia* to supplant it."

But if utopias *do* turn toward the past to find a model of future society, if they *do* reflect the human values absent in the present, and if they *do* turn toward the future in revulsion from the present, then acceptance of the views I am expressing here would be intolerable for many of the radical and revolutionary spirits to whom utopia has beckoned. My views would be intolerable precisely because that which they are hoping to build away from is intolerable. Thus the myth of the general strike will persist for anarcho-syndicalists, the myth of the withering away of the state for communists and, one might add, the myth of a hereafter for the religious.

In conclusion it seems worthwhile to glance at the prospect for those who, while conceding the utility of social myths for the weaker brethren, prefer an attitude which is tough-minded, bloody-minded... and realistic.

Bakunin, in a quotation by George Molnar which I have been unable to find, once proclaimed that "to think of the future is criminal." Kropotkin interpreted the history of our civilization as a conflict between two opposed tendencies, "the authoritarian tradition and the libertarian tradition." Realistically, he added that "Between these two currents, always alive, always struggling in humanity... our choice is made" (Kropotkin 1946: 43). As we applaud Bakunin and Kropotkin for their sentiments, so, too, we may agree with them in their tough-minded moments. And with Zamyatin, when he proclaims infinite revolution, terrible and unending and inevitable.

Plumbing the primitive past and the utopian future leaves us with the present. We have seen that the anarchic and communistic aspects of the past, necessitated by low levels of energy harnessed, have been caught up into social myths and projected into the future, supposedly as descriptions of what the future would be for those living in it. And the myths are reverse reflections, critiques, of the present, for the qualities they mirror from the past are precisely those qualities lacking in the present. We have seen, too, that the myths may have a certain utility in spurring men on to action. For the tough-minded, however, there is an alternative philosophy:

> ...we can take freedom as a character, not of societies as a whole but of certain groups, institutions and people's ways of life within any socie-

ty, and even then not as their exclusive character. Equally, on this view, piecemeal freedoms will always meet with opposition and those who are caught up in them will resist conformist pressures. The "permanent protest" implied by this is carried on without the promise of final triumph but in a spirit of "distrusting you masters and distrusting you emancipators", and with no intention of wanting to make the world safe for freedom. (Molnar 1958: 16)

I am not as pessimistic as Molnar, for I think that here and there we can take some faltering steps in the direction of liberty, equality and fraternity, the great triad extolled by Morgan and White in the primitive world. But we are living in the present, and *to think of the future is criminal*.

# References

Eltzbacher, Paul (1960 edition), *Anarchism*, London: Freedom Press.
Evans-Pritchard, E.E. (1940), *The Nuer*, London: OUP.
Firth, Raymond (1961), *History and Traditions of Tikopia*, Wellington (N.Z.): Polynesian Society.
Geddes, W.R. (1954), *The Land Dayaks of Sarawak*, London: HMSO.
Kropotkin, Peter (1946 edition), *The State, its Historic Role*, London: Freedom Press.
Kuusinen, O.W. (ed.) (no date), *Fundamentals of Marxism-Leninism*, Moscow: Foreign Languages Publishing House.
Marx, Karl and Engels, Frederick (1957). *On Religion*, Moscow: FLPH.
Marx, Karl and Engels, Frederick (1985), *Selected Works*, 2 vols, Moscow: FLPH.
Molnar, George (1958), "Anarchy and Utopia", *University Libertarian*, No. 5.
White, Leslie A. (1959), *The Evolution of Culture*, New York: McGraw-Hill.

# 6. Not any power: reflections on decentralisation

## George Woodcock

I WAS asked to write on decentralism in history, and I find myself looking into shadows where small lights shine as fireflies do, endure a little, vanish, and then reappear like Auden's messages of the just. The history of decentralism has to be written largely in negative, in winters and twilights as well as springs and dawns, for it is a history which, like that of libertarian beliefs in general, is not to be observed in progressive terms. It is not the history of a movement, an evolution. It is the history of something that, like grass, has been with us from the human beginning, something that may go to earth, like bulbs in winter, and yet be there always, in the dark soil of human society, to break forth in unexpected places and at undisciplined times.

Palaeolithic man, food-gatherer and hunter, was a decentralist by necessity, because the earth did not provide enough wild food to allow crowding, and in modern remotenesses that were too wild or unproductive for civilised men to penetrate, men still lived until very recently in primitive decentralisation: Australian aborigines, Papuan inland villagers, Eskimos in far northern Canada. Such men developed, before history touched them, their own complex techniques and cultures to defend a primitive and precarious way of life; they often developed remarkable artistic traditions as well, such as those of the Indians of the Pacific rain forest and some groups of Eskimos. But, since their world was one where concentration meant scarcity and death, they did not develop a political life that allowed the formation of authoritarian structures nor did they make an institution out of war. They practised mutual aid for survival, but this did not make them angels; they practised infanticide and the abandonment of elders for the same reason.

I think with feeling of those recently living decentralist societies because I have just returned from the Canadian Arctic where the last phase of traditional Eskimo life began as recently as a decade ago. Now, the old nomadic society, in which people moved about in extended families rather than tribes, is at an end, with all its skills abandoned, its traditions, songs and dances fading in the memory. Last year the cariboo-hunting Eskimos probably built their last igloo; now they are herded together into communities ruled by white men, where they live in groups of four to six hundred people, in imitation white men's houses and with guaranteed welfare hand-outs when they cannot earn money by summer construction work. Their children are being taught by people who know no Eskimo, their young men are losing the skills of the hunt; power élites are beginning to appear in their crowded little northern slums, among a people who never knew what power meant, and the diminishing dog teams (now less than one family in four owns dogs and only about one family in twenty goes on extended hunting or trapping journeys) are symbolic of the loss of freedom among a people who have become physically and mentally dependent on the centralised, bureaucrat-ridden world which the Canadian Government has built since it set out a few years ago to rescue the peoples of the North from "barbarism" and insecurity.

The fate of the Eskimos, and that of so many other primitive cultures during the past quarter of a century, shows that the old, primal decentralism of Stone Age man is doomed even when it has survived into the modern world. From now on, man will be decentralist by intent and experience, because he has known the evils of centralisation and rejected them.

Centralisation began when men settled on the land and culti-vated it. Farmers joined together to protect their herds and fields from the other men who still remained nomadic wanderers; to con-serve and share out the precious waters; to placate the deities who held the gifts of fertility, the priests who served the deities, and the kings who later usurped the roles of priest and god alike. The little realms of local priest-kings grew into the great valley empires of Egypt and Mesopotamia, and overtowering these emerged the first attempt at a world empire, that of the Achaemenian Kings of Per-sia, who established an administrative colossus which was the pro-totype of the centralised state imitated by the despots of Northern India, the Hellenistic god-kings and the divine Caesars of Rome.

We have little knowledge how men clung to their local loyalties and personal lives, how simple people tried to keep control of the affairs and things that concerned them most, in that age when writ-ing recorded the deeds of kings and priests and had little to say about common men. But if we can judge from the highly traditional and at least partly autonomous village societies which still existed in India when the Moghuls arrived, and which had probably survived the centuries of political chaos and strife that lay between Moghuls and Guptas, it seems likely that the farther men in those ages lived away from the centres of powers, the more they established and defended rights to use the land and govern their own local affairs, so long as the lord's tribute was paid. It was, after all, on the village communities and village councils that had survived through native and Moghul and British empires that Gandhi based his hopes of *panchayat raj*, a society based on autonomous peasant communes.

In Europe the Dark Ages after the Roman Empire were regarded by Victorian historians as a historical waste land ravaged by barbarian hordes and baronial bandits. But these ages were also in fact an interlude during which , in the absence of powerful centralised authorities, the decentralist urge appeared again, and village communes established forms of autonomy which, in remoter areas, like the Pyrenees, the Alps and the Apennines, have survived into the present. To the same "Dark" Ages belong the earliest free city republics of mediaeval Europe, which arose at first for mutual protection in the ages of disorder, and which in Italy and Germany remained for centuries the homes of European learning and art and of such freedom as existed in the world of their time. Out of such village communes and such cities arose, in Switzerland, the world's first political federation, based on the shared protection of local freedoms against feudal monarchs and renaissance despots.

Some of these ancient communes exist to this day; the Swiss Canton of Appenzell still acts as a direct democracy in which every citizen takes part in the annual voting on laws; the Italian city state of San Marino still retains its mountaintop independence in a world of great states. But these are rare survivals, due mainly to geographic inaccessibility in the days before modern transport. As national states began to form at the end of the Middle Ages, the attack on decentralism was led not merely by the monarchs and dictators who established highly organised states like Bourbon France and Cromwellian England, but also by the Church and particularly by the larger monastic orders, who in their houses established rules of uniform behaviour and rigid timekeeping that anticipated the next great assault on local and independent freedom, and on the practice of mutual aid; this happened when the villages of Britain and later of other European countries were depopulated in the Agricultural Revolution of the eighteenth century, and their homeless people drifted into the disciplined factories and suffered the alienation produced by the new industrial towns, where all traditional bonds were broken and all the participation in common works that belonged to the mediaeval villages became irrelevant.

It was these developments, the establishment of the centralised state in the seventeenth century and of industrial centralisation in the eighteenth and nineteenth centuries, that made men for the first time consciously aware of the necessity of decentralism to save them from the soulless world that was developing around them.

Against Cromwell's military state, Gerrard Winstanley and the original Diggers opposed their idea and practice of establishing new communes of landworkers on the waste lands of England, communes which would renounce overlords and extend participation and equality to men, women, and even children.

When the French Revolution took the way of centralism, establishing a more rigidly bureaucratic state than the Bourbons and introducing universal conscription for the first time, men like Jacques Roux and his fellow *enragés* protested in the name of the local communes of Paris, which they regarded as the bases of democratic administration, and at the same time in England William Godwin, the first of the philosophic anarchists, recognised the perils of forms of government which left decision-making in the hands of men gathered at the top and centre of society. In his *Political Justice* Godwin envisaged countries in which assemblies of delegates would meet – seldom – to discuss matters of urgent common concern, in which no permanent organs of central government would be allowed to continue, and in which each local parish would decide its own affairs by free agreement (and not by majority vote) and matters of dispute would be settled by *ad hoc* juries of arbitration.

The British and French Utopian socialists of the early nineteenth century, as distinct from the Marxists and the revolutionary socialists led by August Blanqui, were inspired by their revulsion against monolithic industrial and political organisation to base the realisation of their theories on small communal units which they believed could be established even before the existing society had been destroyed. At that period the American frontier lay still in the valley of the Mississippi, and there was a tendency – which existed until the end of the pioneering days – for the small pioneer societies of trappers and traders, miners and farmers, to organise themselves in largely autonomous communities that managed their own affairs and in many senses of the word took the law into their own hands. In this society, where men responded to frontier conditions by *ad hoc* participatory and decentralist organisation, the European and American Utopian socialists, as well as various groups of Christian communities, tried to set up self-governing communes which would be the cells of the new fraternal world. The followers of Cabet and Fourier, of Robert Owen and Josiah Warren, all played their part in a movement which produced hundreds of communities and lasted almost a century; its last wave ebbed on the Pacific coast in the Edwardian era, when a large Finnish socialist community was established on the remote island of Sointula off the coast of British Columbia. Only the religious communities of this era, which had a purpose outside mere social theory, survived; even today the Mennonite communities of Canada keep so closely to their ideals of communitarian autonomy that they are leaving the country to find in South America a region where they can be free to educate their children as they wish. The secular communities all vanished; the main lesson their failure taught was that decentralist organisation must reach down to the roots of the present, to the needs of the actual human beings who participate, and not upward into the collapsing dream stuctures of a Utopian future.

Other great crises in the human situation have followed the industrial revolution, and every one has produced its decentralist movements in which men and women have turned away from the nightmares of megapolitics to the radical realities of human relationships. The crisis of the Indian struggle for independence caused Gandhi to preach the need to build society upon the foundation of the village. The bitter repressions of Tsarist Russia led Peter Kropotkin to develop his theories of a decentralised society integrating industry and agriculture, manual and mental skills. World War II led to considerable community movement among both British and American pacifists, seeking to create cells of sane living in the interstices of a belligerent world, and an even larger movement of decentralism and communitarianism has arisen in North America in contradiction to the society that can wage a war like that in Vietnam. Today it is likely that more people than ever before are consciously engaged in some kind of decentralist venture which expresses not merely rebellion against monolithic authoritarianism, but also faith in the possibility of a new, cellular kind of society in which at every level the participation in decision-making envisaged by nineteenth century anarchists like Proudhon and Kropotkin will be developed.

As the monstrous and fatal flaws of modern economic and political centralism become more evident, as the State is revealed ever more convincingly as the enemy of all human love, the advocacy and practice of decentralism will spread more widely and on an ever-wider scale, if only because the necessity for it will become constantly more urgent. The less decentralist action is tied to rigid social and political theories, and particularly to antediluvian ones like those of the Marxists, the more penetrating, and durable its effects are likely to be. The soils most favourable to the spread of decentralism are probably countries like India, where rural living still predominates, countries like Japan where the decentralisation of factories and the integration of agricultural and industrial economies has already been recognised as a necessity for survival, and the places in our western world where the social rot has run deepest and the decentralists can penetrate like white ants. The moribund centres of the cities; the decaying marginal farmlands; these are the places which centralist governments using bankers' criteria of efficiency cannot possibly revivify, because the profit would be not financial but human. In such areas the small and flexible cell of workers, serving the needs of local people, can survive and continue simultaneously the tasks of quiet destruction and cellular building. But not all the work can be done in the shadows. there will still be the need for theoreticians to carry on the work which Kropotkin and Geddes and Mumford began in the past, of demonstrating the ultimately self-destructive character of political and industrial centralism and showing how society as a whole, and not merely the lost corners of it, can be brought back to health and peace by breaking down the pyramids of authority so that men can be given to eat the bread of brotherly love, and not the stones of power – of any power.

*Anarchy 104*                                        *October 1969*

# II.  EXPERIENCES

## 1.  Poor people
### Alan Sillitoe

I ONCE knew an American writer in Majorca who, over a bottle of gin and a dish of spiced snails, smoking a two-peseta cigar, would lean back contentedly in his chair after finishing his work in the evening, and exclaim: "Ah! I wonder what the poor are doing tonight?" I didn't try to tell him, because I was poor myself. In any case, he didn't really want to know, because he was joking, and because he also had been poor.

In England there are half a million people out of work, and ten times that number living in real poverty, what I would call below the telly-line, as well as below the bread-line. The gap between the very poor and the normal rich is wider than it has ever been. The adults of these five or six million people form part of those twenty-three per cent who regularly never bother to vote at a general election.

Voting can never make any difference to their plight. It would take too long. They want to get out of it now, this minute, this week at the most. When you live from day to day, how can you believe anyone who says he will alter things in a few years? The years ahead are an empty desert, without landmarks of any kind, beyond the imagination. Poor people live in the present.

The poor lack manoeuvrability. Without money you are born and die in the same place. To travel presents difficulties that are rarely overcome. You are tied at the ankle, and cannot stray beyond a certain distance from the roots of your poverty. The advantage of this is that you become familiar with the environs of your sleeping place, and there may be a chance of living off the land.

Your world becomes small, intense and real. Your senses are sharpened but, strangely enough, this doesn't necessarily mean an increase in intelligence, or the ability to act. Intelligence is often stunted in the fight for order and food. A near-cretin, mustering energy in order to survive, may present a dextrous visage to the better-off, who imagine he must be cunning to survive at all on so little.

The very poor are too busy surviving to want to get on. To get on is something often dinned into them, handed down by the culture beneath which they exist. They are unable to take advantage of it, for to reach next week with clothes on your back, food still on the table, and enough life in your brain to face another week is the most they can do.

The rich, or normally well-off, cannot imagine how much an achievement this in fact is. The rich can accuse them of fecklessness, lack of thrift (qualities that the rich dare not enjoy if they want to stay where they are) but the greatest virtue of the poor is that they have learned how to survive without disturbing the rich.

Apart from the natural failings found in people of any class, they are where they are because of the lack of opportunity to develop intelligence or learn skill. Their life is maintained by patience, tenacity, scepticism and pride. This quality of survival is one that the better-off have forgotten how to use because they do not need it any more: to keep what they already have demands a different mental process.

Films on the telly, or at the cinema, giving examples of people who, one way or another, got on through personal striving, are enjoyed for the story, but believed only as a fairy tale is. That, they say, is not for the likes of us. In a way they are right. The poor not only know their place (maddening as this may seem to many) but they will go on knowing it until they can get out of it on their own terms.

The poor live in isolation, unreachable by private benevolence, goodness of heart, or sound advice. Poverty is a disease, as incurable as cancer, incurable because the resources of the state are not made to do a great surgical operation.

How can one define a poor person? When I had some money in my pocket I was walking down Holland Road and saw a grey-bearded man in absolute rags lying on a piece of wall. Rain was pouring down. I offered him some money, but he waved me angrily away. I should have known better. The poor either earn money, ask for it, or take it. They have a way of keeping their self-respect, in these forms of getting what they need.

There are degrees of being poor. The most common is that of the man who earns twelve pounds a week and has a couple of children. If he is living in London he may pay four pounds a week for a room, and his wife will be unable to go to work because the children can't be left alone. This is not usually regarded as poverty. In such a room you might find a telly or radio. The man will smoke cigarettes, go to the pictures now and again, drink a pint maybe – all in a small degree, after his rations are secure, sometimes when they are not. Orwell did his nut about the diet of the poor, in *The Road to Wigan Pier*. He would do it again if he were still alive. Not for them the simple wholesome stuff. Frozen-this and processed-that, tinned muck, loaves of sliced, wrapped, steambaked pap, margarine and turnip marmalade, tea, flaky pastries made with axle-grease and saccharine, meat like frozen rope – is what keeps people pale and frantic, and just strong enough to work, or strong enough not to. The womb-sweets and womb-custard (as advertised on telly) keep them close to the umbilical cord of the "deeply satisfying".

If a poor family doesn't throw some of its money away each week on fags and the pictures they may go under quicker than if they do. Their morale cracks, and they end up either in the poor-house or the looney bin. This is a reason for the so-called fecklessness of the poor: a visit to the pictures is often better than a hot dinner.

A poor family cannot always find a room to live in. They may be terrorised and thrown out by someone wanting vacant possession of a house in an area becoming fashionable. Sometimes my eye catches an ad in a newspaper, of a house for sale, and the tagged-on phrase "vacant possession if desired" makes me think of two hundred police and bailiffs ejecting a family recently in St. Stephen's Gardens at four-thirty in the morning after a ten-day siege. A poor person can never be sure, from one week to the next, where he will be living. He has mobility within a wall. To get beyond the wall, into the big wide world, he needs an entrance ticket. That means money, and he knows it. The poor live in a vicious circle, work hard, and pay out so much a week in order to live – an eternal HP so as to get the biggest Bingo prize of all at the end of sixty or seventy years: death in a fine coffin.

There are different kinds of poverty then. First is the never-ending sort, which collapses in death, a poverty in which you were born, and from which you were never able to move. Then there is the poverty of the young man, say, who is to become a writer or painter: poverty from choice. This can be awful and degrading but, whatever he may say, it is a lesser form of evil than poverty. It is a stage to something else. It has compensations.

There is the poverty of the man who has known better days, as they say. This is bad enough, but he knows it is not the only state of living. He knows also that there is a possibility of alteration. At least he has had better days.

The worst poverty of all is that which afflicts the man who is out

of work for a long time, through no fault of his own. This is a
destitution of the spirit as well as a destitution of material means –
the man who wants work yet has to see his children never quite
getting enough to eat, who knows that something could be done
about his situation but is powerless to do anything on his own. Such
a man becomes filled with bitterness.

The poor know of only two classes in society. Their sociology is
much simplified. There are *them* and *us*. Them are those who tell
you what to do, who drive a car, use a different accent, are buying a
house in another district, deal in cheques and not money, pay your
wages, collect rent and telly dues, stop for you now and again at
pedestrian crossings, can't look you in the eye, read the news on
wireless or television, hand you the dole or national assistance
money; the shopkeeper, copper, schoolteacher, doctor, health visitor, the man wearing the white dog-collar. Them are those who
robbed you of your innocence, live on your backs, buy the house
from over your head, eat you up, or tread you down. Above all, the
poor who are not crushed in spirit hate the climbers, the crawlers,
the happy savers, the parsimonious and respectable – like poison.

When there is widespread poverty, people help each other in
order to survive, but when poverty is patchy, uneven, and separated
in its unevenness, they lose faith in unity. They acquire a sense of
guilt, and this is worst of all because it is unnecessary, undeserved,
and undermines even further their self-respect.

It creates a good atmosphere though, as far as action from outside is concerned: the government can ignore it. When many other
people appear to be OK and getting on then the poor can imagine it
is their own fault that they are poor. This accretion of guilt far
outweighs the encouragement they are supposed to get from seeing
people less poor, whose example they are expected to follow because they somehow have managed to eke out a better form of
living.

If a poor person slides his hand onto some counter and pulls
down a bar of chocolate he is dragged into the court and made to pay
a hundred times its value. This is the basis of all justice as they see it.
Is there not, they might ask, enough for everybody if all food were
to be shared out? Enough room for us all to live in? You have to go
on working, of course, work until you drop (that's all right, you
have to work, expect to) but isn't there an abundance that, if shared
out, would be enough for us, for everyone? It takes them a long time
to realise that, while there is enough for the poor, there would not
be enough for the rich. Only those who win a football pool see that.

Their folk heroes are those who try, by brains and daring, to get

some share of the rich man's loot. He is superior to those who get it
on the pools, which means the falling in of mere luck. The idolisa-
tion of Robin Hood went out centuries ago. If it hadn't, would
schoolbooks still tell of him? It never quite rings true to them that
someone should, as an individual act, rob the rich and give to the
poor. That was a way of buying off enough of the poor, who would
prevent those not given anything going straight to the source of
wealth – that only Robin could get at. Robin had an unofficial
monopoly of wealth by being able forcibly to tax the rich. There is a
saying: "Robin Hood? Robbin' bastard, more like". He ended up
becoming one of the king's men.

The poor idolise and idealise those who bring off wage or train
robberies and don't get caught. A patriotic Victoria Cross or
George Medal has nothing on the thrill of reading about this. They
don't expect any of the robbers' loot: the mere act of striking is
enough for them.

A man who takes from those who have more than himself is not a
robber. The word "robber" is applied in all its tragic depth only
when one poor man robs another poor man. If the first factor of
poverty is lack of mobility, the second is powerlessness. There is
nothing you can do about it, except endure and survive. If you can't
help yourself, then don't expect God to do so. If God helps those
who help themselves, then how is it possible for him to be on anybody else's side but the rich? God is a Tory, a landlord, a mil-
lionaire, a magistrate. If he's a worker he's the sort of bastard who
started out with five pounds and made five millions. He did it on his
mates' backs, and wouldn't give them the skin off his nose.

For the desperate, which means those who feel their poverty
most, and deserve it least (if such a thing can be said) there is always
the gas oven. But that is your trump card, a fate you often think
about in order to get yourself over the worst times.

If it is used it is only as a last desperate defence. It is the great
individual act of which you are capable – without asking anybody's
permission except that of your own deepest inner self. You don't
sign for it, you do it of your own free will, to spite either someone
you know, or the world in general, or because there is nothing else
left to do but that – for a thousand reasons. It has a dignity nothing
else has been able to give, and few are able to make this last act of
dignity. It is the final freedom which no-one can take from you,
which depends on you alone.

To me, after saying all this, the poor do not have a common
psychology. That would be an inadmissible statement from a writer. They are all individuals for whom the rich – who form the state –

are responsible. And because the rich can never effectively help the poor (they just don't want to know them) then the only solution is a political system which makes such responsibility not an act of charity but a fundamental principle.

*Anarchy 38*                                                      *April 1964*

# 2.  On refusing

## Personal preface to a handbook on selective trouble-making
## Kingsley Widmer

NOT LONG AGO I spoke at an anti-war rally to a few hundred people under the eucalyptus trees in a Southern California city park. I've been doing that, as part of my obligation of public refusal, whenever asked by student or liberal-left political groups for some years now. Indeed, for more than twenty years, though the opportunities to speak against the American political megalomania were rare until the war in Vietnam reached major scale. As usual, my remarks in the park were brief arguments against the destructive hypocrisies of United States institutions and a plea for resisting them.

Though mostly a recital of what should be obvious, I like to think that I added a few touches of the tangible and sardonic to the usual protest oratory. My reception by the largely youthful audience was politely positive. The next speaker, a black-bereted black militant, started about like this: "Who owns and runs this goddam country? White mother-fuckers! Who kills brown Vietnamese? Who kills black Americans? The same white mother-fuckers! We're gonna make a revolution and take this country away from the white mother-fuckers! When he finished his half-hour black mass on white American mother-fuckerism, he raised his right fist above his head and chanted, with the audience enthusiastically joining in, "Power to the people! Power to the people!" Then an exceptionally well-amplified rock group took up the applause, the beat vibrating even the ancient eucalyptus, and overpowered all mere people in the park.

Peace, brother, but that's not my style. I do not object to the ghetto poetry – the metaphors of sexual violation have always, and quite properly, been central to rebellion – nor do I object to the performance's surreal irrelevance to "peace" since protest actions primarily serve as aesthetic rituals for dissident para-communities. But the racist anti-racism, the resentful populist cry for power, and the muddling of tangible rebellion with pretences to revolution, seem finally repressive. Aggrandizing black mother-fuckers would not necessarily be much improvement over aggrandizing white mother-fuckers. That's just the old politics, again, when we need to de-race and de-power in erasing a whole imposed mode of consciousness.

Underneath the generous rage of my fellow speakers I heard the beat of a parochial and sadly reversible revolutionism. Granted, we should support authentic protest, which this also included, whenever and wherever. Purist political fantasies, whether of bureaucratic reformism, proletarian revolution, or technological and educational magic, subserve even greater moral ambiguities. Yet radical intelligence must also be detachment and I felt that the tone and style the occasion serviced were not sufficiently radical. I also later wryly reflected that I may have gotten through more successfully to the undercover military cop (so identified to me by a reporter) who slyly questioned me after my speech than I did to much of the audience. So: Whose radical am I?

Let me answer with a couple of stories which, I ruefully note, must partake of history since for an American radical these days I am old – not only paunchy and suburbanized but necessarily responsive to an accumulated reality. After all, it has been a generation since I first bit the bullet of social bitterness as a field hand and factory worker, as an infantry soldier and prison convict, as a de-classé and dissident. But the ancient radicalism I would affirm has less to do with political "generations" – that ideological sleight of hand to reduce the critical to the merely chronological or a fleeting biology of discontent – than with the persistent refusal of a false social ordering. If radical criticism and refusal mean much, then they must apply beyond the topical and generational, residing finally in a permanent radicalism of social transformation. Only that deserves allegiance.

Society, for example, must still redeem the curse of labour. That will not be done, as our latest piety pretends, by technology alone

since its processes do not contain outraged human awareness –
indeed, technological order discourages and represses any larger
human responsiveness. Yet most of our technologues and economists and political moralists grievously obscure the work issues. Long
ago I lost the knack of understanding such people. Was it when I
hoed beans in a hot midwestern sun for ten cents an hour? Or
unloaded, for subsistence pay, freight cars of coal with a scoop and
wheelbarrow? Or worked twelve-hour shifts running a dangerous
steam filler, in 120-plus degree heat, in a canning factory? No matter when or at what, that bitter sense of monotonous, arbitrary,
body-and mind-wracking labour, without autonomy or reasonable
reward, remains a basic and black reality. May theorizing never
undercut the truths of memory!

Granted, my examples are old-fashioned, though they still apply
to millions of Americans, not to mention most of the rest of the
human world. Because of those experiences, I am permanently deaf
to talk of Gross National Product affluence, or technologically marvellous social order, or any other claim to "advanced" civilization
that does not minimize the sweated drudgeries and maximise the
just solace for those forced to do our unpleasant labours.

Most basically, liberty must always be tested on the labour and
eroticism and vitality of the body. Except in the fantasies of
bureaucratic technology, whose pathological quality is evident in its
current Egyptian monumentality and rocketing lunacies, our struggle remains for the tangible necessities of the human flesh. For
society to honestly recognize the burden of labour means that no
businessman receive higher rewards than the field hand hacking
with a short hoe; that no exalted professional merits as much honour as those mucking out our coal and crap; that no fashionable
entertainer or artist receive as good a treatment as the most menial
labourer or domestic. I know on my nerves, having been both, that
the garbageman deserves to be better paid and comforted than the
college professor. Any contrary social ordering is not only wrong
but certain, by its corrupting denial of basic human reality, to be
pervasively ugly and vicious.

But let me take an example of dehumanized labouring beyond
the essential moral revulsion. A few years ago I practised the trade
of airframe "template maker" in various plants and job-shops in
three western states. After several months of making metal patterns
in one of the largest, and reputedly most "progressive" plants, my
boredom reached such excruciation that some gesture towards critical change was imperative. From the better writings on the subject
as well as from my co-workers I know that my reaction was unexcep-

tional. Many a factory worker, not just a *poete maudet* with a hand drill, finds his routine painful, his conditions of work arbitrary and his sense of life emptied. Above a certain minimum, issues of pay and other "benefits" only concern the condiments , not the life-diet. To those reduced to being controlled functions in a factory (and the similar, if sometimes lavish, dehumanizations of office and business and profession), the alternatives consist of escape, degeneration and counter-assertion.

My counter-assertion no doubt revealed a peculiar naivete. I combined my responses to the tooling shop with some of the studies on industrial organization and came up with a moderate list of rational changes that would help humanize my work. When I then consulted a noted academic specialist on how I might initiate these, he exhibited acute embarrassment. He did provide two pieces of wisdom on how I might modify my life in the factory: I should go back to school to major in Industrial Relations, thus both getting out of the shop and "getting ahead" – the usual American ideal of "opportunity" substituting for justice and meaning – and I should spend my spare time in politics, in liberal-Democratic chores in a Republican suburb. Such counselling passes for "realism" in therapy as well as in politics.

Next, the labour union. With difficulty, I finally presented my critical suggestions to someone at a low level in that hierarchy. My points ranged from making the "breaks" concur with the job (i.e. take a smoke or coffee at a natural place in the work instead of being bound by a rigid plant-wide schedule), through co-operative decisions on work assignments to a procedure for electing foremen. All such proposals were angrily rejected. The union, like most "pressure groups" in a psuedo-pluralistic society, usually bends and bulges only in the accepted ways: I quickly learned that individual and various conditions, such as flexible rest periods, lacked drama and therefore had no chance as bargaining issues; everybody knew that assignments and promotions were purely corporate prerogatives; and that I'd better "get with it". Though too dumb to say it, the union official's tone insisted that arbitrary production requires arbitrary authority, including his own, rather than autonomy for those doing the work.

My even raising such questions was suspect: "Just what *are* your politics?" They certainly weren't going to appear anti-union. Some years earlier I had raised some questions to an official in a different union and obtained my answers from two persuasive gentlemen who wanted me to make contact with the hard realities of the problems and so repeatedly put my head against a brick wall. In addition to my cowardice, I felt some reluctance in pushing things because my experience in a non-union shop, where I was fired for talking too much, inclined me to prefer a union which re-enforced false conditions to no union at all. (The dilemma remains: as president of a college professor's union local, I find that a majority of my colleagues want to aggrandize salaries and the institutional surrogate for themselves rather than radically change education. One can only serve by subverting.)

Then I started arguing my way up the company hierarchy, finally reaching one of the biggest incompetents, the Plant Superintendent. That was a scene of comic pathos in a cubicle high above the assembly line: the thickly nervous factory Major General, on company time, trying to get rid of a loquacious, unshaven, T-shirted third-rate toolmaker inexplicably spending his off-time arguing about perfectly standard shop procedures. The Super came on with phony geniality, then irritated belligerence, and finally collapsed into a self-made-boss intimacy, lamenting that he'd never understood those "industrial psych" courses he had to take in night school, and concluding, hand on my shoulder, "What can I do for you? Put you in for a promotion?" No, I wanted to be able to smoke my pipe at reasonable intervals, to work out with the other template men the divvying up of the jobs – it might even be more "efficient"! – rather than be trapped by engineering numbers and foremen's caprice, and, in sum, we wanted to be a bit more our own bosses and make some changes. Wasn't that reasonable? He agreed but wearily assured me that what I asked would require getting rid of all those goddam personnel people, changing the company and union contractual procedures, and not only reorganizing the whole plant but the prime contractor, the US Government. Such a vicious circle allows only one real rational reform; by its own logic, the system must go.

The standard escapes urged upon me – becoming an "industrial relations" decorator or climbing the shop hierarchy – would only aggrandizingly re-enforce the viciousness. In the long run, such an order must be radically transformed; in the short run, it must be resisted if one is to remain humanly distinct. For both, we need more effective and intransigent ways of negation. That is the main "social issue" of our time. At that point all I could do was give my humble bit: take "breaks" when I damn well pleased, set my own slowed-down work schedule, knock off days, and agitate others to go the same way. Personal intransigence must ground any genuine radical awareness, not least as defence against the self-destructive schizophrenia which sickens our institutions. While neither demands for individuality nor group social justice will be sufficient to give real freedom, equality and meaning to most work in our society, that is where a communal politics must start.

Surely refusal can take more subtle, less naive, ways than mine – though they had better not be too subtle. The essential obtuseness of our institutions to humanely rational amelioration from below can also be put in a harsher light. When I was a convict in a federal prison I found that there, too, that radical intransigence, personal as well as ideological, provided the only pertinent responses. Though prison was less nastily totalitarian than the US Army, the grim, gray tedium – the surface of the basic terrorism which controls all "total" institutions such as armies and prisons and hospitals – forces almost everybody to "hard time" it. Aside from that, my own situation as head convict librarian, combined with the fortuitous double protection of a senior "screw" and an extortionist who was an inmate leader, became downright comfortable, for a prison.

But since the prison system (run in large part by the more corrupt inmates) was grossly unjust, and since I was there for having defied the government, a radical response was imperative.*

In that "correctional institution" usual ameliorist criticisms were undercut by a "liberal" administration. For example, the place was racially segregated but since the "ghetto" sections of the cell blocks and mess hall were the most desirable ones, the Negroes protested any efforts to reduce them to "equal" conditions – a shrewd bigotry which may show a useful future. When I also objected that the educational system only existed on paper and in rare dress appearances of "rehabilitation", my complaints got me the additional job of convict-head of the prison school. As with most official educational roles, the main effect was moral solace since I didn't really do a very good job of teaching aged illiterates. Finally, my recognition of the co-opting pattern discouraged me from very vigorous com-

---

*Though as a combat veteran of World War II I was not legally subject to further military service, I refused, as a point of anti-authoritarian principle, to complete a registration when conscription was reinstituted in 1948. I was convicted of felonious violation of the Selective Service Act and, from characteristic American righteousness (plus some of the Cold War psychology developing then) sentenced to eight months in prison instead of the more logical suspended sentence. While I am now less naive about the American character, I would still emphasize such action as a necessary self-definition against a false society. Radicalism without some such grounding appears to me as often dubiously abstract-sentimental.

plaints about the psychiatric and religious services for fear that I might be led to unnecessary additional lessons in humility.

But what could I do? Certainly I could have joined a prison reform society, after I got out. Or I could have stuck to my intellectual bench and worked out a sociological theory of the imperviousness of "total" institutions to the usual forms of criticism, as correctly do the few good writings on the society of captives. Or I could make the selfish "best of a bad situation", which I had already done though I was not quite self-regarding enough to claim it as a social philosophy. Since the authorities were constitutionally incapable of making more than trivial gestures of justice and were psychotically deaf to cons (except for the Captain of the Guards, all too open to persuasion since he was the biggest crook around), and since the elite among the cons (confidence men, extortionists, and similar professionals) were intelligent but over-adaptable types with power-roles to conserve, the usual elitist and educational theories of change were irrelevant. (There's nothing like a totalitarian institution for checking out the social and political theorists!)

But one discovers another elite, usually submerged: the "brilliant psychopaths", the extreme, "deviant" personalities who lead riots and escapes. While "outside" institutions make elaborate efforts to remove these dissidents – probably because they are usually superior persons in intelligence and competence to those in power – prisons, themselves the place of removal, find it difficult to be inhumanly pure. (Following contemporary educational and psychological programming, prisons and armies their imitators now do attempt to change this by a "scientific" – that is, conservative – process of segregation.) To the degree that most of our institutions parallel the totalitarian ones – and that must be considerable since the total institutions do the basic controlling of the society – we may find that "psychopaths" provide the real possibilities for change. We need not draw any sentimental conclusion that such efforts will always be for the best, only that this is the major route of possibility, still not fully excluded in our carefully modulated and dehumanized orderings. Any serious social-political theory of change, then, must in effect include a Table of Organization entitled "Beating the System: Where To Have the Madmen". If it doesn't, it's the usual bullshit, so out with it.

What I am defending here is what one of my Neomarxist friends condemns as my "lumpen elitism of the desperate poetic imagination". Lovely phrase, but I more than once, and in a variety of roles – from merchant seaman through advertising hack and university professor – discovered the significance of that psychopathic elite not by theory but by need and by natural taste in friends. They are more lively, if somewhat more difficult.

And this led me to one of the few ways of meaningful action in prison. A psychopathic young con, the compulsive captive and congenital hard-timer, mildly screwed-up and was bum rapped with a bad work reassignment. He confided his rage, and break-out plans, to me. As in most institutions in our society, prison job replacement and promotion primarily come about through sycophancy (and related corruption), custodial security, and (at the unconscious level) psychosomatic typologies, not by competence and need and desire. The human discrepancies show up most glaringly in closed systems but, even when admitted, are not likely to be corrected since rational standards for jobs would not only displace convicts whose power situations (as in the bakery and dispensary) were crucial to the illicit structure of business and pleasure but would threaten the pathology of the whole system. If one kiss-ass goes, why not the rest of them? While "advantage" and "avoiding trouble" block revision, the basic warping, not just the usually claimed "self-interest", needs to be assaulted. Change, therefore, requires a psychic as well as practical disproportion. To be *rationally* appropriate, efforts at reform must be *excessive* in apparent style, disruptive not only of identification and advantage but of over-all order. Contrary to the smug pieties of narrow rationality in so much of our social and political thought, nothing less will do. True politics is the art of trouble-making.

I encouraged my psychopathic fellow con to dramatically refuse his new job assignment, and backed him up by "unreasonably" refusing to work myself. Further steps included encouraging the other psychopaths to "act out", refusing to go to the mess hall as the start of a hunger strike, and making demands about everything. These direct actions depended less on the moral suasion often claimed for civil disobedience than on countering "advantage" (a lot of unpleasant extra work for the short-handed screws), on dramatic enlargement (people were pushed into choosing sides almost in spite of themselves), and on the obviously swelling psychic explosiveness. The authorities took the easy out and made the sensible changes in job assignments, and I went back to eating, work and ineffective liberalism. Later, my friend went over the wall anyway. Granted, in this prison such methods had previously been used by "political" prisoners so that my role, and therefore the action, were identified as ideological rather than just sick or selfish. Without such definition, the sequence would have been quite unlikely. What radicals do, the justification for their interminable argument and dramatization, is essentially esthetic: they not only

Perhaps in this case (as also in the army when I several times led buddies "over the hill" but also back again) I took the cowardly way out in not pushing additional demands, fomenting more drastic responses, upping the ante to violent disruption. I may be guilty of excessive moderation, which rationalizes as a search for a continuing refusal rather than a spastic riot, selective rebellion rather than chiliastic revolution. Of course I know that total institutions can only be reformed by being negated, but overwhelming violence may less defeat them than demythification and continuing refusal and rebellion. So, I believe, generally with this social order.

Factories and prisons led to much the same experiential conclusions. But, for a social theory, what of the other institutions? To which I can only reply with a sincerity no longer naive: What *other* institutions? Someone usually suggests "good" institutions, say, schools and universities. Agreed, they may well be more pleasant as well as more honorifically glossy. Probably that is much of the cause of the proliferation of educational institutions these days. After all, the technicians and bureaucrats which they primarily produce could be trained and indoctrinated on the job. But our fancied up bureaucracies serve as half-escapes, selective and pious substitutes, from our most obviously indefensible institutions of control and exploitation.

Everyone, of course, senses that the schools are dominated by custodial functions and indoctrination for submission. And the half-dozen universities in which I have professed can best be compared, in exact as well as broad detail, to factories of a more sloppily indulgent but malicious and incompetent sort. Hired learning, of course, reveals itself more comfortably hypocritical then "total" stitutions but less rationally ordered than "productive" institutions which come up more directly against material nature.

However, all institutions these days, even if we still manage to distinguish those for products or education or pure control, seem increasingly ambiguous as they synthetically merge indoctrination with products and technical services with control. Suggestively, such synthetic organizations may arrive at similar weaknesses so that, say, student revolts can provide paradigms for refusal in all institutions. Presently our "best" institutions would seem to be, contrary to my own libertarian sentiments for small organizations, the large and mediocre. The controls, such as hierarchical anxiety, cannot be taken too seriously, and the purposes and functions are sufficiently confused and inefficient to allow tolerance and autonomy. If we encourage this cynical state, and I see no reasonable alternative in the desire for freedom, then we must try to simultaneously create new life, which would therefore be oppositional social and cultural styles, within and without.

Naturally (to answer an obvious objection) one recognizes differences between various institutions. Anyone who has been in a few jails knows the drastic dissimilarities between the small "county tank", usually a vicious hole, and the large "federal correctional facility", which can be outgamed and resisted like any other bureaucratic institution. But jails remain jails. Control can be nice or nasty without ceasing to be control. So, too, with indoctrination; change in costume is not change in character. (*Mea culpa*: the infantry non-com who once gave compulsory lectures – it was that or punishment – to the troops on "Why America Fights" now gives, for a slightly dishonourable professional living, covertly compulsory lectures on "Conflict in American Culture".) Strategies for liberation must vary – guerrilla tactics don't work well against "nice" repression in "good" institutions (a mistake of some recent student rebels) – so that one refuses the covert order actually present and thus brings to consciousness the functional and ideological similarities of most of our institutions. The most appropriate disenchantment still focuses on "the authorities", the realization that essentially the same people as well as ideologies run the "good" and the "bad" institutions, not only the businesses and the governments, and the factories and the services, but the schools and the jails, and the universities and the armies. In several senses, it is all a "total" order.

I desist from an academic anecdote to parallel those of factory and prison and complete my institutional sketch, though my file on Academic Bureaucracy Baiting swells largest of all. Just a passing illustration. I have usually been shocked by the people I know who become successful, powerful, rich, famous. Not that stupid machine and human toad! So with the news that a former college room-mate of mine had become executive officer of one of the leading American universities. I remembered him as a real dummy, a silly cheater, and a generally inadequate person. Surely I overlooked something which made him more than an ambitiously unprincipled jerk. Didn't he have some sort of special quality? A moral chameleon sensitivity...an unusual energy for trivia...a crypto-homosexual responsiveness to superiors...Any talent to justify my former roommate as a top administrator turns out to be a social and human defficiency. Of course he also has the special craft it takes to identify with institutional ideology and power, and to suck on. I hear that he acts a trifle better than some in his role because still impulsively muddled. Perhaps, to look for the happy side, people partly boosted him up as a substitute for someone much more competent and evil.

Since I've been mostly at the bottom of orders, I admit some puzzlement over those at the top. Might I be mistaking the ways of peripheral examples for the real thing – for the big entrepreneurs, the major organizers, the military masters, the driving techno-logues, the famed authorities? But careful researches lead only to the conclusion that most of the controlling and wealthy and cele-brated turn out to be even less adequate human beings than my successful ex-room-mate. Indeed, many in power can only be ex-plained with antique notions of insanity and evil. Most of our power figures deserve the greatest contempt. Why don't more people say so?

All the usual selfish and sick explanations apply, but some that can certainly be changed include the pretences at objectivity, the pseudo-scientific intellectual fashions, which turn out to be merely conservative manners. Even the better social moralists these days do not often savage the powerful and rich and celebrated, except when their behaviour seems exceptionally unfair. But the unfair-ness is really what all of them are, and nothing more. Even if they were only as you and I, they would tend to be worse because of what one must be as well as do in getting, and staying, on top. More often the powerful are the less intelligent and responsive to start with. One must simply conclude, and act, as if the powerful were no good, which is true. In the long run they must go; in the short run we should refuse them, not least by treating them with the scorn they merit.

Though probably justifiable, the violent destruction of the powerful does not seem very tempting. The sensible arguments against violence apply, the most rational of which is that the wrong people usually get it in the neck. Also, the politics of resentment puts other vicious people on top. The only true radical alternative is not to have any top and right now. Our refusing of power, our de-authorisation, must be both specific and pervasive. Currently, Western societies seem midway towards demythification of power. Not only do we find an increasing amorphousness (where *is* the boss?) characteristic of control in bureaucratic-technological prog-ramming but an undercutting culture in which the hierarchical sub-mission combines with surreal contempt. So silly are our "leaders" – the comic statesmen, the administrative nullities, the rootless rich, the fatuous celebrities – so lacking in social imagination and moral style and even interesting personal qualities, that some humane people hopefully assume that we have already achieved self-rule by default. Unfortunately, in the amorphous order of overwhelming mass-technological power even what little our leading fools do comes out disproportionately destructive. Also from that arises our recurrent disguised authoritarianism, the destructive ambivalence in which many "decent" people yearn for some pretence at authoritative power instead of demanding self-rule. Then we get the fancy statesmen and swinging administrators and charming leaders who would claim to really lead. They, in fact, start our wars and put outmoded rhetoric into counterfeit social ordering, thus inhibiting real change. Should radical refusal here prefer the mediocre fools, just as, in truth, we prefer the large ineffective bureaucracies?

Some choice! Yet, in effect, we must sometimes make it. More importantly, we must make the system make it. If we chose political and economic and institutional leaders by random selection – frequent blind drawings for celebrities and artists as well as administrators and rulers – we would no doubt come out with a better selection than we generally get. We should find ways to encourage such devaluations as steps towards a better social ordering which quite separates real authority – the ability to do, to know, to say, to exemplify – from most prerogative and force. In the meantime, we refuse anything less by resisting all claims to authoritative power. If Oedipus can't find Laius, we move towards the day when he no longer rages when he does find him, and his own guilt. To dissolve the ancient curse means to turn it into a daily dance of life.

You may label the social-politics I have been sketching "sceptical anarchism" (in partial contrast to the positivistic and optimistic sort) or "conservative nihilism" (a persistent unfrenzied negation of false order). In any dramatic sense of society, one recognizes that such action must be played out, so we might just as well be self-conscious about it. Certainly I would not claim for refusal a total politics. But negation prepares for creation. Only the paranoid, on both sides, take destruction as definitive. And by far the most destructive among us seem to be those who never claim it. Not the anarchists and nihilists but the positive saviours advance the great historical crimes. Even on the smaller scene, institutions which cannot bear with considerable refusal deserve to go under. Since we should never reduce the human to equation with its institutions, better them than us. And by so doing we might just possibly move towards that new communal order of human proportions which we so desperately need.

Somewhat elliptically, to lessen the false abstraction of social-political theorizing, I have been refusing some often accepted premises of social criticism and change. Anecdotally, I have been arguing for a community of refusal, a libertarian praxis in which ideological radicalism (the vision of an institutionally transformed society) and personal radicalism (intransigent behaviour and variant life-style) must go together. Their separation still pervades most of what passes for politics. Partly a 19th-century mania for repressively respectable virtue even in opposition – Jacobin puritanism – only now do we see it dissolving with such liveliness as the beat-hippy-underground styles of contemporary radicalization. A polymorphousness of sexuality and imagination and rebellion subverts the rigid sensibility which, leftist or not, can only maintain rather than radicalize our daily institutions. I see it as a new insight, though still alien to the politically-minded, the trend in contemporary Western society that social and cultural rebellion precede rather than follow revolutionary political changes of institutional order.

The revolutionism which seeks organized external mass methods of power usually insists on subordinating social and cultural revolution to political activity. Instead of refusing power, that heightens it, and ends conserving the repressive character and authority of institutions. Revolution and reaction agree in condemning styles of refusal as romantic and utopian and deviationist. Mere politics thus becomes the new displacement of full humanness, generating a new terrorism and totalism of *le peuple* or the proletariat or a political organization or an historical process. Revolutionism is not nearly radical enough.

To turn false institutional order into more fully human proportions requires not so much force as deconversion from the reigning faiths. For as one painfully discovers in doing battle with our controlling organizations, faith, not just power, maintains these institutional mountains. Or, as my farmer grandfather used to put it, "Ta sell corn ya gotta raise corn an' to raise corn ya gotta believe in corn". With most of our traditional deities decrepit, our civilization passionately holds itself together with quite paltry convictions, such as a religiosity about bureaucratic technology. Especially from unadmitted faiths, deconversion cannot simply be reasonable but would seem to require, like conversion, radical experiences and traumatic breaks and imaginative disruptions of consciousness. Thus politics of gesture and fancy and defiance and shock might be more productive in breaking the faith than the usual organizing of the barricades and bureaucracies of dissent. Refusal in our society may need new oppositional styles.

The great unwritten work in contemporary social thought, which I am prefacing, may be "Humanizing Technological Organization" by the descendants of Ned Lud. The radical criticism, the dissident way, the comic resistance, the emphatic difference, the intransigent act, and all the other ways of refusal, must be put both against and inside our institutional orderings. Furthering rebellious life-styles, no matter how weirdly Joachimite they may be, constitutes radical change now. So does institutional subversion, such as that considerable folk lore and practice of "beating the bureaucracy" and "fighting the system". They already exist – and in an expansive state – otherwise our institutions would be totally unbearable since patently not designed for passionate human fullness. Far more than revolutionary postures, the multiform ways of refusal and the continuing demythification and other negations may redeem the curse of labour by transforming its justice, decorrupt authority by removing its force, and humanize power by making it immediate and personal. To prefer libertarian rebellion to megalomaniac revolutionism also affirms the wonderful anarchy of the sexual and social and cultural "revolutions" actually going on around us. Only by way of rebellion comes contemporary community.

The favourite myth of those who would master others is that denial is bad – bad manners, bad policy, even bad psychology. Do they most fear its truth, its effectiveness or its pleasure? By a fraudulent calculus, they also conclude that a total order of human attrition comes out less destructive than a liberating negation. But the simple truth, discoverable here and now, is that a richer human life often comes from a joyous NO!

*Anarchy 104*                                        *October 1969*


# 3.   Black anarchy in New York

## H. W. Morton

ON NOVEMBER 9, 1965, shortly after 5pm, at the Sir Adam Beck No.2 Distribution Plant at Queenston, Ontario, a little four-inch-square electric relay took it upon itself to illuminate a number of anarchist principles. In doing so it selected a method which in and of itself is anarchistic: direct action. Certainly it was far and away the all-time world's champion blown fuse, in that it blacked out 80,000 square miles of the US and Canada, leaving about 30 million people in total darkness. This was an electronic *attentat* – and on a scale one is hard put to overlook. Yet through the darkness, like a beacon, shone such anarchist truisms as decentralism, mutual aid, direct action, and the like.

On the individual level we found people acting so beautifully that even Kropotkin might have been impressed. Naturally there were instances of people acting like capitalists – selling candles at $1.50 (11/-) each, charging up to $50 (£18) for a taxicab ride, gouging pounds of flesh for flashlights, etc. Howevei, as *Newsweek* (11.11.65) pointed out, the "real keynote" was struck by a Negro cleaning woman who led a Manhattan career girl up 10 flights of stairs to her apartment, gave her two candles, and then waved away a $5 tip. "It's OK, honey, tonight everyone helps everyone".

Somehow it seemed as if the whole crazy city had read *Mutual Aid* the night before. Remember, New York is notorious for being this planet's biggest cut-throat rat-race. Furthermore it was not only the town longest hit by the blackout, it was also by far the most vulnerable area. The blackout struck in the middle of the rush hour, hence there were probably 800,000 people stranded in subways and/or subway trains when the power failed. Another 100,000 were stranded waiting for commuter trains. Thousands more were trapped on the upper floors of skyscrapers. Undoubtedly the worst off were the hundreds upon hundreds who were trapped in elevators. Yet there was no panic! Everyone was calm and patient. Neither was there any crime wave or looting – of course for this we have to thank the fact that the police were kept too busy with rescue work and other emergency activities. It was estimated that $100 million (£36 million) was lost in revenue. Certainly one of the hardest hit business interests was the New York Police Force. Therefore I have to give them credit for coming through in the pinch, although several cops of the 24th Precinct failed to appreciate my concern when I walked by in the darkness explaining to my companions in stentorian tones of commiseration that the poor guys were beating their brains out and "all on straight salary for a change". (The 24th Precinct specializes in shooting 14-year-old Puerto Ricans.) All in all some 5,000 off-duty policemen were called up to join the 7,000 already on duty. The Fire Department brought in their off-duty personnel also.

Yet although these men all performed beautifully at tasks of supererogation, the real stars of the show were the people. Piecing together various contemporary reports (cf. *Life, Time, Newsweek, US News and World Report, New York Times,* and *New York Post*) many people actually enjoyed the situation. There was drinking, singing, and necking in the streets. Parties of Frenchmen and US Southerners stuck on the 86th-floor observation roof of the Empire

State Building chorused each other alternately with "La Marseil-laise" and "Dixie", though how many hours they kept this up was not reported. A church sexton handed out free votive candles – even God lost money – while a blind woman led passengers out of a subway station. One 19-year-old girl said: "They should do this more often; everyone is much more friendly. It's a big community again – people have time to stop and talk".

Volunteers directed traffic with flashlights and handkerchiefs. Home transistor radio listeners pitched in to report on develop-ments and incidents so that helpful information could be shared with everyone else. Drivers shared cars with pedestrians. People quietly queued up at pay telephones, restaurants and saloons. They gathered on street corners to listen together to portable radios. One shoeshine boy completed his task by his customer's matches.

There was incident upon incident: the whole situation was fan-tastic. *Time* later mentioned a "crisis-born spirit of camaraderie and exhilaration" and a very prevalent view was that "it brought out the best in people". Of course the fact is that our authoritarian social system cannot help but bring out the worst in people, hence its removal – and bear in mind that the state had well-nigh disappeared – merely allowed them to act as free human beings. After the black-out various politicians, officials, and kindred parasites delivered encomia to the splendid behaviour of their "fellow citizens", never realizing how completely superfluous this splendid behaviour proved their own functions to be. Somehow or other the ruling class is incredibly fortunate: people often see through individual leaders, but rarely through leadership *per se*. One woman said that she had received "so many singular courtesies" during the power failure that her "faith in mankind had been restored". Tragically she didn't say she had received so many that her faith in authority based on force had been lost. Yet that power failure was nearly a power vacuum: we were closer to a true anarchy for those few hours than anything most of us will ever be lucky enough to see again. Incidentally, the Statue of Liberty, because it draws its current from New Jersey, remained lighted throughout the blackout. For the first time in her life "that old bitch" as one of her would-be bombers described her, was almost telling the truth.

To some extent there was a Dionysian quality reminding one observer of VE or VJ Day "when everybody loved everybody". Another commented on "the same air of revelry that often accom-panies a heavy snowstorm". A lawyer in his 32nd-floor office said, "first we just sat around having drinks. Now we're having a seance to communicate with the spirit that caused this bliss. We could have walked down but it's about 600 steps, so we're staying, and we're all getting to know each other". Someone else confessed: "It's a big pain and all, but I sort of hate to see it over. Tomorrow will be just another working day". But the following day, and several thereafter, there was a continued *élan* as people exchanged anecdotes of courage, kindness and adventure. There was something to talk about and we were impressed by one another. Cab drivers, waitresses, secretaries, truck drivers, grandmothers, teenagers, lawyers and bellhops interviewed by the *New York Post* all remarked on the "calm, cheerful, considerate attitude the majority of people maintained". Yet, by way of contrast, there were the inevitable exceptions: an elderly woman paused diffidently trying to cross Fifth Avenue and instantly acquired a four-man escort; meanwhile a panhandler continued to intercept passers-by, concentrating on his own version of mutual aid.

Naturally, the transportation hang-up, vertical as well as horizontal, posed the biggest problem. There were 600 stalled subway trains containing some 800,000 commuters, hundreds of whom were trapped for as long as eight hours, and 60 of whom stayed on for over 14 hours. Furthermore in New York City there were hundreds of elevators stalled between floors in apartment and office buildings, which meant several thousand additional victims requiring rescue.

Nonetheless even in these untoward circumstances the leitmotif was solidarity. As one housewife put it after a six-hour stay in a subway car, "I never thought New Yorkers could be that way. I mean everybody seemed to lose his anger". In one car a passenger was leading people in Calypso songs and handclapping. Couples were dancing when the conductor arrived to lead them out of an emergency stairwell to the surface. The universal report was that there was no panic. As one woman said, "Our conductor would pop in every once in a while and ask 'How's everybody?', and everybody woud say 'Fine'. We really weren't worried at all." Some good samaritans left one train and walked along catwalks to find emergency exits. But then, instead of going safely home, they returned to lead their fellow passengers out. On other trains, talented victims entertained their fellows: in one car there was a tenor; in another, an harmonica player; but the *pièce de résistance* was a bagpiper. Many cars featured communal singing. The most common thing, however, was light conversation interspersed with sardonic humour. Men gave up their seats to ladies who frequently offered them back. In one car a woman fainted but word was trans-mitted from person to person until someone was located with smell-ing salts. Thereupon these were passed back up hand to hand.

Those who had long waits on their hands exchanged whatever comestibles they had in pockets or pocket books: peanuts, wild cherry drops, assorted goodies, or even antacid tablets. One group shared a combination of doughnuts and salami which had been sliced with a nail-file. At midnight the Transit Authority sent in food to those who hadn't yet been extricated. The food-bearers were greeted with a tableau of people sleeping with their arms draped about other people who had been complete strangers five hours previously, and nary a cop in sight!!!

Meanwhile those unfortunates trapped in elevators – 96 in the Empire State Building alone – were enduring their plight with the same sort of equanimity exhibited in the subways. Here too the people entertained one another with improvised games, such as the unlikeliest partners for stalled elevators. This was readily won with the combination of Defence Secretary Macnamara and a draft card burner. In an elevator in the RCA Building one gentleman gave a course in Yoga positions. When foremen chopped their way into one immobilised car, they asked: "Are there any pregnant women in here?" They were answered: "We've hardly met!"

Surface transportation reflected the same sort of co-operation and solidarity. Even though the Transit Authority was running 3,500 of its 4,000 buses it could barely make a dent. Therefore countless thousands hiked home across the bridges or up the ave-nues. Others waited calmly in line at the bus stops, with no pushing or shoving. Nobody seemed to take advantage of the confusion to avoid paying fares, although some passengers couldn't have paid if they'd tried – they were riding on the rear bumpers. Bus drivers themselves were inordinately accommodating, calling out each stop as they approached. In New York this comes under the heading of *mirabile dictu*. At the same time, dozens of private automobiles were loading up at every intersection with absolute strangers.

On the other hand all was not sweetness and light during the darkness. Some people capitalized on others' vulnerability. About 100 windows were smashed in, and about 41 looters were arrested (none in blue uniform). All told perhaps a dozen stores were looted, which is absolutely negligible in a city of over eight million. Even Police Commissioner Broderick conceded that both the crime and the casualty rates for the night were far below normal. (So who needs him?) One enterprising gunman held up a rare-coin dealer by the flickering light of the shop's only candle – a touching vignette to be sure. There were a total of 65 persons arrested for burglary, larceny, or felonious assault – as opposed to a typical 380 for a comparable 16-hour stretch. The sum total of arrests for all crimes was only 25 per cent of what it would have been during an ordinary night. There were very few shoplifters reported, which is nothing short of miraculous considering the open-house policy of the department stores (cf. infra). Moreover there were only 33 vehicle accidents involving injuries, and 44 involving property damage – and this in the world's largest city, completely devoid of traffic lights! There was one bus that ploughed into a crowd of people in Queens knocking down 38 persons, some of whom were seriously injured. The driver – evidently in complete consternation – jumped out and fled. Yet his actions must be viewed in context with the fact that his was only one out of 3,500 buses operating under these weird conditions.

Somewhere along the line a subway motorman found himself facing charges of rape for flashing a badge and leading a young lady to the ostensible safety of his room. Yet later in court he contended that on any number of previous occasions he had led the same young lady to a similar lair to similarly lay her, so who knows... Progressing from debatably to unquestionably false alarms, we find that the Fire Department reported a much higher incidence than usual: 227 rather than the typical 50. This is totally irreconcilable with anarchist theory, so I've decided not to mention it at all.

Easily offsetting those relatively few human beings who acted like capitalists were the many capitalists who acted like human beings. For example many department stores flirted with free access for the evening. Macy's played host to an estimated 5,000 customers and employees for the night – inviting one and all to make themselves comfortable, and serving them all coffee, sandwiches, cookies, and candy. Needless to say, the furniture department on the ninth floor was the best spot for comfort. Meanwhile, across the street, Gimbels was featuring a guitar-playing salesman for the entertainment of its customer/guests. One of the songs they reportedly joined in on was the old wartime favourite, "When the Lights Go on Again All Over the World". Evidently no one was familiar with "We Shall Overcome". Lord and Taylor's turned over its entire second floor to customers for the duration of the blackout, while B. Altman's turned over its first. Altman's, incidentally, has its own power generator, so there was some light by which to enjoy the caviare and specially blended coffee which were among the imported delicacies provided by the gourmet department and served to shoppers and employees. Five hundred stayed there overnight, evidently being unable to tear themselves away from all that

caviare. Bloomingdales turned over its home furnishings department to strandees – one woman slept on an $800 (£287) sofa – and
then capped it off by having its staff serve breakfast to everyone the
next morning. Fina Company had a combination sales meeting and
dinner scheduled for that evening, but they catered it to customers
instead. Bonwit Teller chartered two buses to get its employees
home, and suggested that they hold hands leaving the store so that
none would get lost. Indicative of the prevailing mood was the fact
that the employees danced out of the store together because "someone thought it would be fun". Meanwhile 40 people were bedded
down for the night in the showroom of the Simmons Mattress Co.

The city's hotels came through in grand style. The Commodore
set up 150 cots in a banquet room. Both the Roosevelt and the
Algonquin switched elderly guests and those with heart conditions
to the lower floors. At the Stanhope the manager gave up his own
room, and an assistant manager carried a crippled woman up to the
16th floor. On arrival, she said, "Now I'd like a glass of water," so he
procured one. At the Statler Hilton two bellmen carried a crippled
guest to the 7th floor, but it was not reported what his needs were on
arrival. The Americana passed out blankets and pillows to the 200
occupants of its plush lobby – most of the other hotels merely provided their lobbies as free space. The Sheraton-Atlantic, whose
lobby was occupied by some 2,000 people, considered the evening
somewhat less than a total loss, because as one manager pointed
out, "The bar is doing a land-office business". That hotel's report
seemed typical: 99 per cent of the people were "terrific" but a few
guests tried to sublet their rooms at double the rate.

Unfortunately, utopian free access was much less prevalent in
food than it was in shelter. Nevertheless one meat market in Brook-
lyn donated a whole pig to a neighbouring convent thereby providing roast pork snacks to everybody for blocks around. Two numer-
ically named restaurants, 21 and Four Seasons, adopted a policy
dangerously akin to "from each according to his ability; to each
according to his need". The 21 passed out steak sandwiches and free
drinks without limit, while Four Seasons ladled out free soup. Fully
to appreciate the enormity of this, reflect on the following: in 1960,
when prices presumably were lower, an acquaintance of mine told
me that two friends of his went to Four Seasons for luncheon.
Including drinks and tip it cost them nearly $60 (over £21) while the
band played "Nearer my Veblen to Thee". My wife and I didn't
happen to go there that night so we missed out on the free soup, but
we did enjoy knishes by candlelight at our own expense in a nearby

delicatessen. Many other restaurants, although they didn't give away food, stayed open all night to provide free shelter.

Most downtown offices close at 5pm and were empty when the blackout struck. Those still occupied did whatever they could. Revlon, for example, gave its girls couches in the executive offices and then told them to take the next day off. One of their secretaries, stuck on the 27th floor, ate crabmeat and graham cracker sandwiches, and described the experience with a wistful: "I had a great time". Whether she was alluding to the crabmeat or the couches was not made clear.

All sorts of institutions opened their doors, or in some instances dropped their gangways, as a free public service during the emergency. Final estimates included well over 400 people who had been put up for the night in staterooms of ships in port when the lights went out. Armouries were thrown open to all comers, while railroad stations, airline terminals, and churches sheltered countless thousands.

The 34th Street Armoury alone accommodated 1,500 refugees, offering wooden chairs and what illumination could be furnished from the headlights of a few jeeps parked in the middle of the drill floor. For some unexplained reason no cots were available. Naturally Rockefeller had immediately called out the National Guard, which is always a good safe ploy for masking gubernatorial inutility. According to the *New York Post* the Guardsmen were armed with rifles "unloaded but impressive". To complete the farce they wore packs containing ponchos and gas masks, perhaps out of fear that someone would fart. The Guard's major contribution seems to have been scouring the area around 34th Street and Park Avenue until 1.30am – a full eight hours after the attentat – at which point they finally came up with coffee and French bread for the beseiged. Compare this forlorn, dilatory effort on the part of the military to the ingenuity of the prostitutes in their quest for bread. *Life Magazine* pointed out that these ladies "were among the first to procure flashlights", indicating that the yen is still mightier than the sword.

At the Central Commercial High School, a double session school, the second session runs from 12.30 to 5.50pm. Thus there were 1,000 students being subjected to obfuscation when the blackout struck. Some 400 of these left during the course of the evening as parents arrived to pick them up, but the school officials kept the other 600 in the classrooms all night. These joked, sang, and later put their heads on their desks and slept – readily taking the crisis in stride. Of course they were nowhere near as comfortable as the lucky ones who spent the night cradled in luxurious barber chairs, but they were infinitely better off than the hundreds who sought sanctuary in St. Patrick's Cathedral. These were huddled in the pews without even a hair shirt for warmth, and worst of all, no bogs. Mgr. McGovern later confessed, "We've been sending people over to the New Western Hotel for 80 years", which tends to confirm something many of us have long suspected: God's up shit creek.

Of far more serious import was the situation in hospitals. Here, too, people improvised brilliantly in the emergency. At Bellevue a delicate cornea transplant was under way when the lights went out, but was successfully completed by battery-operated floodlights. At St. John's, under similar conditions, emergency surgery was performed on two people whose spleen had been ruptured in the previously mentioned bus accident. In another hospital a five-hour craniotomy was performed by makeshift light. Final reports indicated at least five dozen babies delivered by candle or otherwise. One man died tragically in the emergency room at Flushing Hospital. He had been in an automobile accident prior to the blackout and was already under surgery when the lights went out. Only two other deaths in New York City were attributed directly to the blackout: one man suffered a heart attack from climbing ten flights of stairs, and a second fell down a stairway and struck his head. Injuries, of course, were much more common: at the emergency ward of Bellevue alone, 145 patients were treated for blackout injuries – broken arms or legs from falls, car accident victims, and some heart cases. Police, firemen, and volunteers rushed dry ice to the city's hospitals to keep stored blood from spoiling, whereas a distress call from St. Vincent's brought forth 30 volunteers from a Greenwich Village coffee house to hand-pump iron lungs.

Although New York offered perhaps the most spectacular, and in view of its well-deserved reputation for ruthless competition, the most unexpected examples of mutual aid, the same pattern was repeated everywhere throughout the blacked-out area. It was solidarity, ingenuity, lack of hysteria, consideration, etc, and little or no government. In Toronto, Ontario, businessmen directed traffic, and in the process unsnarled the city's all-time record traffic jam. Among other things all the street-cars and trolley buses had stopped dead. In Albany, New York, teenagers with transistor radios went from house to house advising residents to turn off electric appliances. In Burlington, Vermont, 200 people hurried with flashlights to the local hospital in answer to a radio plea which later turned out to be a prank. In Springfield, Vermont, a barber finished trimming a customer's hair by the headlights a motorist aimed in his front window. All over the stricken territory civilians patrolled areas, directed traffic, and maintained order. Included among all

these civilian volunteers would have to be the contingent of Boston
gendarmes who rushed out of the Policemen's Ball dressed in tux-
edos. Devoid of badge, uniform and gun these were on identical
footing with the students from Boston University who also pitched
in.

Incident after incident offered irrefutable proof that society can
function without the implicit threats of force and violence which
constitute the state. There was probably more freedom from the
law, however temporary, in that blacked-out 80,000-mile area than
there has been at any time since it was originally stolen from the
murdered and/or defrauded Indians. And it yielded compelling evidence of anarchist theories. As Kropotkin once stated: "We are not
afraid to say 'Do what you will; act as you will', because we are
persuaded that the great majority of mankind, in proportion to their
degree of enlightenment, and the completeness with which they
free themselves from existing fetters, will behave and act always in a
direction useful to society".

Such then might be the blackout's confirmation of Kropotkin.
What reinforcement does it offer Bakunin? Actually a good deal,
but I'll cite only one case – a frequently distorted quotation which
Max Nettlau once described as "a clarion call for revolution in the
widest sense". Written in 1842, some 20 years before Bakunin became an anarchist, in fact before he could even be considered a
conscious revolutionary, it appeared at the conclusion of an article
entitled "Reaction in Germany", under the pseudonym Jules Ely-
sard: "The urge to destroy is a creative urge". Bakunin's detractors,
both in and out of the anarchist movement, invariably swoop down
like vultures on that line. However Bakuninists might suffer less
dismay (and, let's face it, embarrassment) if they viewed it in context with a heart-warming article which appeared in the Financial
Section of the *New York Post* the day after the blackout: "Without
power, Computers Died and Wall Street Stopped".

On the other hand, if the blackout provided all sorts of verification for decentralists, anarchists, Kropotniks and Bakuninists, what
comfort did it offer to pacifists? The answer is, damn little. As both
James Wechsler (*New York Post*) and Brad Lyttle (*Peace News*)
pointed out, the same sort of unfathomable but infallible electronic
technology which blacked out 30 million of us temporarily is exactly
what we're relying on to prevent an accidental World War III black-
ing out three billion of us permanently! Small solace to me is the fact
that the whole god-damned Pentagon will come down as local fall-
out: my urge to destroy is not quite that creative. What with the hot
line conked out, and the blithe "assurance" from the First Regional

Army Air Defence Commander that despite the blackout "all of the Army's missile sites on the Eastern Coast are operative", it was obviously a case of genocide continued as usual. Bring on the Dark Ages!

The final object lesson of the blackout? The predictable, virtually automatic, responses of various members of society when confronted by crisis: soldiers fall back on their weapons; clergymen fall back on their prayers; doctors fall back on their antibiotics; bureaucrats fall back on their desks; and politicians fall back on their asses. But people fall back on one another, and in that fact must remain all the hopes – however minimal – for the survival of the human race.

*Anarchy 67*                                                    *September 1966*


# 4.  Notes from Notting Hill
## John O' Connor

*In my Eden our only source of political news is gossip. In his New Jerusalem there will be a special daily in simplified spelling for non-verbal types.*
–W.H. Auden: *Vespers*


IF WE imagine a world in which economic necessity no longer had importance in determining peoples' relationships with each other, it would be one in which the full spectrum of political stances and groupings still existed, except that they would now be formed in accord with the demands of different temperaments for their different satisfactions.

A society in which the distortion of material things no longer applied has been used as a postulate before, but it has usually been thought of as an almost ideal situation in which the only conflict would be the beneficial friction between ideas and philosophies. It becomes clearer every day, however, that as people are released from the more brutal necessities of economic survival they begin to differentiate themselves from each other in any number of new ways and form those classes based on age, race, sex (and sexual orientation), which present themselves at first as politically and economically oppressed minorities before revealing their intentions to make a bid for power – control of what I think has been called the OFFICIAL REALITY[1].

A declaration by any of these oppressed minorities that it intends to rebuild the world in its own image, can be excused by the anarchist, who instinctively sides with the underdog, as being the excess of an overheated imagination which hasn't in the past been able to put into practice its more practical and modest desires (the most important of which is simply the wish to live without interference) and to believe that the chest-beatings will subside a little as soon as this equality is granted. But I think we cannot ignore the fact that this doesn't follow as a matter of course. The battle of policies and ideas which are a subterfuge for the range of emotions which these new classes represent is creating a state of confusion which will make the capitalist's desire to control the economic life of his workers seem a touching and childlike materialism.

I believe, however, that this "confusion" has a dialectic which hasn't yet been put into the kind of cast iron system in which Marx fixed our economic drives...that until a system is created,[2] or revealed rather, in the movement of ideas in a society, we face the likelihood that the struggle between these different "classes" will continue to create the divided consciousness that ensures the advance of totalitarian government. The worst mistake we can make at this time is to believe that every class of people producing anti-authoritarian literature is at the service of the revolution. There are people who have a hatred for the well-integrated personal authority which would give the necessary density and texture to a self-determining community without central government.

I intended to write a straightforward account of the Notting Hill district of London, with a description of the different community action and political groups of that area. (The *Observer* recently quoted it "the most fashionable social laboratory in the country", and quoted someone who said that living in the area was "like living under a microscope".) But I find that I can't approach the question of poverty in our society without trying to define what I think is its new position. It might seem from what I have written above that I am going to claim that the only people who are poor today are poor by temperament – which I'm not. There are certain families living in Notting Hill and Ladbroke Grove whose morality is the kind of religious materialism which capitalism seeks to encourage. (Capitalism doesn't even induce a genuinely realistic materialism, but – more horrible than that – an attitude to consumer goods that has requisitioned the imagination.) There are poor families who will not, on principle, wear secondhand clothes, or eat the cheap but unpretentious foodstuffs. On the market it's possible to buy, for ten shillings or so, a pair of handmade shoes that somebody must have paid ten pounds for, and died unexpectedly, leaving them in perfect condition. The sense of self, that our society tries to awaken, has to belong to something other than capitalist morality to feel capable of exorcising the ghost of past ownership.

When I see newspaper headlines which refer to Notting Hill with words like "misery", "twilight zone" and "hell", I have to keep in mind that there are people in the area who see themselves as unable to reach the first rungs of a ladder which stretches far above them, and to whom these terms apply: but I feel little urge to join one of the political groups trying to help them onto the bottom rungs of this particular ladder. Far more interesting, in a society that might very well "clean up" all its ghettoes sooner or later, is the existence of people who *choose* to live in this area rather than anywhere else in London. A housing survey which George Clark organised discovered that 77% of the people interviewed wanted to stay in the area after rehousing. To them, the families as well as the young dropouts, South Kensington is the nightmare area which has come to be part of the foreign territory that stretches away from the boundaries of the Grove, just as the social worker comes into North Kensington and sees only bad housing conditions. Now that the demand for the rehousing of the people of Acklam Road has been agreed to (thanks to the vigorous agitation inspired by George Clark), it is worth while pointing out that the residents of Cromwell Road tolerate a noisier and filthier piece of "motorway" outside their front doors without ever coming to the conclusion that there is anything they can do about it. And another point worth mentioning is that the reason why so many children are involved in road accidents in Notting Hill is because mothers insist on their *right* to let their children wander around or go to the shops on their own. If you walk round South Kensington or Chelsea, you will rarely see any young children out on their own. This isn't because play amenities are that much better. Children still have to be taken backward and forward between the parks and squares that do exist. And whereas in a "better" area it costs from £3 15s to £4 10s to put a child in a day nursery (provided they can be given a place from long waiting lists), there is at least one nursery in Notting Hill that will take any young child for four hours a day at a nominal five shillings a week, apart from the half dozen groups for older children that have been run by students and volunteers during the summer.

Obviously community leaders and social workers, plotting to get bigger grants from the local council or the GLC, need to stress the bad aspects of the area, but in many ways the place has that lived-in look, and liveable-in feel about it that makes it more bearable than most of the districts of London. The density of relationships, which again ensures the safety of children in the streets, is very high in the area. People know the names of their local councillors and policemen (mostly the notorious ones) and there is always somebody who knows somebody who wants to sell/buy an old sewing machine or a large wooden trunk, and so on.

So the real horror of society, which is alienation and destruction of community, deprivation of meaning rather than deprivation of food and shelter (a situation in which the best anarchist slogan would be DECENTRALISE EXPERIENCE) – is less severe because of a persistent sense of place and stubborn sense of self which, even if they only result from the kind of mutual aid and independence that is forced on people in any disaster zone, ought to be the subject of a more optimistic sociological study for its own sake.

The Christian and the Marxist have both enlisted the poor as being closer to their respective salvations than any other group in society, and, if we accept the existence of a dialectic in which all the stances and strategies are aimed at greater control of the Official Reality, they must be enlisted again as being one of the groups that are closest to snatching control of their own thoughts, and coming closer to self-determination. Together with the conservatives (by which, at best, I mean the people with a particular view of human nature rather than people with money or sexual repressions!),[3] they are a class of people who pay little attention to the manufactured attitudes and new puritanism surrounding questions of race, violence and sex in society.

The middle-class amenity groups, the footpath preservers, the consumer protection groups and the people who manage to foil plans for new airports, as well as the community groups in poor areas, are the two classes of people left who are showing some kind of local opposition to central government. Some of the best criticism of centralised government and ignorant totalitarianism is at the moment coming from the right. I've noticed, for example, a big improvement in the expression of ideas in the *Daily Telegraph*, and a bad decline in the *Guardian*, and in the next couple of years I think the *Telegraph* will come to occupy the place which the *Guardian* held for so long. (Beginning as an outlaw, of course.) Because the right-winger – again I don't mean capitalist or policeman or anything like that – senses that the middle-ground of thought in society (as represented by the intelligent young lecturer in sociology or economics, the top-class journalist or reviewer, as well as thousands of schoolteachers and students) has been lost, he is being forced to tighten up his ideas. A correspondent to the *Telegraph* has no authority – the latest report from the latest committee or social study group, etc. – he can bring forward to support his own feelings on a topic. Whereas the correspondents in the *Guardian*'s letter column consistently evoke the findings of a committee rather than their own common sense, in suggesting what improvements can be made in society. This is a complete reversal of the position, probably as little as fifteen years ago, when the libertarian took it for granted that every schoolmaster was conservative and authoritarian by nature, and that any committee would be bound to oppose his ideas.

It is one of the victories of a permissive society that this middle ground of thought in society now expresses its ideas in libertarian concepts such as "participation", "decentralisation", "spontaneity" dn so on. The price to be paid for this is an increasing slackness and lack of meaning in the use of these words which is going to lead to their expulsion from this territory by a set of terms, outlawed at the moment, but regenerating themselves by the necessity to be self-referential.

This year the Notting Hill Carnival, which has been run for five years by Mrs. Rhuane Laslett and the Community settlement, was cancelled because of fear of "growing racial tensions in the area". She is quoted in the *West London Observer* as saying:"We would have felt a tremendous sense of responsibility if there had been any incidents, and we thought that until problems had been resolved it would be better to call it off". I'm afraid that most people living here wouldn't know what she meant by that. The women who depend on the Nigerians and West Indians for their living, taking care of many more problems than the local social worker, are the people most ready with the term "black bastard" at the slightest provocation, without bringing to mind the word "prejudice" or images of gas chambers. The weight of commonsense in a community, the density of its relationships, can keep in check any outbreak of prejudice or violence. Ideally, people ought to be allowed their prejudices and quirks, which never get out of hand until they are abstracted from everyday circumstances by establishment politicians, or their opposite numbers who belong to the "revolution". To ask an individual to consider what his private thoughts would mean if ten thousand people had the same thoughts and banded together in some way, shows the lack of trust in the social maturity which exists in Notting

Hill more than in many communities where talk of racial tension
might have more meaning.

As it happens, the carnival was taken over by members of the
Notting Hill Youth Project, and renamed the People's Carnival for
the day. It was a great success, a self-conscious and rather militantly
joyful celebration of the two famous local victories that centred
around Powis Square and Acklam Road. It's wonderful to see
crowds of people surging past their own homes and down the centre
of the streets which belongs to them. It's a kind of tribal assertion of
territorial rights that people everywhere should get a chance to
indulge in once a year.

This brings me back to the idea that it is this sense of identity and
sense of place which is being undermined by all those who attach
themselves uncritically to the centrally organised crusades of the
day.

"The ideas of a time are like the clothes of a season, as much
imposed by some superior will which is seldom explicit. They are
utilitarian and political, the instruments of a smooth running government".

Wyndham Lewis wrote that in 1926 in a little-known masterpiece
of social criticism called *The Art of Being Ruled*. It is so relevant to
the new kind of political battle that is being fought at the moment,
that I suspect the publishing and literary fraternities of suppressing
the book for fifty years. Lewis was the first to write social criticism
which paid serious attention to the fashions in ideas and policies and
life style, which have become the subject of so much attention in the
last few years. He was the first man to set foot inside the global
village with his assertion that the popularity of Charlie Chaplin was
due to the spread of the philosophy of Bergson. This strikes us as
nothing more than a novel idea now, one of the hundreds of such
notions that exist in an atmosphere when it seems commonplace to
discuss the Beatles' lyrics and Mahler in the same breath. But
Yeats, who read Lewis's *Time and Western Man* towards the end of
his life, records that it struck him as one of the most novel and
striking ideas he had come across. Since, by the time he read Lewis's
book, Yeats had explored every (for him) strictly separated labyr-
inth of art, popular culture and politics, Lewis's thought must have
seemed true enough to threaten one of the barriers Yeats had
erected round his ideas.

One of Lewis's prophesies describes an attitude, a political
stance even, that we have heard a lot of recently. "In a society, the
political and social machinery of which could be logically reduced,
for the purposes of grasping it in its simplest, most radical workings,

to such a figure as the above, what type of being would be pointed to as the ideal of human perfection? Obviously a child of some sort – of the same race of 'little children' as that of which Christ proposed to build his heaven. But Christ's charm would be absent. The grace and gentleness of his evangel would not come to mind on reading the harsh and fussy text-books of this political faith, prepared for the mechanisation and fixing of the new child type".

I don't know if Lewis expected a recognisable part of the established power groups to begin preaching this doctrine, but it is now being preached by somebody I like to call a freakout philosopher who rightly regards himself as an avant garde in the wish to create this new kind of political being. There is an exhilarating freedom to be found in submitting to something called Experience, drifting on the surface of life, tossed here and there by delightful and spontaneous accidents. But it is the freedom of the adult slave and the freedom, whose existence only a self-determined individual can ensure exists, of the child.

Seeing the hierarchically structured personality of an adult, with purpose, will and ego in control, and so preventing a beautiful and passive understanding of existence coming to the surface, our freakout philosopher recommends a reversal of this state of affairs, reminding us that this structured personality is a reflection of the structure of states which are causing all those dreadful wars. But since choice, hence self-determination, is based almost by definition, on some repression of parts of the self and the outside world, he is recommending the dismantling of the centralised and integrated personality which has become its own dictatorship and aristocracy, and no longer needs government and authority in the outside world.

Lewis tells us that the first kind of freedom, the one based on choice and self-rule, man finds too difficult to achieve, and begins to seek the second kind, "the great patent of ecstatic submission, the feminine type of freedom and self-expression", and Lewis adds that "the first requisite for it is a master". Seen in this light then, Paul Goodman's appeal to the young to accept the help of the "professional" is futile, because every underground magazine in England or America is filled with the kind of writing which sets out to undermine the values of the professional – of which Goodman himself is a good example – by its distrust of objectivity and stress on the dionysian freedom of ecstatic submission, and by its aversion to the structured mind which, the closer it comes to defining real freedom and how it is to be achieved, threatens to impose a more intolerable authority on the young rebel's mind than a clumsy government does.

A government that knew what was happening would be happy to sit back in its own invulnerable position and watch the internal structure of society disintegrating, the ground falling away till it is left alone on a high rock hidden by mist. The authority of its own henchmen is threatened of course, but they are becoming less important to it, and a totalitarian government would ditch its right-wing support in the community, as soon as the destructuring process had gone far enough to ensure the lack of cohesion in any assault on its position from the left.

There is an awful wisdom in being impotent and helpless in the face of events, and the blind stupidity of revolutionaries in the past who thought that they could change society and did, needs to be cultivated in very small areas of existence before it is ready to face a larger world. If anything, it is a too great awareness of the complexity of society which is undermining people's sense of their own realities, and the deliberate stupidity of a person who thinks he can take his fate in his own hands seems to be worth a cheer whether that person is a hard-bitten old reactionary or an unashamed lumpen who hasn't heard of the new impossible situation we are all in. It's in this situation then, where people take their identities from the Official Reality and not from a community existence that the politically motivated social worker is the small entrepreneur of the new dialectic.

I heard that the people who run *Bit*, the underground information service, were worried recently about the decline in the number of telephone calls being made to them. Fewer people wanting advice, fewer people with problems perhaps: but politically oriented organisers with a vested interest in other people's helplessness beginning to feel vaguely irrelevant.

Because of a self-consciousness about the need for spontaneity and participation that these people have, you can walk around the *Bit* or *Release* premises and some of the underground newspaper offices without being challenged too directly as to your purpose. It's best to lurch in looking puzzled and stand reading notices stuck on the walls in a compulsive and slightly unbalanced way, so that after a quick glance at your back, they will write you off as best left alone and carry on with what they are doing. If they suspect some kind of impudent observer in the room, among the transcendent junkies and fifteen-year-old problem runaways, the games with telephones, urgent messages and impossibly worsening situations (common to all offices, I suppose) will tend to become more subdued and so less interesting.

On one line there is a mother in Kent, wondering if her daughter has shown up in London, then somebody runs up the stairs to say that there's a big bust at No. 11 and the police are holding over twenty. As another telephone rings – by which time you have turned round to watch, you can't help noticing the touch of manic glee. Christ, another problem? It's one of those days! as it is explained by the person on the other end that there is a bloke in the room next door to her who says he can see black spiders the size of LP records trying to get in at his window. What can she do about it?

Still holding his head, the man who took the call passes this last problem to a political female with a sincere voice who says to give him a cup of hot lemon juice with plenty of sugar in it and to ring back in an hour if the spiders haven't gone away by then.

I'm not suggesting that it is possible to expect social workers, or young people who run community and information services and so on to be completely disinterested, and not to seek their own emotional satisfactions and mental stimulation by helping people with their problems. But as with any other kind of organisation – even the most informal, participatory and unstructured kind, a person with a desire to lead or to represent, can only demand dependency and insiduously begin to encourage it. There's nothing some of them love more than an authentically hopeless wreck.

By way of gossip, I've heard stories of community helpers fighting each other for control of a problem which both of them claim they found first. The housing organisation woman, for instance, who rang up another organisation in the area which had already found accommodation for a homeless family, warning them to leave her homeless families alone.

A form of humanitarianism, and for younger people a more libertarian-based humanitarianism, has become the secular religion, which means that the political left have inherited that huge body of people, the well-meaning philistines, the good people with irreproachable ideals who were a plague round the church for centuries. It took decades of political and literary activity to expose the hypocrisy and reactionary role of the "Love, Peace and help-your-neighbour" attitude of the charitable Christian, and I'm depressed to think that it's going to take as long before it is generally seen that a certain kind of modern community worker and socially concerned man or woman is the same person in a different disguise.

A typical extract from one of the numerous reports of one of the youth projects in the area (which I've invented however) will read:

"When Jimmy first appeared at one of the informal gatherings we had begun to hold, because of lack of funds, in the largely improvised environment of a school hall, he displayed a brazen self-sufficiency which was obviously a brave front to hide the turmoil of adolescent difficulties. He wouldn't join any of the groups we had arranged to talk over the racial discrimination in the area, and to answer queries about any of the kids' sexual difficulties that might turn up in the conversation.

"One of the female students who had joined us that summer was enlisted to approach him but she was unable to coax him into telling her about himself and his problems. (It was known already, in confidence, that his father was a drunkard and that his mother had taken up with a black man who was still taking money off another woman in the area.) His usual reply to such attempts was: "Who, me? I'm all right."[4] And he spent most of his time around the record player, shouting remarks at the girls and generally disrupting the work we were trying to organise.

"But the fifth time he came, a night when he seemed upset about something and had stopped making fun of the girls, another volunteer was able to achieve some success in getting him..."

When I think of people with problems and difficulties, I remember Kerouac's Dean, running into the road holding his gangrenous thumb in the air. Well, perhaps it's an unpleasant truth, but a society with its head on fire doesn't pay attention to the agony of its separate parts – its poor included – knowing that if it can do the basic things well, the details will fall into place. This isn't a very helpful attitude at the moment, and the community worker probably is doing the best possible job in a situation in which the only synthesis of consciousness there is, forms itself round a shared helplessness. I've only to see a crowd of mothers painting their own "GO SLOW" sign, erecting their own play street barriers, or emptying their dustbins into the road as a protest, to want to change my attitude completely. But I suspect that if the optimism and confidence which will risk radical change was to appear in the future, you would find the Jimmies and the sharp spades who shut the door in your face when you are trying to complete a housing survey, of more use than the people who, at present, are willing to group themselves together and present authority with a challenging list of complaints.

*Anarchy 117*                                              *November 1970*

# Footnotes

1 Two novelists, William Burroughs and Colin Wilson, seem to have come up against the idea of thought control. Colin Wilson is a political writer in a way that hasn't been understood yet. His attitude to literature is completely utilitarian – to a prosaic extreme. He has little interest in aesthetics, words and rhythms never lead him astray from his ideas, and in a sense he hasn't bothered to become a "writer". He sees himself as writing in the English progressive rationalist tradition that Wells and Shaw belonged to. If he doesn't apply himself as closely to everyday politics as those two writers did, it appears to be because he is doing the kind of "pure research" which points to a new dialectic.

2 I suspect that the "new Marx" will be a psychologist and literary historian who uses the whole field of art history as his raw material.

3 Interesting, in connection with the idea that temperament is becoming more important than money in determining political attitudes, is the stress, among people who call themselves the "underground", on the latter qualification for a reactionary attitude rather than the possession of money.

4 This is a false note in my invention, because it is here that a social worker will put a four-letter word into his report to illustrate depth of experience and the informal character of relationships inside the group.

# III.  WORK

## 1.  The gang system in Coventry
### Reg Wright

THE GANG system as operated in Coventry is modern and yet traditional. Its roots lie among the bloody-minded craftsmen who, centuries ago, sent the King to hell – and paid for it afterwards. They worked in *groups* – guilds. Later on in Coventry there was a prosperous ribbon-weaving industry. Semi-domestic *groups* by the thousand sent beautiful silk ribbons, flags and banners all over the world. My grandmother started work at 6 years of age, winding silk for the weavers. She told me: "We didn't look upon it as 'work' – we enjoyed it." She also carried tea (an expensive luxury) to the weavers. Ribbons were followed by watch manufacture. Again highly specialised family and neighbour *groups* made the various parts of the watches which were assembled by the master-watchmakers – who also worked in *groups*. It was all very informal and satisfying. The watchmakers always had a 'Saint Monday' – boozing all day, taking Tuesday to get over it, and working Wednesday, Thursday and Friday. Saturday morning they "cleaned up the shop". They grew most of their own food, kept pigs and fowl, grazed horses and cows on the commons (which were never enclosed – only built on in recent years), and nearly always married young – not because they had to, but because they liked it. Watchmaking died out from lack of standardisation – undersold by machine-made watches. The making of parts *was* highly specialised, but to make a cheap product an elaborate system of standards and gauging was necessary, as in engineering today. (Peter Kropotkin described a similar set-up among the Swiss watch-case makers of Jura – how they sat around and worked and talked and were natural anarchists.)

Next came the manufacture of sewing machines, and then bicycles. Inventions by the thousands, mostly by unknown men, made bicycle-making into a precision manufacture, one of the bases of production engineering as we now know it. Again men formed groups around the job. Mechanics came from all over England and they learned that group work paid. As employers became capitalistic, groups were broken up, but they always re-formed, and re-demonstrated their virtues.

And so it has continued to the present day: right through the making of cycles, motor-cycles, cars, aeroplanes and machine tools, there has been a continuous warfare between the group idea and the individualistic-minded employer and his officials. Those firms today which have the knack of the gang system have a huge advantage over the others. Wages are higher (which attracts better workers), they turn out a good product, make larger profits and are very adaptable. Technical methods and tools used are the same in the American type mass-production plant, *but* the human aspect is vastly different. Each worker contributes an effort, an idea, a pooling of knowledge and experience that is not readily forthcoming in the autocratically managed plant. Work is easier and people are happier. This is *not* a eulogy of capitalism – there are rows – fierce disputes that break the monotony of regular work. Disputes are often due to the clash of opposite mentalities – middle-class individualism in management *versus* working-class collectivism. Domestic disputes between gang members are settled on the spot – purely private scraps! Idle people are very severely dealt with by their mates – *never* from above. There is no 'idealistic' talk about these things, but the benefits are obvious. Rough talk and aggressive attitudes are usually poses – the real man underneath is usually quite reasonable. People rarely leave and the labour turnover is very small indeed. There are no secrets about earnings or wage rates – everybody knows all about everyone else. The facts of output required and achieved are common knowledge. A car model will be in production for five years or more, a tractor for ten. Regular work, year in year out is thus essential – which can be horribly monotonous.

One of the compensations can be the company of other people. In addition to the firm's social club activities, most gangs organise their own, some of them surprising. The firm's official sick-club *reduces* the amount of benefit paid to members as illness is extended. To counter this each gang pays an increasing amount to the person as the period grows longer, on the basis that "the longer he is away from work the more his need grows". In another firm a man has been away in a mental hospital for over five years – he is still a gang member, recognised by the management and the trade union. The latter grants his wife periodic sums from surplus funds – the firm can provide for his rehabilitation should he be cured. He still *belongs*.

In another works, sheet metal workers were making car wings by hand (for high-class sports cars) and one man spoiled fifty – a week's work – through misreading a drawing. The gang had a meeting, took the foreman out to the pub, fifty men made one wing apiece, the scrap ones were 'lost' and no-one was any the wiser. The middle-class works manager would have had a baby had he known, but the gang saved him the inconvenience. There are thousands of such stories that could be told daily. This is the natural cohesion of workers when they are not stampeded by clever and cunning people. They don't profess to be good – just ordinary. Girls and boys enjoy ganging-up and so do men and women. And in Coventry the gang system has been *forced upon* employers who, at first reluctant, now concede it. But each new generation of clever young managers has to relearn the same old lessons. They start off determined to "put the men in their place" and end by accepting the gang system – even boasting about it as though it were their own creation.

Gangs are self-recruiting, nearly all new members being "recommended" to a trade union for the formalities. 'Green' labour (*ie* people with no special skill) is put on simple repetitive jobs and when the stage of boredom is reached are moved to increasingly complex operations. In effect the man or woman serves an apprenticeship of sorts while earning full pay as a gang member. No distinction is made between them *as people*. They are all paid the same regardless of skill. The clever man will do the clever job – because he can, and because he likes it. The not-so-clever (or even stupid) man will do the job that is within his powers. It has been proved long ago, that distinctions cause much more trouble than they are worth. Both management and men are agreed on this. Such agreement is tacit. These things I describe are not even mentioned – they have become social custom, commonplaces. Melman in his work continually refers to the excellence of the gang system but the fundamentals of it, the human sense of it seems to be beyond him.

The whole method has evolved directly *from the work*, from the human and technical need for co-operation. The tough men who have given their whole lives to it have seized on every significant thing or event and turned it to their purpose, *our* purpose. Bit by bit a new form of industrial society is being built. However bad it may still be, it is far better than most autocratic systems and it teaches people better ways by practice and not by exhortation. When the gang system has worked out and stabilised a new step forward, then the local trade union officials come in and register the facts in an official agreement with the firm. One such man (known to me personally as a very clever negotiator) stepped in and formalised the entire scheme at the Standard works. It was a major achievement, and would have been, at the highest professional level. This man was self-taught, in workshop and trade union. There are *some* trade union leaders who try to claim credit for themselves for all that is done – they don't deceive *us* but the newspapers lap it up. *They* think and write of trade unions as the *leaders*, whereas in reality the achievements are those of the members and their ideas.

Technically the gang system is a method of payment for piece-work – a form of collective contract. In *practice* it follows the natural tendency of men to group up around the job. Gangs can be of any size from three to three thousand – the latter being the approximate size of the Ferguson tractor team. Half-a-million tractors were turned out in ten years with practically no supervision – one gang for the entire works and yet there was still the piecework urge – still the initiative from below, in addition to the technical progress from above. This is the essential difference between the Midlands attitude to the job and the uniform and fixed wage system elsewhere, especially in the south of England. In the Midlands the *men* have the initiative and are the driving force – the rest of the staff have to keep pace, to provide for and assist the production team. Everything is done to make the job easier, every hint and suggestion from whatever source is heeded and used if possible – especially if it takes the strain from the job.

Thus men's energies are conserved for other things than work. But it is still work! Automaton is a misnomer – there is just continuous production, some automatic, some semi-automatic, and much of it by hand. Greed is abolished because any increase in wages or betterment of conditions is due, and is *known* to be due, to the men's own effort and creative ideas. The result of continuous struggle and creative effort is *seen* in the finished product and enjoyed *via* the pay packet. People of lethargic temperament may loathe and dread the very idea of all this, but the workers concerned "don't die on the job". Neither do they worry or conjure up images of destruction. They are vigorous and healthy and are busy home-making and rearing families.

In other factories *small* gangs may be grouped around a machine that is being built, or an aeroplane component. In a car factory it will be a production line, or a group of machines. When the product is very complex and costly and is produced in small numbers the gangs will be very clever in adapting their skills to a variety of jobs. Individual skill of a very high order will be applied to a prototype and to the first few production 'jobs'. The individual will be guaranteed his money by the gang while he undertakes exploratory work – others will follow him, each taking a portion of the work and becoming specialists in it, while others will improvise special tools and gadgets to make it into a "production job". The variety of work and gangs is infinite.

The gang system sets men's minds free from many worries and enables them to concentrate completely on the job. It provides a natural frame of security, it gives confidence, shares money equally, uses all degrees of skill without distinction and enables jobs to be allocated to the man or woman best suited to them, the allocation frequently being made by the workers themselves. Change of job to avoid monotony is an easy matter. The "gaffer" is abolished and foremen are now technicians called in to advise, or to act in a breakdown or other emergency. In some firms a *ganger* will run, not the men, but the *job*. He will be paid out of gang earnings, and will work himself on a small gang. On a larger gang he will be fully occupied with organisation and supply of parts and materials. A larger gang may have a deputy ganger as a second string and also a *gang-steward* who, being a keen trade unionist or workers' man, will act as a corrective should the gangers try to favour management unduly or interfere with the individual in undesirable ways. Gang meetings are called, as necessary, by the latter and all members of the gang are kept informed and may (and do) criticise everything and everybody. All three are subject to recall. Constructive ideas on the other hand are usually the result of one or two people thinking out and trying out new things – this is taking place continuously – to the general advantage of the whole gang.

The fact of taking responsibility in any of these capacities is educative in every sense, and I have often been amused to see someone who is a notorious "gaffer's man" being persuaded into taking the gang steward position which will bring him into contact with other stewards whose ideas he will unconsciously absorb. He will attend meetings with management representatives at all levels and usually completely changes his ideas. Experienced stewards, with grim humour call this "educating the so-and-so's!" Some stewards have been known to use variants of this method in educating management representatives.

Similarly in car factories. A gang of 100 or more will have a *charge-hand* paid by the management. He will stand out from the gang, only working in the event of difficulty arising – any hold-up of breakdown. The *gang-steward* will stand out with him and settle with him all points of difference on the gang's behalf. He also will work as necessary. Sometimes they are idle (educating each other!) and at other times they will work like fiends, to keep the flow of work going.

Gang stewards form a reservoir from which *senior* stewards are recruited. There are thousands of such men and they are quite often engineering experts, usually holding their own with any rate-fixer, cost expert or other managerial type. Occasionally fools are appointed – the blustering wordy windbag – the 'rebel' who just fights – and the exponent of an ideology. Some ideologists are first-rate stewards but do not realise that their actions may be the reverse of their ideological aims.

There are many local variants of the scheme – some good, some indifferent. As in any other aspect of life, much depends on the quality of the people concerned, and on their experience, ideas (that is, theories or ideological or political standpoints) do not enter into any of it – a person can think what he likes, say what he likes, *except* that he does not *do* anything against the gang or the trade union. He is expected to be a trade union member – even if only as an outward and visible sign of toughness. In terms of the old working-class motto, "he is either with us or against us". There is no half-way. Incentives are three: to get as high a rate of pay as possible (depending on output), having achieved a certain stability in that, there is a general urge to speed up production gradually so that hours of work can be reduced. The final aim (a continuously successful process) is to make the job itself, and the surroundings, as good as possible.

All these urges are *everyone's* concern. In such a production set-up it is natural that people in full health and vigour are needed, and sickly people are strongly advised not to take a job there. In a temporary indisposition it is usual for the person to be given some help, or if that is not possible, a transfer to a light job that is not urgent.

Most of this has been forced upon employers, but one must give credit to those managers who have genuinely tried to help the urge to better conditions. On the other hand one frequently finds amongst managers a tendency to "swing to the right". This may be the result of a new director or manager coming in from the outside, usually from firms with American ideas; occasionally he will have a strong political (Conservative) urge. Sooner or later he shows his hand – forthright and dictatorial. From that moment the "worker decision-making" apparatus works against him. His "education" commences. Once I finalised the process by warning the particular manager "You must always remember that a thousand men will wear *you* out quicker than you can wear *them* out". It worked. The moment something actually happens or is pending, there is a ferment right through the plant and the decision-making is carried out at shop-floor level, even to the point, if necessary, of contradicting or disowning the stewards' proposals.

It is difficult to convey in writing a whole way of industrial life, a subtle, yet obvious, development of capitalism, a different and better way of running large-scale industry. It *is* better – a vast improvement – a continuance of an age-old method in a modern setting. *It has all those elements that could develop into a successor to capitalism.* I can imagine some clever people dismissing all this as nonsense, mere sentimental drivel, etc, and going on to *prove* that it is only a temporary thing that could be wiped out when required, by a powerful managerial capitalist class, etc, or that when "the slump" comes and the workers are thrown out on the streets, etc. (all of which is outmoded thought). My answer is that if "disaster" comes to capitalism, we have at least done some preliminary rehearsing for the new play we may be called upon to produce. If capitalism goes on for a long time without disaster, we shall have tried to make life as good as we can for as many people as we can. If there is some day a general desire to push capitalism over, we shall do our share. I think we are quite as clever as the "intellectuals", only we have applied ourselves to the daily task instead of to theoretical disputation. As engineers we have changed the world, as social engineers we nave improved our part of it as much as we can. We feel that we are reasonably well-equipped to go very much further, and if we do we shall need the co-operation of all those technicians and organisers who are at present on "the other side", and we know that *some* of them are already with us.

*Anarchy 2*                                                        *April 1961*


# 2.   Anarchism and trade unionism
## Gaston Gerard

THE QUESTION of the position anarchists should take in relation to Trade Unions has been the subject of perennial debate within the anarchist movement. It is not, however, a question which admits of

a permanent or definitive answer. Because of differing circumstances and changing conditions, each generation of anarchists must
think out its position afresh in the light of existing tendencies within
its own national trade union movement. The present time seems an
opportune one for a re-assessment of the anarchist position in relation to the British trade union movement and what follows is to be
taken as a tentative contribution towards this end.

# I.

A useful starting point for discussion is provided in the two articles
by Errico Malatesta on the subject published in 1907 and 1925
respectively.* The first was written at a time when the movement of
revolutionary syndicalism was making great strides on the Conti-
nent. In France, where the classic revolutionary syndicalist movement found its most complete expression in the days before the first
world war, this movement was very much a product of anarchist
activities. Largely in reaction against the notorious policy of "propaganda by deed", many of the younger anarchists, led by the re-
doutable Fernand Pelloutier, joined the syndicates with the object
of developing their revolutionary potentialities. Such work seemed
to them to offer a constructive alternative to a policy of negation
and destruction which, however justifiable it might be in theory,
had done much to discredit the anarchist movement in the sight of
the world at large. In their enthusiasm for the new policy, however,
many of the anarchists abandoned any purely anarchist activity on
the ground that the syndicate in its various forms was not only the
most effective means of overthrowing capitalism but also contained
in itself all the essentials of a free society.

Such an attitude amounted in effect to an identification of
anarchism and syndicalism and it was against this attitude that
Malatesta directed his attack. He was not opposed, it should be
noted, to anarchists participating as individuals in labour organisations. On the contrary, he thought that such participation was
necessary; but he insisted that it should be participation and not

---

*"Anarchism and the Labour Movement", originally published in FREE-
DOM, Nov. 1907 and republished in the same journal 23.2.1946; "Syndicalism and Anarchism", published in *Pensiero e Volonta* April-May,
1925 and republished in FREEDOM, 11.10.1952

identification. This position, which he reiterated in his second article, he supported on two main grounds. First, that anarchism was
not equivalent to syndicalism. If it were, he argued, then syndicalism was merely a new and confusing term. In fact, however, it was
not; only certain syndicalist ideas were genuinely anarchistic; others
were only authoritarian ideas under a new guise. Experience had
shown, he argued, that labour organisations, however revolutionary they might be in their initial phases, had a twin tendency to
degenerate into reformist and bureaucratic bodies. And this
tendency was owing, not so much to *personal* factors, such as the
corrupting influence of power, as to certain *institutional* factors.

It was, and is, a fundamental article of syndicalist theory that
syndicates or unions perform a dual role; a negative role of defending the workers' interests under capitalism and a positive role of
acting as the nuclei of the future society. Malatesta's point, as I
interpret it, was that the first role – the defensive role, and in the
short run from the ordinary worker's point of view, the most important role – inevitably dominates the second role, and in so doing
paves the way for reformism. To fulfil their defensive role, the
unions have, for example, to submit to an element of legal control.
In addition, they are compelled to widen their membership as far as
possible with the object of achieving a 100% organisation in their
trade or industry. In doing this, however, the conscious militant
minority becomes swamped by the non-militant majority, with the
result that, even if the leadership remains in the hands of the militants, the revolutionary ideas one started with have to be toned
down. The revolutionary programme becomes nothing but an empty formula.

Malatesta's conclusion, therefore, was that whilst anarchists
should remain in the unions, combating as fiercely as possible these
degenerative tendencies, they should not identify themselves too
closely with syndicalism. "Let us beware of ourselves," he said.
"The error of having abandoned the Labour movement has done an
immense injury to anarchism, but at least it leaves unaltered the
distinctive character. The error of confounding the anarchist movement with Trade Unionism would be still more grave. That will
happen to us which happened to the Social Democrats as soon as
they went into the Parliamentary struggle. They gained in numeric-
al force, but by becoming each day less Socialistic. We also would
become more numerous, but we should cease to be anarchist".

# II.

How far are Malatesta's arguments applicable to the British trade union movement and how valid is his conclusion today?

A review of the history of British trade unionism shows that there is ample evidence to support the view that labour organisations tend to degenerate into reformist bodies. Contrary to popular belief, trade unionism in this country has not always been reformist; it has in fact passed through several revolutionary, or potentially revolutionary, phases. It was in the early days of the movement that syndicalist ideas first saw the light of day. The Grand National of 1834 was the first expression of the One Big Union idea, and it was William Benbow who first elaborated the theory of the general strike – or grand national holiday, as he called it. In its beginnings at least British trade unionism was as revolutionary as one might wish. After the collapse of the first revolutionary movement, the trade unions settled down to win reforms within the existing system – reforms which in the hey-day of its 19th century prosperity British capitalism could well afford. Then in the 1880s with the onset of the Great Depression and the rise of competitors like Germany who challenged British capitalism's industrial supremacy, revolutionary ideas once again came to the fore in trade union circles. These ideas were associated particularly with the rise of what was called the new Unionism – the attempt to organise the unskilled workers. Many British anarchists of the day considered that this New Unionism offered great scope for anarchist influence. William Morris' Socialist League, for example, addressed one of its first manifestos to the trade unions urging them "to direct all their energies towards confederating and federating with the distinct end of constituting themselves the nucleus of the socialist commonwealth" and making clear that the aim of socialism was the abolition of "that great bogey," the State. Similarly a writer in *Freedom* in 1892 urged that "Unions are free spontaneous associations of working men waiting to do anarchistic work". In point of fact, however, the New Unionists, despite their more militant policy, their vague talk of workers' control and a general strike, and their disavowal of the friendly society functions of the old union of skilled workers, proved to be less not more anarchistic than the old unions. It was the New Unions which were the first to become infected with Fabian State Socialism and it was the New Unions which forced the pace in the movement towards the creation of a political Labour Party.

The reason for this apparent paradox is illuminating. *Just be-*

*cause* the workers they enlisted in their ranks could not afford to finance "coffin club" activities, and did not possess a monopoly of any particular skill, the New Unions were predisposed towards political action. Too weak to secure their defensive objects themselves, they turned to the State to do the job for them – to introduce a legislative 8-hour day, old age pensions, unemployment benefits and the like. At its birth the Labour Party was largely a means of achieving the defensive objects of the trade unions – and this, despite its "Socialist" programme, remains its primary function today. To tell trade unionists therefore to renounce political action is to ask them to renounce what they have found to be a powerful defensive weapon and to rely on their own unaided efforts – and to risk the possible loss of reforms that have already been won.

The third and to date last revolutionary phase of British trade unionism was the period roughly 1910–1926 when syndicalist ideas were again in the ascendant. British syndicalism was born partly of disillusionment with Labour Party policies and was partly the result of Continental and American influence. The movement achieved some success in spreading the idea of workers' control among the rank-and -file trade unionists and , in fact, to the extent that this idea is alive today in the British working-class movement, it is largely owing to the syndicalists of this period and their middle-class counterparts, the guild socialists. But the syndicalist movement proper collapsed partly through internal dissensions consequent on the creation of the Communist Party and partly through the lack of success. The savage counter-attack of the British ruling class during the General Strike of 1926 dealt a body blow to British trade unionism. Syndicalist ideas were discredited – most unjustly since the General Strike was certainly not syndicalist-inspired – and after 1926 the policy of political action once again began to dominate trade union thought. Nothing that has happened since has seemed to justify to the majority of trade unions a return to the policy of relying on direct action in the industrial sphere. In terms of their own practical objects, trade union leaders have no incentive to revert to direct action methods. The political ruling class is now agreed on the maintenance of the Welfare State which represents the limit of the utopian aspirations of the average trade unionist. As a guarantee of its maintenance the official trade union movement has been granted a secure niche in the organisation of the State and in return for this concession it throws its weight against "irresponsible" and unofficial strikes.

It is possible that if the Welfare State were threatened either by a reactionary government or by a new slump, this might provide the necessary stimulus for a new revolutionary phase in the history of British trade unionism. But there are no signs that a real slump is likely to occur in the forseeable future or that our ruling class is so inept as to allow a repetition of mass unemployment on the scale experienced in the 1930s. And what is more important, there is no reason to believe that, if trade unionism did take a revolutionary turn, this would be anything more than a passing phase. There is nothing in the history of British trade unionism to suggest that in the long run it is ever likely to be more than a reformist institution. Looked at historically, revolutionary methods and policies on the part of British trade unionism have been no more than one way of winning reformist concessions from the ruling class. Trade unionists have, in effect, been saying to their masters: "If you don't grant us our modest demands, just look what we'll do!"

# III.

The other tendency – the tendency towards bureaucratisation – which Malatesta discerned is also amply illustrated in British trade unionism. "Every institution," he wrote, "has a tendency to extend its functions, to perpetuate itself, and to become an end in itself". When this tendency becomes dominant, bureaucracy, the *de facto* rule of officials, is the result. This stage in the life of an organisation is marked by the emergence of a new type of leader – the organiser, who replaces the more demagogic type: the Morrisons replace the Keir Hardies, the Bevins and Deakins replace the Ben Tilletts and the Tom Manns. In theory the officials remain responsible to their members but in practice it is the officials who run the show.

This tendency which Malatesta noted has since been elaborated into a sociological hypothesis, known as the law of oligarchy. First formulated by Robert Michels in his exhaustive study of "Political Parties" (1915) , it has a general application. Put in its most general form, the hypothesis states that in any organisation, however democratic it may be, once it has reached a certain size and degree of complexity, there is an invariable tendency for the officials to gain effective control. The ostensibly democratic constitution thus merely serves to mask what is in fact the rule of a narrow oligarchy. It needs no great knowledge of British trade unionism to appreciate the fact that the movement has reached the oligarchical stage. The facts published in Dr. Goldstein's book on the TGWU confirm the view that Michel's "iron law of oligarchy", as he called it, holds within the trade union world that we know today.

# IV.

Increasing awareness of the twin tendency in trade unionism towards reformism and bureaucracy has suggested to many contemporary anarchists that participation in trade unions is value-less and that instead attention should be concentrated in building up a new trade union movement on avowedly syndicalist lines. This, as I understand it, is the policy of those who call themselves anarcho-syndicalists. Such anarchists propose that the new movement should adopt principles of organisation which would ensure that it would not develop in the way the "official" trade union movement has developed. The new unions or syndicates are to be based on industries rather than on crafts, thus avoiding sectional conflicts between the workers themselves. There is to be no political action; instead, reliance is to be placed exclusively on direct action. By this means it is hoped to avoid mere reformisms and the danger of unions being used for the ulterior ends of political opportunists and careerists. Special measures are to be taken to avoid the danger of bureaucratisation. There will be a minimum of organisers; no organiser will be regarded as permanent; and no organiser will be paid more than a rank-and-file worker. By these means, it is hoped that control will remain with the rank-and-file: the danger of control falling into the hand of a hierarchy of officials will be avoided because there will be no officials in the sense understood by ordinary trade unionists today.

In theory all this is perfectly correct but nevertheless the policy of seeking to create anarchist organisations – for this is what it amounts to – is, I believe, mistaken. In the first place, the time is not propitious. Such a policy is likely to bear fruit only in a period of revolutionary crisis and after the ground has been well fertilised by years of propaganda in favour of such general objects as workers' control. In this respect, it will take years of intensive effort before the climate in the world of labour is as favourable towards revolutionary activity as it was in, say, the early 1920s. In the second place, the theory of anarcho-syndicalist organisation fails to show how it can counteract the institutional factor noted by Malatesta. The means proposed for ensuring rank-and-file control can only be successful if membership is confined to workers who are more or less conscious anarchists. But if this was done, the numbers at the present time and in the forseeable future would necessarily be small and the unions so organised would find themselves unable to fulfil satisfactorily their first role – that of defending the interests of their members under the existing régime. If, on the other hand, membership was not limited – the unions would soon become swamped by reformists and the anarcho-syndicalist principles of organisation would cease to operate. The reformists might allow the organisation to keep its revolutionary programme but it would be no more than a paper programme. In this connection it should be noted that many existing unions still have the revolutionary object of workers' control written into their constitutions. In short, the anarcho-syndicalist is faced with an inescapable dilemma at the present time: he can either choose to keep his organisation revolutionary, in which case it will be small and ineffective in defence; or he can choose to make it large and effective for defensive purposes at the sacrifice of its revolutionary potentialities. In addition, a policy of creating separate organisations would divide and confuse the workers even more than they are divided and confused at the present time and this in itself would be used as a strong propaganda point by the existing union hierarchy. And, finally, there is the undeniable fact that the effort expended by anarcho-syndicalists in propagandising their policy has had little effect. The hopes placed by the anarcho-syndicalists in the unofficial workers' committees that have sprung up since the war have not been fulfilled.


# V.

In the present circumstances, therefore, it seems to me that Malatesta's main contentions still hold good that those anarchists who are prepared to act in the industrial sphere should work within the existing unions rather than propagate the idea of a new union movement. This is not to say that the time will never come when the workers should be encouraged to form new and revolutionary unions but that time will be in the future *after* the ground has been well prepared in the present unions. In short, the position anarchists should take in relation to trade unionism today is to participate in them as rank-and-file members with the two-fold object of (i) making anarchists by spreading anarchist ideas and explaining to their fellow-workers the root causes of their disillusionment with the trade union leadership and policies and (ii) acting as a prophylactic against reformist and bureaucratic tendencies.

The first object is fundamental in the sense that it is now clearer than ever that an anarchist society can be brought about, not by mass movements, however "revolutionary", but only by individuals who have consciously adopted an anarchist philosophy and faith. As William Morris was never tired of asserting in the days when "socialism" was still an honourable word, the only way to make socialism is to make socialists – a truth which his Fabian opponents never began to understand.

The second object, if less fundamental, is of the utmost importance in the immediate future. The unions began as free associations of workers to promote their economic interests. Increasingly since the war, however, they are being incorporated in the mechanism of the State. Such incorporation means in practice that instead of defending their members' interests they are tending more and more to act as disciplinary bodies and as agencies for restraining the workers. The insistence on greater productivity at all costs – with no questioning of what is produced and to what end – and the present talk of regulating strikes are significant pointers to the fact that British trade unionism is treading the same road as its Soviet counterpart. Unless the present tendency is halted soon, the much vaunted independence of trade unionism will be no more; and one further step will be taken towards the totalitarian state. In a situation such as this and granted that the most desirable course of action is not practicable – in this case, the speedy building up of genuinely anarchist unions – there is only one sensible alternative for the revolutionary: to do his utmost to reverse the present tendency. For it is obvious that independence of the State is a prior condition for any further development of labour organisations along anarchist lines. By opposing the reformism and bureaucratic control of the existing trade unions, anarchists could play their part in stopping the drift towards totalitarianism. Such a role is less heroic than attempting to foster anarcho-syndicalist unions, but in the long run is likely to be more fruitful.

In an age like our own when all the major currents are running towards "the closed society", the revolutionary might well be satisfied if he can achieve the limited object of keeping open the door to freedom.

# 3. The relevance of syndicalism

## Geoffrey Ostergaard

TO DISPLAY anything other than an academic interest in syndicalism at the pesent time is to lay oneself open to the charge of being a social troglodyte. Syndicalism, as a movement of any size and influence, flourished in the first two decades of this century and, since then, apart from a brief and cruel flowering in Spain during the Civil War, it has been a spent force. Avowedly syndicalist groups and organisations still exist in many countries but their memberships are numbered in the hundreds and thousands rather than in the tens of thousands and millions; and a dispassionate observer would be forced to place them firmly in that half-submerged political world inhabited by "the socialist sects". Periodically, attempts are made to regroup the scattered forces of syndicalism in preparation for a new offensive: there have been several such attempts in this country since the war of which the National Rank-and-File Movement launched two years ago is only the latest. But it seems unlikely that such attempts will lead to any significant movement in the forseeable future.

Why, then, should we bother our heads with syndicalism? Why not leave the subject to the historians? It is clearly one of the failures of history, a movement that didn't "come off". With our eyes on the present and the future, why concern ourselves with the past, especially the unsuccessful past? As T.S. Eliot has reminded us, "We cannot revive old factions or follow an antique drum"; and perhaps we ought not, even if we could.

There are at least two good reasons for not adopting the viewpoint implicit in such questions. One obvious reason is that the present and possible future cannot be understood without an understanding of the past. And by "the past" I mean not only the "successful" past – that part of history which most obviously leads to the present; I include also the "unsuccessful" past – that part of history which, from the viewpoint of the present, seems to have led nowhere. It is a point often overlooked, even by intelligent historians, that there is as much, if not more, to be learned from the failures as from the successes of history. This, as I shall try to show, is particularly true of syndicalism. An understanding of why syndicalism failed and a pondering on the implications of that failure can illumine our understanding of the present in a way that no account of "successful" movements could do.

A second good reason for not dismissing syndicalism out of hand is perhaps more debatable, since it stems from the values inherent in my own political position. Looked at in the round, the world socialist movement since 1917 has been divided into two camps: the social democratic camp, on the one side, and the Bolshevik or Communist camp, on the other. These two camps have been and remain sharply divided over the question of the road to the socialist society. The social democrats have opted for the constitutional and democratic road, while the Bolsheviks have been prepared, if necessary, to take the revolutionary road. But despite this and other differences, both social democrats and Bolsheviks are united in believing that the road to socialism lies through the acquisition by their respective parties of the political power of the State, the institution claiming, within its territory, sovereignty and a monopoly of the instruments of coercion. In this respect, both social democrats and Bolsheviks differ from the socialists of what might be called the third camp: the camp of the anti-state or non-state libertarian socialists. Not much has been heard of this camp in the last forty years. Historically, it has comprised a variety of groups and movements both constitutional and revolutionary. These include the so-called pre-Marxist "utopians"; the co-operators; the anarchists in all their different hues; the guild socialists; and, of course, the syndicalists. Apart from the doubtful exception of the co-operators, the list looks like a list of "failures". But it is my conviction that, between them, the adherents of this camp have provided both the most realistic analysis of capitalist society and also the most penetrating insights into the essential conditions for the realisation and maintenance of a free, egalitarian, classless and international society.[1]

At the present time we are witnessing the decomposition of social democracy. The social democratic road, it is now becoming clear, leads not to socialism as traditionally understood, but to the managerial-bureaucratic Welfare-cum-Warfare State. In one important area after another, Bolshevism is gaining ground at the expense of social democracy. Bolshevism, at least, has demonstrated in a way that social democracy has never done, its capacity to make a revolution, to establish a new social order. What, alas, Bolshevism has not demonstrated and shows no sign of demonstrating is its capacity to create a new social order remotely resembling that of the classical socialist ideal. If the future does indeed lie with Bolshevism, so much the worse for the socialist dream!

From this perspective, the libertarian socialist tradition takes on a special significance for the present generation of socialists. It may be – and we have cause enough to be sceptical – that there is *no* road to the truly socialist society. The whole ideology of socialism over the last 150 years may come to be seen in the future – if mankind has any future – as yet one more ideology preparing the ground for the rise of yet one more historic ruling class.[2] But, *if* there be a road, I am convinced that it is the third road which the syndicalists helped to pioneer. I believe that the socialists of this generation will have to take a long step backwards if they are ever to move forwards again in the right direction. They will have to reassess the whole libertarian tradition from Owen to Sorel and from this re-assessment draw sustenance for a new third camp movement.

                    *          *          *

The most striking feature of syndicalist thought and action is the importance it attached to the class struggle. The classical syndicalist movement emerged at about the same time as the first great revisionist controversy at the turn of the century. Led by Bernstein, the revisionists questioned, among other things, Marx's analysis of class development and his theory of the state. They argued, in effect, for what I have called the social democratic position – the view that socialism could be achieved gradually by a broad democratic movement acquiring, peacefully and constitutionally, control of the existing machinery of the State. This amounted to a right-wing revision of Marxism. Syndicalism, in contrast, was a revision of Marxism to the left. The struggle between the proletariat and the bourgeoisie was seen by the syndicalists as the very essence of Marxism – "the alpha and omega of socialism", as Sorel put it. All their energies were devoted to the relentless pursuit of this struggle: the class war was to be fought to a victorious finish with no compromise given or taken. Any form of class collaboration was regarded as an anathema. Like the Marxists, the syndicalists saw the State as a bourgeois instrument of coercion. Where they parted company from the orthodox, however, was in their opposition to any form of the State. Marx argued that the task of the proletariat was to destroy, in the course of the revolution, the bourgeois state and to put in its place a proletarian state, which would be the prelude to the eventual liquidation of the coercive apparatus of society. The syndicalists, influenced in this respect by the anarchists, insisted that the State *as such* must be destroyed by the revolution: to build a new state on the ruins of the old would simply result in the perpetuation of class rule over the proletariat in a new form.

This view implied a rejection not only of parliamentary action – the contesting of elections for bourgeois parliaments – but also of political action in the narrow sense of the term. The syndicalists insisted that the class war must be waged, as they put it, on the *terrain de classe* by direct action. Fighting the class war involves, of course, political action in the wider sense of a struggle for social power. What distinguished the syndicalists was the view that this struggle for social power, the struggle to achieve proletarian ascendancy, did not involve setting up a specialised political organisation, to wit, a political party. On the contrary, quite the reverse. To try to achieve socialism through such an organisation would be fatal to the very aims of the proletariat.

It is important to grasp this point and the reasoning behind it if we are to make any sense of syndicalism. To Bolsheviks, rejection of party organisation will appear to be the fatal error of the syndicalists. The so-called Marxist revolutions of our century have been carried through only by use of the instrument of a highly disciplined proletarian party perfected by Lenin. No Communist party, they would argue, means no revolution, or at least no successful revolution. How, it might be asked, could the syndicalists have made such a stupid mistake?

This, of course, is a begging question. But, leaving aside the suggestion that the syndicalists were in error, it is relatively easy to see how they arrived at their position. In a sense, they did so because they were more Marxist than Marx himself and certainly less heretical than that arch political determinist, Lenin. For those who accept the materialist conception of history, political power is essentially a derivative of economic power. A class that possesses economic power will necessarily, sooner rather than later, acquire political power. If, then, one sets about acquiring the latter and is able to do so, one need not worry overmuch about the former. For the proletariat, as for the bourgeoisie, economic power means power within and over industry. If the workers can win control of industry, the battle for supremacy is won. James Connolly put the syndicalist point succinctly when he wrote, "The workshop is the cockpit of civilisation... The fight for the conquest of the political state is not the battle, it is only the echo of the battle. The real battle is being fought out every day for the power to control industry".[3]

But there is more to the syndicalist case than this. Taking seriously the theory of the class struggle, the syndicalists worked for a clean-cut, uncompromising proletarian victory. Socialism for them meant the replacement of bourgeois culture and institutions by proletarian culture and institutions. Their whole conception of socialism was a thoroughly working class conception:[4] they had no patience at all for middle class socialists, not even for the guildsmen who were closest to them and who, with their statist ideas, were, as they put it, "incapable of conceiving a commonwealth which is not designed on the canons of bourgeois architecture".[5] When Marx in his Address to the First International had said that the emancipation of the proletariat must be the work of the workers themselves, the syndicalists thought he meant it. They did *not* think that emancipation would come through the organisation of a self-styled proletarian party led principally by men of bourgeois origin who for one reason or another had taken up the cause of the workers. Bourgeois socialist intellectuals – students, professors, publicists and the like – had only a limited auxiliary role to play in the strategy of the revolution.[6] Their task was to make explicit what was implicit in the social situation of capitalist society: it was most definitely *not* their task to instruct the proletariat, to guide them and to lead them in to correct courses of action. Any movement which allowed itself to be directed by bourgeois intellectuals, even *déclassé* intellectuals, would, they believed, end up either by compromising with the *status quo* or by establishing a new form of class rule.

This perspective led the syndicalists to juxtapose the concept of class against that of party.[7] As social formations, these two are quite different. A class is a natural product of historical development, comprising individuals who occupy essentially the same position in the economic order. A party, in contrast, is an artificial aggregate, a consciously contrived organisation, composed of heterogeneous elements drawn from all classes. A class is based on homogeneity of origin and conditions of life, and the bond of unity is economic. A party, however, represents essentially an intellectual unity; the bond uniting its members is ideological. When an individual is approached on the basis of class, the focus is on his role in the economic order, a role which separates him from members of other classes; and the opposition of class interests is high-lighted. When, however, an individual is approached on the basis of party, the focus is on his role as a citizen and elector in the political order, a role he shares with members of all classes; and inevitably the opposition of class interests is muted. Parties may and often do express class interests but, more important, they also serve to moderate and to contain class antagonisms.

The syndicalists, of course, appreciated that classes as such do not act. Social action involves the actions of individuals in organisations. Organisation, therefore, was an admitted necessity: in this they differed from the classical anarchists who minimized the im-

portance of organisation and pinned their hopes on the possibility of
spontaneous revolutionary uprisings. But, if the class struggle was
the basic reality, why, asked the syndicalists, create an organisation
– the party – which would inevitably from its very nature undermine
that struggle? Why, indeed, when the proletariat *already* had an
organisation of its own: the trade union, an organisation based on
the working class, confined to members of the working class, and
created by the workers for the purpose of defending their interests
in the daily struggle against their capitalist masters. True, the trade
unions had been conceived, even by their creators, as mainly ame-
liorative instruments, as a means to win for the workers concessions
within the capitalist social framework. But there was no *a priori*
reason why their role should be so limited. Given proper direction,
it was argued, they could be transformed into revolutionary instruments.

A single-minded emphasis on the potentialities of the trade union is in fact the most distinctive single feature of syndicalism. The
syndicalist saw the trade unions as organisations with a dual role to
perform: first, to defend the interests of the workers in existing
society, and secondly to constitute themselves the units of administration in the coming socialist society. From a long term point of
view, the second role was, of course, the more important. It was a
role that did not begin on the morrow of the revolution. The syndicalists did not simply assert that the basic unit of social organisation
in a socialist society would be the trade union and draw up blue-
prints in which the unions, federated at the local, regional, national
and international levels, would take on all the useful functions now
performed by various capitalist bodies. The revolutionary role became operative at once. The task of the unions was to struggle *now*
to divest the existing political organisations of capitalist society of
all life and to transfer whatever value they might have to the proletarian organisations. This part of the syndicalist programme was
summed up in Sorel's words: "to snatch from the State and from the
Commune, one by one, all their attributes in order to enrich the
proletarian organisms in the process of formation".[9]

It is an egregious error to accuse the syndicalists, as some Bolsheviks have done, of ignoring the problem of power. Not only did they
not ignore the problem; they proposed the most realistic way open
to the workers of acquiring power. It is true that they were mistaken
in their belief that the unions could perform the dual role assigned
to them. To be effective as defensive organisations, the unions
needed to embrace as many workers as possible and this inevitably
led to a dilution of their revolutionary objectives. In practice, the

syndicalists were faced with the choice of unions which were *either* reformist and purely defensive *or* revolutionary and largely ineffective.[10] But in the context of modern society, their general strategy of power was surely correct. They proposed to begin to acquire power at the point where, according to the logic of Marxist theory, they ought to begin – in the fields, factories and mines. And they did so because they were convinced that, unless they did win power within the social base of capitalism, there would be no *proletarian* revolution, whatever other kind of revolution there might be. The syndicalists said, in effect, that the revolution must begin in the workshop. Their message to the workers was much the same as Goethe's to the emigrant in search of liberty: "Here or nowhere is your America". Here, in the workshop, in the factory and in the mine, they said, we must accomplish the revolution or it will be accomplished nowhere. So long as we are a subject class industrially, so long will we remain a subject class politically. The real revolution must be made not in Parliament or at the barricades but in the places where we earn our daily bread. The organisations that we have built up to carry on the daily struggle must be the foundations of the new order and we must be its architects. The law and morality that we have evolved in our long struggle with capitalism must be the law and morality of the future workers' commonwealth. All other proposals are but snares and delusions.

The syndicalist strategy of revolution, therefore, involved a struggle for social power through direct action based on the workers' own class organisations. The tactics of direct action included sabotage, ca'canny, the use of the boycott and the trade union label and, of course, industrial strikes. What is common to all these means is a determined refusal to acknowledge the legitimacy of bourgeois rule. It was not, argued the syndicalists, a proper function of the unions to make agreements with the employers. Negotiations, agreements, contracts all necessarily involve bargaining and compromise within the framework of capitalist contrived rules. The function of the unions was not to participate with employers in ruling the workers but to impose, as far as they were able, the will of the workers on the employers. The only contract the syndicalists cared to consider was the collective contract conceived as part of a movement of "encroaching control" – a system by which the workers within a factory or shop would undertake a specific amount of work in return for a lump sum, to be allocated by the work-group as it saw fit, on condition that the employers abdicated their control of the productive process itself.[11] After a period of vigorous pursuit of such tactics, the workers in their unions would, it was envisaged, have won sufficient power to make a successful General Strike possible. Such a strike, since it was only the *form* of the revolution, could not be planned in advance: the conditions had to be ripe for it. It would probably begin as a local or national strike confined to a single industry. Class solidarity would lead to its extension to other industries and rapidly it would build up to a strike general in its dimensions.[12] The mass symbolic "folding of arms" would, in effect, be a total withdrawal of the workers of their consent to a system of class servitude. The legitimacy of the capitalist order would be shattered and in its place would emerge a proletarian social order based on the unions.

*          *          *

For a movement that is generally labelled a failure, there is surprisingly much in syndicalism that is relevant for our age. Most significant of all, perhaps, is the fact that it did fail. In retrospect, syndicalism appears as the great heroic movement of the proletariat, the first and only socialist movement to take seriously Marx's injunction that the emancipation of the working class must be the work of the workers themselves. It attempted to achieve the emancipation of labour unaided by middle class intellectuals and politicians and aimed to establish a working class socialism and culture, free from all bourgeois taints. That it failed suggests that, whatever else they may be, the socialist revolutions of recent decades are not the proletarian revolutions the ideologists would have us believe. In this connection the eclipse of the syndicalist doctrine of workers' control, in the USSR no less than elsewhere, and the subordination of trade unions to political parties and their quasi-incorporation into the machinery of government, take on a special and ominous significance. We are, indeed, living in a revolutionary epoch in which dramatic changes are taking place in the composition and structure of the ruling class. But in both East and West the emerging rulers, displacing the old capitalist class, are not the workers but the managerial bureaucrats whose privileges and power are based on their command of organisational resources. In the West the rule of this new class is being legitimized in terms of a rationalized corporate capitalism operating in a mixed economy; in Communist countries, the formula of legitimization is avowedly socialist and the economy is state-owned and managed. But, in both, the rulers, like all ruling classes known in history, accord to themselves superior rewards and privileges; and the mass of mankind continue to toil and to spin for inferior rewards and for the privilege of keeping their rulers in a state to which they show every sign of becoming accustomed. The new society, rationalized managerial capitalism or bureaucratic state socialism, is in many respects a more tolerable society than competitive capitalism. Given industrialisation and modern economic techniques, mass poverty can be and is being abolished. For this reason, in all advanced industrial countries the acute class divisions that marked 19th and early 20th century capitalism are becoming blurred and it is no longer possible to locate in the social arena a simple straightforward contest between two main classes, the proletariat and the bourgeoisie. At the same time, the techniques of social control available to the rulers in the shape of the mass media of communications and the mass political parties have enormously increased their power *vis-à-vis* the ruled. All in all, the emerging managerial-bureaucratic society possesses historically unparalleled potentialities for maintaining a stable system of exploitation. There is only one major flaw in the system: its patent inability to solve the problem of war in an age when, for technological reasons, war has become a truly deadly institution.

The omnipresent threat of nuclear annihilation now clearly vindicates the anti-statism of the anarchists and the syndicalists. For war is a function of the state and of the state system into which mankind is politically divided. The emerging new social order has modified the bourgeois state system: it is no longer a system of many balancing sovereign nation-states but rather a system of two superstates each surrounded by their satellites plus a group of uneasy non-aligned and relatively undeveloped states. The state system has been rationalized but not rationalized enough: for, within the framework of a state system, nothing short of one world state would be adequate to solve the problem of war in a nuclear age. And a world state – set up by mutual agreement – is just not on the political agenda of the great powers. The reasons which led the capitalist ruling class in their several states to engage in mutually destructive wars still operate to make possible, and perhaps almost inevitable, the final war between states dominated by the managerial-bureaucrats. The great tragedy of our epoch is the lamentable failure of the socialist movement, with its fine promise of universal peace and brotherhood, to appreciate that an indispensable condition for achieving its objective was the liquidation of that supreme bourgeois institution, the sovereign state. Failing to appreciate this, the socialists after one hundred and fifty years of endeavour have succeeded not in making socialism but only in making socialist states. Not surprisingly, in this situation the socialist leaders have found what the anarchists and syndicalists always predicted they would find: that it is impossible for socialists to accept the responsibility of governing in existing states without thereby becoming defenders of them.[13] The role that they occupy as state leaders inevitably impels them to act like state leaders, even to the extent, as in the case of the USSR, of making them subordinate, in the interests of the Soviet State, the revolutionary Communist movements in other countries. That the Soviet leaders have not always and everywhere succeeded in this subordination, with the result that we are now witnessing the development of national rivalries within the international Communist sector of the world, is no consolation. It makes only more obvious the fact that socialist revolutions within states, even socialist revolutions within all the states of the world, would not solve the problem that now faces mankind. If the USA were to sink into the ocean tomorrow, the state system in the rest of the world would not, for example prevent the possibility of war sooner or later between a Communist China and a Communist Russia. To think otherwise is to put far too high a value on the beneficient effects of a common ideology, to ignore the material interests that divide one state from another, and to overlook the disastrous increase in nationalist sentiment that is a feature of the contemporary world.

It may be that, from the point of view of sheer survival as a species, mankind has already passed the eleventh hour. In the present context of human affairs, Lenin's cryptic phrase, "We are all dead men on furlough", takes on a new significance. In the contemporary crisis, there is only one sensible course open to those who wish to survive the next decade: to join the struggle to control, or better still to overthrow, the nuclear warlords, militarists and political bosses in all states. This struggle in an inchoate form has begun and is already gathering momentum in many countries. And it is no accident that the most determined participants in the anti-war movement have found themselves adopting the classic stance of the syndicalists: direct action. A direct action movement always has been and always will be an anathema to the rulers and would-be rulers of mankind. For direct action involves a refusal to play the political game according to the rules laid down by our masters. It is a grass-roots, do-it-yourself kind of action which recognises implicitly the truth of what Gandhi called 'voluntary servitude'; the fact that, in the last analysis, men are governed in the way they are because they are content to be so governed. When sufficient numbers of the governed can be persuaded to withdraw that consent and to demonstrate by their actions that they do not recognise the legitimacy of the rulers to act in their name, the government must either collapse or radically change its policies. When the bishops and the editorial pundits warn the participants in the recent Civil Disobedience campaigns that they are undermining the foundations of social order, we should take heed. Civil Disobedience, pressed to its logical conclusion, involves just that. All we need to add is that it undermines the *present* social order which has brought mankind to the edge of the abyss and prepares the way for a new social order in which power will by retained by the people.

There is thus a clear link between the syndicalist movement of forty years ago and the present movement against nuclear weapons. The link is there both in the political style and in several of the basic values of the two movements. The differences, of course, are obvious too. Syndicalism was a proletarian class movement: the anti-war movement appeals to the sane-minded in all classes. In terms of revolutionary potential, the present movement is perhaps of greater significance. The immediate issues involved are simpler and more dramatic than those raised by the syndicalists and the crisis is more compelling. If mankind survives the present crisis, some of the other issues raised by the syndicalists, notably workers' control as a means of ensuring a wide dispersion of social power, will again come to the fore – are indeed already doing so.[14] It is, therefore, I think, no extravagance to claim that the spirit of syndicalism, dormant so long in this country, is once again in the air. In this, if anything, lies a hope for the future. The serious anti-war radical would do well to breathe in full measure the syndicalist spirit of militant direct action.

# Footnotes

1    Towards the end of his life, GDH Cole placed himself squarely in this third camp. "I am neither a Communist nor a Social Democrat because I regard both as creeds of centralisation and bureaucracy, whereas I feel sure that a Socialist society that is to be true to its equalitarian principles of human brotherhood must rest on the widest possible diffusion of power and responsibility, so as to enlist the active participation of as many as possible of its citizens in the tasks of democratic self-government" – *A History of Socialist Thought*, Vol. V, p.337.

2    The idea that socialism may be no more than the ideology of the future ruling class is not a new one. It was first elaborated by the Polish revolutionary, Waclaw Machajski, in his book *The Intellectual Worker*, published in Poland in 1898. Hints of the same thesis may be found earlier in some of Bakunin's writings. For a discussion of Machajski's

ideas, see Max Nomad's *Apostles of Revolution* and, more especially, *Aspects of Revolt*.

3    *Socialism Made Easy*, 1908.

4    See the editorial, "Syndicalism – a Working Class Conception of Socialism" *Freedom*, Nov–Dec 1912.

5    Socialist Labour Party, *The Development of Socialism* (c.1912).

6    That intellectuals have only an auxiliary role to play in the socialist movement is a major theme in Sorel's writings.

7    cf. A Gray, *The Socialist Tradition*, 1947, p.414.

8    The wealth of empirical data on the social class basis of most majoi parties should not blind us to this important truth. It is not an either-or matter: either parties express class interests or they do not. **Within** a political system, parties frequently express class interests (though not necessarily according to the Marxist category of classes); from the point of view of **the system as a whole** however, for the reasons adumbrated by the syndicalists, parties tend to mitigate class conflicts and hence to preserve the socio-political system. Communist parties implicitly recognise this fact in the special measures they adopt in an attempt to preserve their revolutionary character, eg, subordination of the parliamentarians to the party caucus. These measures, needless to say, are not always successful.

9    *L'Avenir socialiste des Syndicats*, 1898.

10   For a discussion of this crux, see Gaston Gerard, "Anarchism and Trade Unionism", *The University Libertarian*, April, 1957

11   W Gallacher & J Paton, *Towards Industrial Democracy*, 1917.

12   The syndicalist vision of the revolution is well described in E. Pataud & E. Pouget, *Syndicalism & the Co-operative Commonwealth*, 1913.

13   The popular radical notion that socialism is continually being "betrayed" by leaders more interested in their own than in working class emancipation is sociologically naive. There is no reason to believe that socialist leaders, **as individuals**, are any more corruptible than most other men. What is corrupting is their acceptance of certain roles which, if they are to be performed at all, impel them to act in ways that radicals define as "betrayal". It is as difficult for a socialist statesman not to betray socialism as it is for the rich man to enter the kingdom of heaven – and for the same kind of sociological reason.

14   See, eg, *The Bomb, Direct Action & the State* (1962) published by the Syndicalist Workers' Federation.

# 4.  Work and surplus
## Keith Paton

## I.  Work and surplus in neo-slave society

ECONOMICS – the dismal science, the liturgy of scarcity. "Perhaps the most telling achievement of the established order of thinkers has been the obscurantist isolation of the so-called subject of economics from the rest of life as we recognisably live it" (David Bazelon). Hence invocation of "the Needs of the Economy" is met by ordinary people not with hilarity but with mere suspicion. We need to learn the "gay science of how to use the social wealth for shaping man's world in accordance with his Life Instincts" (Marcuse: *Eros and Civilisation*).

One who made such an attempt was Stuart Chase in 1920. He calculated the number of useless jobs in America thus:

| | |
|---|---|
| Manpower going into illth (harmful wealth): | 8  m |
| Idle manpower on any given day: | 6  m |
| Production Methods Waste: | 4  m |
| Distribution Methods Waste: | 2½ m |
| TOTAL: | 20½m |

which represented a manpower surplus of 50%. That was way before the Cybernetic Revolution. But even then "the horn of plenty is overflowing, but a dead man reaches up to seal its mouth, and the fruits fall as slowly as before" (Chase: *The Tragedy of Waste*).

"The validity of paper in the absence of scarcity is unthinkable without conscious control of its quality and/or value. When scarcity is in short supply, so to speak, paper leads to a literal form of madness – a distortion or denial of reality in order to preserve the illusion of the absent condition. And when the power of great corporations is a part of the situation, reality itself gives way to the illusion – and a weird, glistening, new kind of scarcity appears as an enamation from beyond the historical grave. It is Scarcity Regained

144

– one of the ugliest of all human creations... I suggest that the Paper Economy is nothing but a destructive perpetuation of existing power relations beyond their period of historical utility" (David T. Bazelon: *The Paper Economy*).

How to define "*socially necessary* labour"? The Lords and Dukes thought retainers in fancy uniforms were absolutely vital. The classical economists pointed out that they were only *feudally-necessary*, ie to maintain the remnants of a dispensable power system: But somebody like a patents office clerk – now there was a really useful job! But Marx pointed out that he was only *capitalistically-necessary*; from the standpoint of socialism patents offices are futile rubbish. "The bourgeois finds to his amazement that the rationalist attitude does not stop at the credentials of kings and popes, but goes on to attack private property and the whole system of bourgeois values" (Paul Baran: *The Political Economy of Growth*).

And for the anarchist, the rationalist goes on to attack Chiefs of Police, Commissars, Bureaucrats and all State functionaries. "In answer to an oral question (House of Commons, *Hansard* 14 April 1969) Mr. Crossman informed the House that for the half year from September 1968, £1,900 was spent in clerks wages alone in checking fraudulent claims for free prescriptions in Manchester, 6,600 forms were checked, 43 patients were found to be not in any of the exemption categories and £8 was recovered for the taxpayer". (*Poverty*, CPAG, No. 11, Summer 1969). Wonder why it took the clerks so long? Bloody shirkers, wasting the country's money!

Profits – for so long the bogey of left-wing thinking. Surplus value, long-term decline thereof. Which is crap. Baran and Sweezy showed that under monopoly conditions, there was a long term tendency for the rate of profits to *rise*, for the break even point to come at ever lower levels of capacity utilisation (30 to 40 per cent in the US Steel Industry). In a closed system this means slump: profits which can't find investment outlets aren't produced and show themselves up negatively in the under-capacity and unemployment rates. So it's necessary to open the system: first War, then the Permanent War Economy, then Imperialism (far too lucrative – makes the surplus crisis worse), then the Colonisation of Everyday Life (Tuppaware parties!), advertising and the implantation of pseudo-wants. Dead labour escapes through our heads (which must first be moronised). Thus "the notion of exploitation proper to modern capitalism must include not only the difference between what one produces and what one receives, but also the difference between what one ought to be able to produce (were it not for waste production) and what one ought to receive (enough, but not an addictively increasing enough). In short, exploitation under modern capitalism is the difference between potential social productivity and overall quality of life (including both work and consumption)". (*Consumption: Domestic Imperialism*, Movement for a Democratic Society Pamphlet No. 1)

Surplus is where it's at – not surplus value. Baran gives the example of a bakery where productivity rises from 2 loaves per man to 12.5 loaves *per usefully occupied worker* and the rate of exploitation remains constant at 50%. But how much else has changed! In Period One 100 bakers make 200 loaves and get the equivalent of 100. In Period Two the wages are still half of the total produced (500 loaves-equivalent out of 1,000 loaves) but the payroll now conceals 20 surplus bodies employed thus: five to constantly change the shape of the loaves, one to mix obsolescence powder into the dough, four to design new wrappers, five in advertising the "new improved versions", one to watch rival companies, two as legal watchdogs and two as public relations "experts" (Paul A. Baran: *The Political Economy of Growth*, Preface to 2nd edition). For the US, Baran and Sweezy estimate profits at only one-third of the potential economic surplus.

The other big theme of (conventional) Marxism is the "contradiction between the (social) forces of production and the (private) relations of production". Written under scarcity competitive capitalism. Technology was Technology and "it" got introduced. Not so in Monopoly Capitalism. Most Marxists only examine one half of the equation, the social relations of production. If they understood the scientific and technological potential of today they would see:

(1) that Technology doesn't exist (if ever it did): only specific technologies in chosen combinations with specific other technologies (which is why the phrase "Technological Society" is so ideological);

(2) that the diversion of technological application into socially useless channels goes way beyond both Space and Arms; and consequently,

(3) that *the* "productive forces" (*per se*) are completely indeterminate and inert and hence to talk of Technology "coming into conflict" with anything is to be in danger both of reifying the notion and of anthropomorphising the reality.

Consider where we would be if from 1950 "we" (ie they) had put the same resources into (a) agriculture instead of Arms, into (b) oceanography instead of Space, into (c) free and ecologically sane transport systems rather than Cars and Aeroplanes, into (d) health (understood in its widest sense) rather than anti-illness. One could go on for ever. I don't know for sure, but I'd be prepared to bet that the US Army spent more on the logistics of toothpaste than the whole world spent on developing Leaf Protein extraction technologies.

Nevertheless the "forces of production" do provide a partial yardstick or baseline for measuring (a) the waste *in* capitalist society (inefficiencies within a given productive process) and (b) the waste *of* capitalist society (the process, the products themselves). (A yardstick is a less misleading analogy than a baby struggling to be born. It's also less hopeful. Yardsticks are passive and indeterminate to use.) Moreover, the forces of production may *potentially* have social implications – if only for enlightened capitalist planning. To substantiate, I'd like to take five areas from *Organisation, Automaton and Society* by Robert A. Brady which is a Big Book on the scientific revolution in industry. Without some heavy factual background it is hard to know what such writers as McLuhan, Marcuse and Fuller have in mind when they refer to technology. And harder still to criticise them.

**A.   Unitization:**   This refers to the way mining operations at a single field have to be co-ordinated. In oil, because of the technologies of surveying and drilling available, it is possible to double or triple the recoverable percentage of oil in place by manipulating relative pressures of gas, oil and water. But this requires control of the relative variables over the whole geological field, not just down one well. Thus wherever oil is being extracted by several unco-ordinated wells, the cost to be laid at the door of capitalism is not just the overheads of superfluous wells, but relates to the (at present irrevocable) squandering of half the available oil.

**B.   River Valley Development:**   Any single-use proposal might be uneconomic, eg to build a dam to control floods. Development is feasible if it is multi-use, eg the flood control halts erosion which keeps the soil fertile for agriculture; the dam can be fitted with hydro-electric turbines; fishing and recreation can take place on the lake, etc. The problem is to create a non-exploitative basis for planning on the scale needed (determined by the size of the river system). We can certainly charge up to capitalism all the TVAs that haven't happened.

**C.   Standardisation:**   Brady considers this so important that he talks of the Standards Revolution on a par with the Materials Revolution or the Energy Revolution. Standards apply to such things as screw threads and size-intervals, prescriptions for lenses, scientific nomenclature, testing procedures, ratings and safety provisions, labelling, etc. Standards may extend only within a firm, or they may apply to a whole industry or nation; or they may be worldwide, thanks to the work of the International Organisation for Standardisation, a kind of clearing-house for standards and specifications which has Technical Committees for everything from ball-bearings to frozen food packages, statistical treatment to tyres, rims and valves, electrodes to cloth widths, yarn counts to colour fastness tests... The point is that incalculable waste and inefficiency is saved by appropriate standardisation. (Think of spare parts.) Yet despite the considerable progress in some fields where the scientists and engineers have had their way, as a general rule economists and industrialists have dragged their feet. The difference between actuality and historically realistic possibility in this sphere is huge and may be charged up under the head "Potential Economic Surplus".

However the question arises: "What about the danger of regimentation, of monotony, of lack of variety?" This fear is realistic only if standards are applied too restrictively and in appropriate areas. Basically standards should increase the meaningful variety available to the consumer by cutting down only on phoney variety. Standardisation in colour does not mean that the world is reduced to a dull muddy brown colour, ie uniformity. Standardisation means that the artist or designer is working with a large variety of hues determined by standard positions on the spectrum; his palette is purer but his freedom to combine and select is not interfered with – indeed it is enhanced. Again the standardisation of building components in partially prefabricated (modular) construction can lead to great savings in building costs but not at any architectural price – the standard door-frames can be fixed at just noticeable threshold differences.

**D. Distribution:** The implications of standardisation run clean counter to the rule of the Market. Instead of the market reaching back and messing up engineering (so that the head of the General Electric calls GE a marketing organisation), production priorities penetrate forward and clean up distribution. This implies an end to all phoney product differentiation and constant model-changing, which in turn implies the stabilisation of production at a socially determined optimal number of meaningful model-types, eg aspirins, car body shapes, grades of petrol. (Again we should remember that where uniqueness of design is important as in, say, dress-making, standardisation can still be helpful, *e.g.* yarn-counts, flame-proofness, colour-fastness, colour values, etc.) Instead of the magic of brand names and secret processes, we get meaningful variety and open information flow as regards material and processing standards involved. This means relevant labelling, standard packaging, the facilitation of repairs and replacements, the virtual abolition of the advertising industry, except for a minimal consumer education role. It also means a vast reduction in distribution costs, for example the diseconomies associated with transportation, ordering and stocking small quantities of artificially differentiated equivalents. Brady goes so far as to suggest that "distributing is building inefficiencies into our economic system almost as rapidly as other production processes are attaining new efficiencies)" (p. 356).

**E. Research and Development:** Another key area lies in research. At present basic research in most areas is liable to be "classified", while applied technological research is either for armies or for corporations and hence equally liable to be kept secret. This means that not only is science held back but also that duplication of effort occurs at many points and an army of security men are needed to stave off another army of spies. Suppression of innovation and patenting systems also result in huge waste wherever the "marginal profit" (Baran) from introducing a new technique is too low.

Technological development is also resisted by ordinary workers however. Thus Lincoln is probably correct in the *The Restrictive Society* when he points to an increase of 15 to 20 per cent in annual production which could result from "switching off the deep freeze of restrictive practices". This too should be entered under Potential Economic Surplus, which is a different notion from the Planned Economic Surplus of a socialist society where the workers might choose to "overman" machines, take leisurely tea-breaks, oppose shift-work and other such practices which so offend Lincoln's mind-less technocratic sensibility. First we must calculate what "we" *could* produce (maximal surplus), before we decide what we *shall* produce (optimal surplus).

The question is, however, whether this aspect of disguised surplus should be laid at the door of capitalism, or at the door of some other factor such as a putative "traditional conservatism of the worker". I think it is clear that resistance to automation in, for example, transport, is a perfectly rational response for men who would otherwise find themselves, deskilled and past their peak, on an already overful unemployment dump. If those dockers, drivers and railwaymen at present engaged in staving off the Container Revolution (another example of standardisation) were free to choose between carrying on the fight and embarking on some project they could see the point of such as constructing a socialised environment, then, provided their wages could be safeguarded, most of them would be only too pleased to start task forces to build community centres, adventure playgrounds and swimming pools on every housing estate in the country, beginning with their own!

*     *     *

One of the main reasons for the abolition of overt slavery was that plantation slaves were incredibly inefficient compared with so-called free men. Wage slaves and bureaucratic slaves are almost as inefficient. This "inefficiency" is not something wrong with the people involved, some psychological quirk of "laziness" or "stupidity", but forms part of the praxis of the slave, representing as is does a perfectly functional adaptation to an intolerable situation: Who wants to work his balls off in the hot sun? Better to be thought innately stupid and lazy, than to be expected to harvest two or three times as much cotton! And the same applies to Council workmen having tea-breaks and rests every five minutes under the indignant but muslin-hidden gaze of the idle middle-class.

At this point we can separate out four distinct aspects of waste: (1) X is a typist and accounts clerk; (2) she has no control over her job situation; (3) she is exploited economically; (4) she works in an advertising agency (which advertises for the firm that makes the vans that Securicorps uses in the employment of the computer firm which programmes the missiles which destroyed the house that Jack built). In other words, futility right down the line! As a typical typist (2) she is doing someone else's work (a man's), she is bored and inefficent and actually works for only 40% of a 7½-hour day. Occasionally she has the flicker of an idea as how to streamline routine accounts, but she doesn't bother to work on it, much less pass it on. Mostly she just doesn't think. (3) represents conventional surplus value and will undoubtedly go into supporting parasites or expanding the number of busy useless jobs somewhere along the line. (4) indicates that even if she worked her guts out and was a constant dynamo of creative feedback in a profit-sharing co-operative, real welfare wouldn't increase in the real world – whatever the book-keeping consequences. But supposing even that the job was a useful one with a social point to it, routine office work as such (1) could undoubtedly be automated. From the standpoint of rationality, i.e.

an anarchist-socialist society establishing priorities in 1950, whose scientists and technologists had been exploring the problems of office work automation, we can see that by now even the typing and accounts function is historically contingent. Incidentally this does not presuppose the dragooning of scientists into studying unworthwhile problems. Scientists would find as much intellectual challenge and theoretical and practical spin-offs from inventing a speechtypewriter as from sending hunks of metal into Space.

Advertising is so obviously useless because wrestling over halves of a per cent of the market doesn't expand the number of useful things produced overall for everyone. Obviously it has a highly important stabilising economic role, via resolution of the "surplus" disposal problem. But we should also realise advertising's role in steadying the whole social system: "the productive apparatus *sells* or imposes the social system as a whole" (Marcuse). A whole pecuniary philosophy, a pecuniary truth-criterion, a pecuniary aesthetic, have developed in association with modern advertising, as Jules Henry shows in *Culture Against Man*. Alienated work isn't so bad if it will lead to being able to recoup your soul in a shining phallic automobile. You need to recoup your soul in your automobile if you have first lost your soul in work. "The organisation of work and the organisation of leisure are the blades of the castrating shears whose job is to improve the race of fawning dogs" (Vaneigem).

Advertising is of course a traditional boo word on the left. But take the man who worked on the assembly track which made the Securicorps van which guards the avionics computers which help to blow Jack's house to bits. Is he necessary? Or take his mate who makes private cars. As a production worker his whole life is sold to the motor car – in common with most of the 480,000 motor vehicle-manufacturing employees, the 431,000 car retailers, petrol fillers and garage employees, and the legion of car insurance and licence clerks, traffic wardens, policemen, chauffeurs, road and multi-storey car park builders, etc. Which works out at over a million able-bodied grown men being taken for a ride by cars.

Anyway, what are they for, these objects, these hunks of metal? For the actual physical culture of the commodity-spectacle, society has been neglected. Consider the car – ideology on wheels! Consider the city – ideology in concrete! What is the traffic jam but the daily staging of the most profound symbol imaginable of near total alienation? "The whole of urban planning must be understood as a sector of the publicity propaganda effort of our society. It is the organisation of participation in something in which it is impossible to participate... The aim of traffic control is the organisation of universal isolation. This is why its perfection is the major 'problem' of the modern city. It is the negation of the human encounter. It exhausts the energies needed for real communication." (*Unitary Urbanism:* Situationist International)

But let us return to these disguised unemployment figures. The *Annual Abstract of Statistics* (Central Statistics Office 1969) gives 25.2m. as the total work force. (Naturally they don't count housework.) The armed forces absorb 400,000 directly, 120,000 civil servants in the Ministries of Defence, a further 150,000 industrial defence staff: equals 670,000. Add all those engaged in manufacturing engines for bombers for Vietnam, Polaris submarines and other such useful toys and we are certainly over the million mark. Add thousands of civil servants in national and local government: (e.g. 30,000 in Employment and Productivity; 83,000 in Inland Robbery; 45,000 Home Office and Courts; most of the Dept. of Health and Social Insecurity cohorts of 71,000; thousands of civil service office cleaners and regulation office carpet fitters; many local government employees numbering 770,000) and again we are pushing the million mark. Add nearly the whole of retailing and wholesaling and that makes at least 2m. Add 675,000 under the heading Insurance, Banking and Finance; 92,000 engaged in rendering accounts; 110,000 engaged in "legal services"; and most of 152,000 in private domestic service; and again that makes a million.

("Most of" and "many" in the way I interpret these figures means that although these jobs, as such, would be abolished altogether with government, there are some useful functions here, which would still have to be carried out on a co-ordinative basis by someone: *e.g.* a welfare society, as opposed to the Welfare State, would have *neighbourhood responsibility* for the aged, sick and helpless.) Then there are 467,000 in "other services" which looks suspicious, so add half to half of the equally suspicious "service trades" of hairdressing (163,000) and laundries (141,000), making 375,000. Allow a 20% marginal futility ratio in Food, Drink and Tobacco (823,000) on the lines of Baran's bakery and Brady's critique of advertising. Similarly allow a 20% useless work rate in chemicals (506,000); metal (580,000); textiles (690,000); clothing (492,000); timber and furniture (321,000); sand, pottery, glass and cement (351,000); and "other manufacturing industries" (348,000). Allow at least 30% in printing, publishing and paper, and almost 30% in engineering and electrical goods (2,281,000). Reminding ourselves that we have counted military end-use waste again in our admittedly cavalier calculations (or else shipbuilding (180,000) would have had a large discount), we arrive at a total for manufacturing industry (less cars and arms) of 1,650,000 useless jobs. Add 20% of construction workers (1.6m) involved in Centre Points, Supermarkets and building new estates when old communities could be rehabilitated at half the cost, including land opportunity cost, though not counting those involved in roads (already counted). Add another 20% for the non-development of building technology and we get 640,000. Add 100,000 for surplus railwaymen (out of 300,000); 100,000 for all the bus conductors; 60,000 surplus dockers (out of 136,000); 40,000 in air haulage (replaceable by co-operative local distribution service, long distances by rail) and we get approximately 600,000 surplus transport workers.

Add the idle rich, living off their shares, those in jail and the unemployed (500,000) and we get 750,000. Then add the various totals:

| | |
|---|---|
| Cars | 1,000,000 |
| Arms | 1,000,000 |
| Government | 1,000,000 |
| Distribution | 2,000,000 |
| The City, the Law, their servants | 1,000,000 |
| Services, service trades | 375,000 |
| Manufacturing (excluding arms and cars) | 1,650,000 |
| Construction | 640,000 |
| Transport | 600,000 |
| Idle rich and Lumpen | 750,000 |
| TOTAL | 10,000,000 |

Guesses as they are, and even allowing for a certain amount of double counting, I must emphasise that I have been guessing conservatively:

(1)   I have not included the unreal "slack" which could only be taken in by everybody working flat out as a robot would do – or an artist seized by inspiration.

(2)   I have not included some mining clerks, caterers, electrical supply, students, teachers, parsons, doctors, and in doing so I have conceded some pretty big assumptions.

(3)   I have not included many discounts for the creative rear-

rangements within concerns that would result from delegate co-ordination and workers' self-management, principally because the latter processes also take time as we shall see in Section II.

(4)    Apart from cars and arms, relatively few assumptions have been made about the end-products to be produced. For example, under the heading "chemical industry" so as not to judge the economy by any too "utopian" alternative society, I have assumed that illness will still be prevalent, and that chemotherapy would go into the cure of the illness (or suppression of the symptoms?) – in other words I deducted for the nonsense of hundreds of competing brands of similar medicines, but not for drug medicines as such.

Recently I had an *en passant* conversation with a minister of religion:

*Him*: Dreadful business about X (friend of mine) being caught shoplifting, isn't it? Its the downward slope...

*Me*: (suppressing mirth) I agree that being *caught* shop-lifting is a bad business, but I don't see what's so terrible with shop-lifting. For example, take the Paris Metro. I understand that it now costs more to collect the fares than it does to run the Metro. So to avoid paying fares would be perfectly in accordance with the technological potential of the situation. Similarly, take the buses. Why can't they be free? And if all the conductors and all the other useless workers were enabled to diversify across to useful jobs, making goods with a high elasticity of demand, then we wouldn't need shop-girls and store detectives to stop X taking groceries!

*Him*: I agree that collecting bus fares all day doesn't really make sense. But then what about all the unemployment if you suddenly sacked the busmen?

*Me*: That's your problem if you believe in this society. I don't. Apart from the fact that, as an anarchist, I would never want to be *able* to sack anybody, as far as I'm concerned the bus-drivers have arms and legs and would be glad to occupy themselves usefully and pleasantly in a decent society. Until then, I support the busmen against unemployment. But I also want to communicate my concern for the meaning and point of work and then people might get angry at a society which only offered them unemployment or malemployment.

Here was a man who one day reads prayers about work being a sacrament ("creation's solemn mass which is said every day through human labour") and the next day is quite prepared to say that bus-conducting is a useless job, but there's no alternative!

But it isn't only ministers who "live in an economy of abundance but think and behave in an economy of scarcity" (Stuart Chase,

1920). Numerous lefties, including a proportion of anarchists, maintain schizophrenic attitudes by dodging the issue of the social meaning of work. Ouvrieristes manage to say *both* that capitalism is an arms economy, leads to useless production, waste, etc, *and* that workers are the ones from whom all the wealth flows. To admit that many of workers are as much bound up in the total surplus irrationality of our society as any advertising agency, "spoils one's rhetoric", as Paul Goodman would say.

Nevertheless, to be honest, we should agree with Baran and Sweezy that, "by far the greater part of the sales effort is carried out not by obviously unproductive workers such as salesmen and advertising copy writers, but by seemingly productive workers, tool and die makers, draughtsmen, mechanics, assembly line workers".

Having reached a rough figure of ten million surplus workers, let us consider how we are going to "spend" them in the creation of a better society. (And notice how our language is such that even as we try to formulate libertarian meanings, there is a constant downhill slope towards centralist language. I meant of course "how we will *spend ourselves* and how we believe that people in a post-revolutionary society should themselves decide to deploy themselves so that there is no longer a ten million malemployment figure.)

# II.  Work in a free society

Would work exist in a free society? Is total automation possible? Is it desirable? On what scale would post-scarcity society operate? Or would we still have scarcity?

We can distinguish two major positions: *Play (plus Work)* and *Play/Work*. These positions tend to be associated with the following clusters of variables.

| **PLAY (plus WORK)** | **PLAY/WORK** |
|---|---|
| **Work** | Progressive pervasion of (re- |
| Progressive abolition of work, | duced) "work" by play. |
| leading to "pure" spontaneity, | Expressive/Instrumental com- |

"pure" creative and expressivity, "pure" relating.

ponents in behaviour difficult to separate. A question of relative emphasis on play or work side. Affective togetherness rooted in common doing.

**Technology**

100% automation as rapidly as possible. Liberation by technology from technology. Means plus Ends.

Optimal automation involves consistency with desired scale of operations, conformity with ecological niche, etc. Means/End.

**Unification Scale**

Totally articulated techno-political system. "Global Village". World culture. World democracy.

Only partial integrations to preserve systematic redundancy. Integration through diversity. Many different appropriate scales. Loose world federation.

**Representative Thinkers**

McLuhan, Fuller, Norman Brown

Morris, Goodman, Lewis Herber.

The usual line on work and play is Marx's description of the breakdown of the division of labour: "Production as a whole" being "regulated by society" (*sic*), it becomes "possible for me to do one thing today and another tomorrow, to hunt in the morning, fish in the afternoon, rear cattle in the evening, criticize after dinner, in accordance with my inclination, without ever becoming hunter, fisherman, shepherd or critic". To us this may appear a picture of leisure and hence to support the play (plus work) position: the machines look after production and we go fishing. However in Marx's day fishing *was* production: the hares, fish and cattle would actually be eaten, if not by the same prolific specimen of free society, then at least by his fellows (or by the estate-labourers in the case of the aristocratic way of life Marx must surely have been using as a model). In other words this wasn't a question of unarticulated or "pure" creativity – something would actually be created, and something socially necessary moreover. Nor would this fishing be a mere extra, a whimsical supplement in the interstices of the main apparatus of production. Distinctions between productivity and creativity would have appeared undialectical to Marx.

Marx saw that the abolition of physical toil might become possi-

ble: man would relate to the process of production "as supervisor
and regulator". This would require the reappropriation of "his own
social productivity, his knowledge and his mastery over nature
through his social existence – in one word; the development of the
social individual". But again, to understand the passage we need to
think of chemists poring over tomes in dingy laboratories, of
geologists making surveys and publishing their results, of scientific
congresses and technical delegations. Marx was not thinking of a
vast increase in the quantity of "free time": time is a reification for
the series of actual projects engaged in, activities carried out *on
something* or *in relation to someone*. By "development of the social
individual" Marx was certɑ ʼnly *not* thinking of sensitivity groups. By
"practical-sensuous existence" Marx was not meaning sensory
awakening classes at Esalen: more what Tolstoy felt as he joined in
the harvesting. Marx would have been amazed (if not shocked!) at
anyone advocating a life full *only* of togetherness as such, the re-
eroticizing of the body, the resurrection of the social-individual
body, the conquest of the reality principle, "*poésie faite par tous*".

One of the best advocates of the Play (plus vanishing work)
position is Norman O. Brown: "My utopia is / an environment that
works so well / that we can run wild in it / anarchy in an environment
that works / ...The environment can do all the work / Serious
thought, / thought as work, / in pursuit of *Wirklichkeit*, / is about
over / *Wirklichkeit*, the German word for reality, / the reality principle / The reality principle is about over. / Thought as work can be
buried in machines and computers / the work left to be done is to
bury thought; quite a job / To put thought underground / as
communication-network, sewage system, power lines / so that wild-
ness can come above ground / technological rationality can be put to
sleep / so that something else can awaken in the human mind /
something like the god Dionysus / something which cannot be prog-
rammed. / The ordering of the physical environment will release
unparalleled quantities and forms of human disorder / The future, if
there is one, is machines and madness".

Definitely a beautiful trip. But compare the Play (plus work)
position with a representative of the Play/work position, William
Morris. Morris defined art as "that which is, or should be, done by
the ordinary working man while about his ordinary work". Morris
looked for the *abolition of alienation in work*, not for the abolition
of work itself. If we ignore side-assumptions about the *conquest* of
nature and the *manliness* of work, we can groove just as much with
the following: "Nature will not finally be conquered till our work
becomes a part of the pleasure of our lives... The hope of pleasure in

the work itself: how strange that hope must seem to some of my readers! Yet I think that to all living things there is a pleasure in the exercise of their energies, and that even beasts rejoice in being lithe and swift and strong. But a man at work, making something which he feels will exist because he is working at it and wills it, is exercising the energies of his mind and soul as well as of his body... If we work thus we will be men, and our days will be happy and eventful".

Purposeful applied activities do not constitute the Toad Work, if the purposes are our own and worthy of our application, if our body/mind *enjoy* the activity (in the full sense of enjoy, as in "enjoy Him for ever"). The expressive and instrumental components in life are only partially separable – the aim being to *expand the expressivity of life*. This cannot happen in a natural or social vacuum. Likewise in our primary groups, we can get only so far along the path of liberation in leisure affinity groups. When even our "work" relationships can be suffused with the flow of Eros, then alienation is really coming to an end. The aim is not a premature "unity", appeals to any solidarity ethic for its own sake, and certainly not the phoney "togetherness" (like the advertisements for bourgeois marriage and drinking chocolate). Togetherness "comes" when it is rooted in common activities, in shared experiences of activities other than experiencing togetherness. (What Reich meant by "work democracy".)

The play/work position can be seen either as the permeation of technology by values ("the interpenetration of means and ends" – Goodman) or as the "translation of values into technical tasks – the materialisation of values" (Marcuse). The point is so crucial that it is worth noting them in more detail.

Although Marcuse has explicitly attacked the idea of work becoming play – on the not very good grounds that such a conception is "romantic" (perhaps the dispute is about words), he has also called our technology over-developed, and this, among other things, marks him off from Fuller and McLuhan:

"If the completion of the technological project involves a break with the prevailing technological rationality, the break in turn depends on the continued existence of the technical base itself. For it is this base which has rendered possible the satisfaction of needs and the reduction of toil – it remains the very base of all forms of human freedom. The qualitative change rather lies in the reconstruction of this base – that is, in its development with a view to different ends. I have stressed that this does not mean the revival of "values", spiritual or other (cf. Maslow or Rogers even in the US), which are to supplement the scientific and technological transformation of man and nature. On the contrary, the historical achievement of science and technology has rendered possible *the translation of values into technical tasks* – the materialisation of values. Consequently, what is at stake is the redefinition of values in *technical terms*, as elements in the technological process. The new ends, as technical ends, would then operate in the project and in the construction of the machinery, and not in its utilisation... Industrial civilisation has reached a point where, with respect to the aspirations of man for human existence, the scientific abstraction from final causes becomes obsolete in science's own terms". (*One Dimensional Man*)*

This, I think, puts him very close to Goodman who covered the same ground in a very much simpler style in his mind-blowing *Communitas*. After rejecting modern architecture and aesthetics for tending to lose the "human scale" and "the intimate sensibility of daily life", Goodman goes back to Greek antiquity and proposes what he calls a neo-functionalist aesthetic: "form follows function, but let it subject the function itself to a formal critique. Is the function good? *Bona fide*? Is it worthwhile? Is it worthy of a man to do that? What are the consequences? Is it compatible with other, basic human functions? Is it a forthright or at least ingenious part of life? Does it make sense?... Is the use as simple, ingenious, or clear as the efficient means that produce it? Is the using a good experience?" (P. and P. Goodman: *Communitas*) These may seem simple questions here on paper, but start applying them to the objects, habits and life-styles about you and you'll find them deeply subversive. Nothing freaks a committee so much as to ask "What's the point?"

The Play (plus work) position is associated with a world-integrative position, which itself derives from an awareness of the fantastic potential of modern technologies (or could-be-technologies, in the case of suppressed applied science). For instance, Brady shows how automation has a sweep and logic extending ever out from the machine, to intraplant integration, to continuous flow between factories and between industries and economies, extending back to resources and forward to consumption. Each "rationalised" process throws into relief new diseconomies in the form of flow fractures. Brady's ideal appears to be whole industries

---

*This is what gives ecology its "critical edge" as Lewis Herber has shown in his beautiful "Ecology and Revolutionary Thought" (ANARCHY 69) and "Towards a Liberatory Technology" (ANARCHY 78). Simply to survive with our machines and techniques we are forced towards an organic value system and praxis.

and economies linked to become one huge machine turning over 24 x 365 hours a year.

Economic advantages in the large scale are generally considerable – provided the planning is totally rational. However, when ordinary mortals are involved the actual economies of scale have been much exaggerated. Moreover many presuppose a capitalist context, eg continual shift-work, buying and selling economies, greater security against business uncertainties, research and development on a private basis, market research economies, the economies of skilled specialist managers. (See E. Goodman *The Impact of Size*, Ch 3 (Action Society Trust).) A national division of labour has the hidden cost of increasing distribution costs. Problems of adjusting supply and demand become acute. Finally, highly integrated large-scale automation is generally associated with extreme product specialisation by different plants. This means that it costs a great deal to turn out new products when demand for the first product falls off. (I mean, of course, when people no longer want more of the things in question – economics is full of reificatory language.)

Moreover, when external diseconomies are brought into the picture, over-complex gigantism invariably comes off worst. For instance, time taken to get to work should be counted in any real assessment of working hours. Moreover the ecological external diseconomies may be considerable: waste generated by several dispersed factories may be absorbed by the environment without long-term damage, whereas the same amount of production concentrated would probably destroy important local balances.

Culturally too, the automated world project would be disastrous. Ye Olde Worlde Englishe Culture for tourists is pitiable because it has lost its roots in the on-going realities of English life. A world-integrated technological and political system would result in a homogenisation of life-styles, language and culture which any amount of mass-produced African headcarvings, filmstrips on ancient India and school-trips to Morocco would only intensify. The point is to let diversity grow *at base* (in technics and in social organisation) and not to be fooled by a diversity of commodities and spectacles.

Brady himself quotes a technological objection which is interesting: "Tomorrow's generations, with far more people to be supported, must depend on extremely intricate technology. After any breakdown in the energy and processing cycle, the future generations might not be able to put in the tremendous quantity of energy to start the cycle once more". Put crudely (too crudely), how to mend electric power failures with electric-mains powered machinery? Although he does consider some variety in energy-source and energy-medium, Brady's faith is always in better and wider planning, planned unification of grids, etc. However he nowhere seems to have realised that large-scale rationalisation inherently cuts down diversity and hence increases instability in the long term. Huge integrated technologies are amazingly vulnerable to sabotage and seizure of control. Programming for all risks imaginable still leaves the unforeseen breakdown to challenge technocratic hubris. If scale and confidence are increased on the basis of the sum of the risks appropriate at smaller scales, the system as a whole must lose stability over time. For "chances in a million" never happen. Until they do.

A highly integrated world-political system is vulnerable, for similar reasons, to power-breakdowns of a different kind. Even on a smaller scale of say 50 million, the problems of overall political integration even in a (fully) democratic way are acute. A general rule for scale increase seems to be that interstitial energy increases $x^2$ as scale expands x. As an institution expands, functions that could be sustained on an informal basis by the members concerned become hived off into time-consuming and inefficient committees, which later need committees to liaise them. A logical next step is to hire teams of managerial consultants to sort out the muddle, and then consultants to sort out the consultants.

At what point are the hours saved through large-scale automation lost again through the time needed (in delegate committees, conferences, journal writing, etc, etc,) in order to stop the scale getting out of control (bureaucratic degeneration)?

At one extreme there is the crofter who is his *own* estate manager, agricultural consultant, co-ordination committee delegate, tool repairer, insurance agent, distribution department, etc. Also there is the kibbutz where only one-eighth of energy expended might be interstitial (eg kibbutz meetings, accounts and inventory) and the result still be democratic.

At the other extreme there is the sort of World Unification of the Fuller or McLuhan kind, whereby we might be totally liberated from physical labour and technical-thinking work only to be enslaved to the necessity to exercise constant political vigilance about procedures and proposals. Hours and hours would be needed in horizontal and vertical connections, and just as long would be required in studying the issues stemming from the vertical connections, so that the delegates would know which way to vote on the various problems facing the world and its continents. For those who think such a totally neurotic level of involvement unnecessary, consider:

(1)    that if World Oligarchy was once formed, that would be that...
(2)    that with the huge scale any wrong decisions would ramify exceedingly widely, that every decision would be a matter of life and death...
(3)    that technological omnipotence would need to be informed by scientific omniscience, hence fantastic capacities for relevant information collection *and processing* would be necessary among ordinary World Citizens; otherwise irreversibly suicidal decisions would be made, or at the least, the advantages of productivity through scale would be nullified by decision-making which, though quite possibly intelligent, was *incompetent in relation to scale...*

Even integration at the national level, if it was to be *efficient* and fully *democratic*, would scarcely leave time for a fuck – let alone for the Resurrection of the Body!

Something more modest is required, something looser and more communal. This does not mean that for particular purposes a *loose* World Federation is undesirable. (I am aware that this is presupposing the destruction of imperialism.) Co-ordination would still take place – indeed it would increase when freed from governmental-nationalist rivalries. Conflicts of interest would still take place, especially over raw materials and food supply. This would lead to "unnecessary" inefficiency and unequal development, but if the price for removing it were overtoppling with the insanities of governmentalism, it would make sense simply to rely on persuasion and/or learn to live with the particular problem (eg shortage of copper). Likewise at the national level: it is possible that the South-East would try to maintain its relatively privileged position (in GNP terms at any rate). The remedy could only come: (1)    through the deprived regions supporting those South-Easterners who were trying to ferment opposition and reverse the relevant decisions at regional level, and/or (2)    via sanctions and unpleasantness transmitting themselves to South/Easterners, informally via the various cross-cutting associations which they shared with people in other regions. In short *there can be no cast-iron guarantees and any attempt to create national guarantees cannot itself be guaranteed and is hence the biggest risk*. The same applies in such questions as States Rights and the South in the USA. A similar thought pattern is at the basis of the question of homeopathic medicine (see Brian Inglis:

*Fringe Medicine*) and "losing life to find it". Life just *is* dangerous. Faith to flow with it is the best non-guarantee available. Existence cannot be totally pacified.

A world of small loosely-federated regions and communities, then, would still take advantage of co-ordination in relevant areas. Thus, in the area of standards and specifications, although Brady argues from the advantages of standardisation to the need for planning powers, he himself admits that a huge range of appropriate standards has already been built up voluntarily, often by humble engineers acting out of professional competence. Kropotkin's example of the European standard railway gauge could be updated and multiplied a hundredfold from the work already carried out by the International Standards Organisation.

Such a modest and partial degree of integration would leave enough PLAY in the system for serendipitous advance, for experimentation and retreat, even for sheer anti-technological cussedness, where desired. It would be capable (1) of evolving progressively refined adjustments according to the unique pattern of local natural resources; (2) of evolving a variety of unique design idioms; (3) of evolving pluriform and increasingly refined patterns of complex multi-level industrial and political structures.

One such pattern might involve a general one-step or two-step localisation of functions, as compared with the present:

**Level One:** Increase in do-it-yourself, kit-construction, repairs: spread of domestic tools and machinery.

**Level Two:** Neighbourhood workshops, [*] redevelopment of craft work at high technological level: also communal task forces, eg build-it-ourselves projects for community centres, swimming baths, adventure playgrounds, etc.

**Level Three:** Small multipurpose community factories able to create a variety of products by flexible tooling (and/or programming) on versatile machines over which men can remain in control. [**]

**Level Four:** Medium-sized largely automatic factories for intra- and inter-regional relative specialisation (and for export sector?), evenly spread throughout the country. For production both of

[*]See original articles on "The Community Workshop" and "Towards a Do-It-Yourself Economy" in ANARCHY 30. Also "Tenants Take Over", ANARCHY 83.

[**]See Lewis Herber "Towards a Liberatory Technology", ANARCHY 78. Also Paul and Percival Goodman: *Communitas*, Chapter Six.

finished goods, and for servicing of community factories and work-shops with standardised materials and parts, machine tools, etc.

Such a system might be inefficient (in the short term especially) in raising every citizen's gross standard of commodities, but that would not be its purpose. Compared with the possibilities of world and nation-wide continuous flows, this system might conceivably result in definite failures of co-ordination, but never in irreversible breakdown. And so what if hundreds of men can't work because of a supply breakdown? It's a lovely morning, let's go for a walk...

A crucial goal would be *transparency of operation*, with reference to (1) the machines and consumer durables (built for ease of use and repair), and (2) the economic (that is social) interrelatedness of society. The general idea would be to have an economy of *things*, not generalised money (Goodman).

To give some idea of the radical consequences of *"breaking through to the point of it all"* (and to give some idea of the difficulty – for it surely wouldn't happen as easily as I'm going to suggest it would), let us consider a factory of 5,000 employees, 1,000 of whom are managerial and minor bureaucrats. The factory is a car factory. After the carnival of revolution come the appeals to return to work. To get into the habit of responding to orders/exhortations to raise the GNP would be to sell the pass straight away. On the other hand production must eventually be got going on *some* basis or other. What basis? Return to *what sort of work*? For what? So what?

So instead of restarting the assembly track (if the young workers haven't already smashed it) they spend two months discussing the point of their work, and how to rearrange it. Private cars? Why do people always want to go somewhere else? Is it because where they are is so intolerable? And what part did the automobile play in making the need to escape? What about day to day convenience? Is being stuck in a traffic jam convenient? What about the cost to the country? Bugger the "cost to the country", that's the same crap as the national interest. Have you seen the faces of old people as they try to cross a busy main road? What about the inconvenience to pedestrians? What's the reason for buying a car? Is it wanting just to HAVE IT? Do we think the value of a car rubs off on us? But that's the wrong way round. Does having a car really save time? What's the average hours worked in manufacturing industry? Let's look it up in the library: 45.7 hours work a week. What's the amount of the family's spending money in a week that goes on cars? 10.3% of all family income. Which means more like 20% if you've got a car because half of us don't have one. What's 20% of 45 hours? Christ, 9 hours! That's a hell of a long time to spend "saving time"! There must be a better way of getting from A to B. By bus? OK, let's make buses. But what about all the pollution and that? What about those electric cars they showed on the telly once? Etc, etc.

The most basic project would of course involve *TRANSINDUS-TRIALISATION*. After a month of intensive discussion and research in complexly cross-cutting groups, the following sort of consensus for eventual self-redeployment might emerge:

*Number of workers*:    185
*Point:*    Car refurbishing (to increase use-value of models already on the road, eg by adding exhaust filters).
*Scale of use*:    Community.
*Technical mode*:    Varied – little end-product specialisation due to variety of makes and problems.

*Number of workers*:    1850
*Point*:    Buses, for connecting train and monorail termini with where people want to go.
*Scale of use*:    National (also part regional, part export, and part giveaway – voluntary overseas aid).
*Scale of making*:    Large regional factory, plus several smaller parts factories in communities in the region. (Also, not included in the 1850, parts from outside the region.)
*Technical mode*:    Regional factory not on shift work or automatic track. Gangs of men who see whole buses through to completion, including distribution. Smaller parts factories make standardised parts, therefore high level of automation.

*Number of workers*:    740
*Point*:    Overhead monorail cars.
*Scale of use*:    Regional (and small surplus exchanged with other regions), *i.e.* on a national basis.
*Scale of making*:    Small regional factory and smaller parts factories.
*Technical mode*:    As above except only quasi-automatic machinery (eg Leaver and Brown drilling machine).

*Number of workers*:    555.
*Point*:    Electric cars and scooters for disabled people and inner city travel especially.
*Scale of use*:    Regional.
*Scale of making*:    Two small community factories of 250, making the engines. Glass fibre and plastics factory for bodywork.

*Technical mode*:   Glass fibre and plastics factory at high level of automation.

*Number of workers*:   370.
*Point*:   White bicycles for communal use.
*Scale of use*:   Community.
*Scale of making*:   Neighbourhood workshops for kit construction and frame manufacture – parts from community factories, regional factories.
*Technical mode*:   Automation for ball bearings, hubs, in community factories. Regionally produced standard steel tubing. Made into bicycles by neighbourhood craft work and kit construction.

*Number of workers*:   925.
*Point*:   Construction of dignified housing with built-in communal potential, communal centres and workshops.
*Scale of use and making*:   Task forces attached to neighbourhoods.
*Technical mode*:   Great variety of work – some construction standardisation with prefabricated modules, but no standardisation of design.

*Number of workers*:   375.
Dropouts from organised work – some do minimal work (say 5 hours gardening a week). 15% dropout ration at first, reduces to 7½% as many drift into congenial milieux. This 7½% largely compensated for by the number of casual *drop-in* workers at community and neighbourhood levels, especially in communal construction work. Kids and old people like to make themselves useful.
Important to create a reasonable subsistence existence for non-workers, otherwise theft, antagonisms, stigma, etc. Antagonisms diminish when people enjoy their own work, and therefore don't resent "skivers". Diminished fear of not-working leads to more rational attitude to the point of work: OK to take plenty of breaks, etc.

\*              \*              \*

But there are other questions on the agenda:

A.   *Materials use*:   Supply, alternative uses? end-use specification?
B.   *Ergonomic Redesign*:   Men in charge of machines, degree of optimal automation, machines fitting in with men (no night work).

C.  *End Product Design*:    Transparency of operation and repair; functionally appropriate ranges of variation.
D.  *Standards and Specifications*.
E.  *External Liaison Functions*:    With parallel industries in different parts of the same country or region; with transportation, etc.
F.  *Distribution*:
   (1)    Eg buses; distribution to community councils on basis of size which make exact allocations of basis of *need* to neighbourhood councils;
   (2)    Eg electric cars; distribution to neighbourhood councils on basis of social *need*;
   (3)    Eg bread; no problem for distribution – bread free – bakeries decentralised and guaranteed flour by farmers on return for neighbourhood and community products;
   (4)    Individual consumer goods (eg record players) can be earned by presenting work tokens allocated according to hours worked and need of home circumstance;
   (5)    Other consumer goods can be had on a "come and work for it" community factory basis.
G.  *Aid*:    Voluntary extra work undertaken by a factory or area. Town-twinning. New Delhi needs buses, provide them by voluntary work.
H.  *Voluntary Extra Work*:    As work becomes more and more pleasurable, as technology and society develop to allow more and more craft aspects to return at high technological level, the idea of *voluntary extra* over the (reduced) fixed working week becomes feasible. Even the fixing of the working week becomes superseded. The aim is to confuse work and non-work, on the terms of play.
I.  *Work Hours*:    Reduced to 30, 20, 15, 10 hours per week. Can be taken at different points of the day, week, month, year, or spread out evenly. All figures approximate. No time-keeping. Deliberate blurring between personal and productive time.
J.  *Variety in "Work"/Play*:    Large scale/craft production; active/passive; indoor/outdoor; brain/brawn, etc. It follows that the figures given earlier for, say, buses, contain hours done by different people. Most importantly, it would be accepted practice for women with young kids to relieve the husband in the factory, so that he could take his fair share of looking after the kids, house work, etc.
K.  *Other-Educative Functions*:    Open to community, therefore to children. Thus every factory worker is a potential "environmental studies" instructor, if a child comes up and asks him how something works.
L.  *Self-Group Educative Functions*:    The factory as university.

Students and lecturers are themselves members for variety from *their* "jobs". Factory discussion groups, internal radio, magazine, etc.

M.   *Discussion, Research*:   Directly related to important policy decisions, working out social "costing" procedures, previously known as money accounts.

N.   *Managerial Functions of Control*:   Abolished.

O.   *Worthwhile Managerial Functions*:   Absorbed. Self-management as a re-appropriation of capacities.

# III.   The implications for revolutionary strategy

Consider the example of the bored typist in the advertising agency. In the face of such a mountain of shit (the superfluous substance) right down the line, what can one say to her? The "your boss is exploiting you" approach seems almost an insult, as does "you want workers' control, don't you?" To pamphleteer at the factory gates, urging more strikes, more pay, more participation, is to hit the problem at a tangent. Work is the problem. *Work is the essential contradiction* which establishes the total dependence of the worker on a system which utterly rejects him as a person.

Factories producing the unwanted commodities of a fetishised world have no relevance, nor have supermarkets controlled by their workers, nor mental hospitals controlled by their inmates. In our society (but not in the society we want) "alienation is work itself, the commodities produced and the structure of relationships that arises out of this imposed need to buy, to sell, to profit". (*King Mob* 6)

"Psst! Why work? You know it doesn't make sense!"

# IV. EDUCATION

## 1. The children and psychology
### Paul Goodman

WHAT IS most significant, it seems to me, is the earnest attention paid to the Children and Family as a subject, the desire of parents to be informed and thereby do their best, rather than following their wit and impulse; or to say this another way, what is significant is the importance assigned in our society to Psychology itself, for Psychology is still by and large the family-psychology that Freud made it, discussing the problems of jealousy, infantile dependency, authority, submissiveness and rebelliousness, and sibling competition: and problems of spite, moral prejudice and other reaction-formations springing from instinctual deprivation. This interest in the Children is of course hopeful, for the increase of wisdom cannot fail to remedy abuses, and has already done so quite spectacularly.

But this interest is also itself a symptom of an unfortunate social situation. Earnest folk pay such special attention to the children, and in general to their Inter-personal Relations, because there is not enough objective man's work or woman's work to put themselves to. I do not mean that there is not enough absolutely (it's a large universe); but that in our present social and technical arrangements there are not enough exciting and *available* and unquestionably self-justifying enterprises, where a lively human being can exercise initiative and use his enormous psychic and physical powers to anything like capacity. This problem goes, I think, deeper than any of the current differences in political or economic arrangements, and I cannot think of any immediate change that could alleviate it. We are in a phase of collective enterprise that does not, and probably cannot as yet, much use and stimulate such remarkably gifted animals as individual people, especially if we consider them (as children) before they are discouraged and become rusty, and in addition to our powers all the knowledge and equipment of our culture. So more and more are likely to blow off steam in religious exploration; and the brunt of the burden falls on pre-occupation with the Children and Interpersonal Relations, for these at least are things that one can individually try to do something about.

Good parents work to preserve-and-give more available energy to their children; the children in turn grow up and find they have not much field of action for this energy, but they can expend some of it on their children.

The helping of children has the prime advantage that it can be disinterested, compassionate, and *noblesse oblige*; it is our nearest equivalent to the old chivalry. The bother is that, except for those who have a calling, who are born teachers, it is stultifying as a steady occupation. We also need some dragons to kill and planets to visit, or goods to produce that people unquestionably need. A psychiatrist friend of mine says that the right care of children is: let them alone and be around; where "be around" means I suppose, to provide safety, audience for the exploit, consolation for the hurt, suggestion and material equipment for the next step, and answers when asked. This simple formula will not fill up a twenty-lecture seminar on Children.

## The family as battleground

As our families are, the children in both their present satisfaction and the free growth of their powers, are certainly crushed, thwarted, pushed, hurt, and misled by their hostile and doting grown-ups. Frankly, I doubt that you can find one child in a dozen who is not being seriously injured, in quite definite and tangible ways, by his family. I would say this indignantly, as an indictment of the Family and *ecrasez l'infame*, let's fight to get rid of it! If I thought that the available substitutes were not even more disastrous. But consider also the other side, that the parents are tied to and tyrannized over by the little Neros. You cannot put them in their places for several reasons: 1.   You can't, try it; 2.   It's bad for them to slap them down, and if they are injured it bounces back on you in the end; and 3.   Most fundamentally, in the good cases you can't deny the imperious demands of the children because most, and perhaps all, of the hard things they really want are justified: they want space, excitement, sexual freedom, noble models to grow up to, wise saws of experience, real arts and crafts to learn, animals to hunt, an unknown to explore, and comprehensible answers to direct questions. But it is not the case that our housing, our economy, our style, our frontiers, and our sciences are amenable to these justified childish demands. Our arrangements have become so objective that few grown-ups and no children any longer have an available objective world. So a sensitive parent feels justly guilty; he tries anxiously, in impossible conditions, not to rob the children of their natural rights as the free heirs of nature and man. Do not many of us suffer from what we could call a Lear-complex? We are abashed by the free unspoiled power of the very young, we have no right to withstand it, we resign and give up our own rights.

As a striking example of parental guilty good intentions, notice in community planning, how every adult requirement of quality, style, and efficiency, is sacrificed to suburban utilities of safety and playground.

# Being master with authority

Contrast it to make the point clear – with a master and his disciples, whether an artist or an artisan or a scholar: he uses the kids for his purposes, he says do and don't with a clear conscience, because his soul is fixed on the work; he teaches them out of his compassion to prevent error and advance the future. They, in turn, are neither humiliated nor browbeaten nor exploited. They are growing into the work and growing through him because he is a master of the work; and the compelling proof of all this does not come from authority but from the work. Now regarding the Family as a school of growth in the art of personal life and of exploration and inspiration towards a career, what experienced mother or father feels like a master of the subject and can command and forbid with conviction, except in some elementary issues of health and safety and perhaps grammar and manners? (As Yeats said, "The best lack all conviction – the worst are full of passionate intensity.") We do not know the method to reach the goal we do not know. This is often expressed by the sentence, "I don't care what my children do or become, so long as they will be happy." An honest, humble, and sensible sentence, but it puts parents in the impossibly anxious position of trying to fulfil an indefinite reponsibility. So instead of improvising with wit and love on a foundation of experience and unquestioned personal achievment, they necessarily rely on Psychology and Mental Hygiene.

Another cause of preoccupation with the children is that children have become the only colourable excuse for existence of the monogamous family. Economically, women make money and own most of it. As a way of life, with the general breakdown of the old sexual conventions and the weakening of the old inhibitions, monogamous marriage is felt as a trap and a frustration; people are exposed to, and allow themselves to feel, temptation but are not able to take satisfaction, so there is plenty of resentment and guilt, projected resentment. Frankly, again, it is my observation that if many marriages (maybe most) could be simply dissolved after a few years, the partners would suddenly become brighter, rosier, and younger. And again I would therefore urge, change the whole institution, except that the situation is not simple: we are still in the toils of jealousy of our own Oedipus-complexes, and in the present social fragmentation the companionship of marriage, such as it is, a safeguard against isolation and loneliness. (The Family was a bulwark of the private economy, and now it is a refuge against the collective economy.) But these grounds for the continued existence of the institution cannot stand much ethical scrutiny, considering the cost. It is the children that make the effort unquestionably worthwhile; and of course with the two or three children now standard, the burden of justification that must be borne by each little darling is great indeed.

## Salvation through sex-technique

As a defence against it, it has become the highest aim in life of an entire young generation to "achieve" a normal happy marriage and raise healthy (psychologically healthy) children. This is, what was always taken as a usual and advantageous background for work in the world and the service of God, is now regarded as a heroic goal to be striven for. This is preposterous. Yet, I should like to repeat it, the sentiment is deeply justified by the fact that at least this goal *can* be personally striven for; it is connected with real, not merely symbolic satisfactions and responsibilities; and the same cannot be said for other goals for most people, which are either fictions of prestige and power, or are managed collectively. Consider, as a test, when the goal cannot be achieved or when the marriage cracks up: it is the exceptional case where the person's work or social role is important enough and real enough to occupy his thoughts and keep him going with manly fortitude. Viewed in this light, the thousand manuals of sex-technique and happy marriage have the touching dignity of evangelical tracts, as is indeed their tone; they teach how to be saved, and there is no other way to be saved.

The well-intentioned loving and resentful parents make a vocation of the children until finally they can send them off, at increasingly early times, to nursery-schools and schools. Perhaps the schools will provide "exploration and inspiration toward a career". But the situation of the teachers in the schools is fundamentally no different. For always the question is, What to teach? What is realistically *worth* teaching? The curriculum becomes poorer and poorer, because an honest educator cannot seriously believe that the solid sciences and humanities are life-relevant to the average of this mass of pupils. Nor is so-called "vocational" training the answer. (The name tends to be applied precisely in the absence of vocation.) Neither the jobs trained? for nor the kill-time training add up to what would enliven a human soul. The answer of the school is again Pyschology; what the teacher has is not a subject-matter but a Method, and what he teaches is Interpersonal Relations. The only art that is essential is to read simple words, for production and distribution depend on reading. (So there has been universal free primary education for a hundred years, and the earmark of the delinquent who won't fit into the economy is that he won't or can't learn to read.) But the savage and intolerable irony is the current raving for more mathematics and physics, lest our bombs, radar, and rockets fall behind Russia's – these beautiful studies that have been transcendent goals for many of our best! now advocated so basely and the professors greedy for the subsidies and students on any conditions.

# Success without achievement

Brought up in a world where they cannot see the relation between activity and achievement, adolescents believe that everything is done with mirrors, tests are passed by tricks, achievement is due to pull, goods are known by their packages, and a man is esteemed according to his front. The delinquents who cannot read and quit school, and thereby become still less able to take part in such regular activity as is available, show a lot of sense and life when they strike out directly for the *rewards* of activity, money, glamour, and notoriety, which will "prove" in one fell swoop that they are not impotent. And it is curious and profoundly instructive how they regress, politically, to a feudal and band-and-chieftain law that is more comprehensible to them. The code of a street-gang has many an article in common with the Code of Alfred the Great.

It is disheartening indeed to be with a group of young fellows who are in a sober mood and who simply do not know what they want do with themselves in life. Doctor, lawyer, beggar-man, thief? Rich man, poor man, Indian chief? They simply do not know an ambition and cannot fantasize one. But it is not true that they don't care; their "so what?" is vulnerable, their eyes are terribly baulked and imploring. (I say "it is disheartening", and I mean that the tears roll down my cheeks; and I who am an anarchist and a pacifist feel that they will be happier when they are all in the army.)


# The psychology of abundance


This a sad picture. Naturally; for it is always sad when you write about something, rather than do something. (Poetry is not sad, it is an action.) I do not think there is cause for indignation, nor for despair. Not for indignation, because so many people are doing their best and many of these difficulties that have arisen are surprising and must simply be addressed patiently. Not for despair, for my feeling is that we are in a strange transition: to finding some kind of collective arrangements that will be rich with animal vitality and creative spontaneity and will be without Interpersonal Relations. Of course I cannot imagine such an apparently contradictory thing or I would be writing that instead of this. Meantime we psychologically-informed parents are doggedly (and out of our own hides) contributing to the explosion of it. By the millions – soon by the vast majority – we have let up on toilet-training, we have been liberating sexuality, we have honestly relinquished an old-fashioned authority because we do not know right principles. Then in the new generation there is more and more health and available energy, and less and less to do with it; more and more unprejudiced, not-class-ridden and good-humoured kids who are, yet, more and more stupid. This is the psychology of abundance that goes with the economy of abundance.

With the alleviation of the anxieties of poverty, there naturally loom vaster and at first vaguer anxieties of destiny. Our present task, it seems to me, is just to get rid of a few more ideas, to get rid of *Life* so we can have a little life, and finally to get rid of Psychology so we can have a little contact and invention. As Laotse said, "Good government is to empty the people's minds and fill their bellies."

*Anarchy 11*                                            *January 1962*

# 2.    The character builders
## Harold Drasco

THE SYMPOSIUM on Adventure Playgrounds which formed the seventh issue of ANARCHY might well have been complemented with a discussion of what is, in one sense, one of the same problem's other faces: education through adventure in open country. For the directions in which this work has been moving should enlist the attention of anarchists. Anyone uninformed in these affairs might assume that what we could call the informal sports – camping, mountaineering, sailing, and their derivatives – that these normally non–competitive activities must be admirably free from the tendencies we make note of in education and in social affairs. Since the war, however, instruction in these skills has become involved with public and private money through the establishment of permanent centres by the Outward Bound Trust, the Central Council for Physical Recreation, several Local Education Authorities, and other interested bodies. And already we can distinguish libertarian and authoritarian attitudes at work.

Of these ventures the Outward Bound Trust is the most publicised and makes claims for its four-week courses different in kind from those made by the other centres. It has indirect liaisons with the Services and the Churches. A glance at any literature about the work of the Trust will help to identify its position provisionally. The vocabulary is characteristic: relating to its aims – spiritual awareness, leadership, loyalty, character training, self-discipline, clean living; to its methods – competition, supreme exertion, shock treatment, honours and merit badges. It doesn't seem essential to outline the whole mystique of Outward Bound here but you can see immediately that there must be points for discussion in this area. Taking it for granted that were we to resolve the more obvious of the semantic problems in the stated aims – matters of definition in such abstractions as "character", for instance – we might still find grounds for hostility, it seems necessary to suggest briefly what values the activities themselves, from any viewpoint, might be agreed to have.

To begin with, we must remind ourselves that most of the adolescents attending these courses are unacquainted with the natural world to an extent difficult for us to grasp. There are factors that have operated towards and against this but for proof talk to a representative group of them for about ten minutes. It isn't necessary to raise a complicated theory of value in order to insist that simple sense-experience, in and for itself, is good. And at this lowest level there is the sheer visual shock of this new world, its colours and space, whether you care to describe it in aesthetic or physiological terms; the feel of rock, snow, heather; the silences and sounds; the new information for every mode of sense perception. For some reason this never seems to be emphasised despite the fact that we admit discoveries of the senses to be the basis of knowledge. And in synthesis, the earth, after all, is our planet and its landscapes, experienced directly, can arouse sensations only remotely stirred by second-hand parade upon the screen. Of course, some of this applies to older people too. Any week-end you can see families getting out of their cars for a roadside picnic with the trepidation of the first astronauts disembarking on a new star: suspiciously on the watch for dangerous rain, untrustworthy animals, the risk of getting dirty.

Then there are the skills acquired. It is a surprise to many to find how peculiarly natural such an activity as canoeing, for example, feels even today. In the same way, the apparently specialised equipment of the mountaineer – ice-axe, rope, climbing boots, piton hammer – is often felt to have an almost instant familiarity; perhaps because these articles are really only types of the basic instruments of man's emergence. For whatever reason, and scores could be advanced, it is observable fact that these skills satisfy richly, that in some way the body recognises them. To many youngsters they are ecstatically exciting. Indeed, with increasing frequency and with justice the question is raised: why is so much money and effort spent on teaching children games which the majority never practise after leaving school? It can't be supported with the reasons used to justify algebra or Greek. On the other hand, if an interest is awakened these informal sports can be, and often are, followed as participant, not spectator, until late in life; because, sooner or later, it becomes apparent that satisfaction in these sports has small reference to any external standard but relates rather to an internal balancing of ability and desire. Also, aside from pleasure and apart from fitness, there are indisputable benefits to the general health, sometimes visible at the end of a week.

Then there is the social aspect. There can be no easier way of demonstrating the necessity for co-operation than by an expedition in rough country, a microcosm in which the consequences of actions are seen immediately and without complication. Indeed, simplified to a level appropriate to any age-group and mentality, we can show as if with the force of an experiment: we must love one another or die. If wisely arranged, the communal life of the centre can support this lesson strongly.

Ought not these possibilities to be enough in themselves? Many of us would maintain that with some obvious resultants they are more than enough. But at this point we must dissociate ourselves from the theorists of Outward Bound. For what is the connection between these benefits and the promises not to swear, not to smoke, not to drink? What has "clean living" got to do with this? Why should it be thought necessary to teach co-operation competitively? Why the cult of leadership, the sermons and homilies, the heavy expense of spirit? Clearly, because we are in Montgomeryland, the Trust is training Christian soldiers, and, to a larger or smaller extent, is simply using the sea and mountains instrumentally. It is using these activities, like it or not, in a way analogous to that in which Germany used them: to fit the child to the State. A different idea of the State, a different idea for the citizen, but beneath it the same principle.

It appears that, aside from any disagreement about what defines character, we can now make two major criticisms of the work of the Trust. Firstly, owing to the stress on extreme fitness, competition, the "conquering of self", and so forth, it seems that in many activities the youngsters are pressed far past the point of enjoyment. Anyone who has talked to a number of unaccompanied Outward Bound parties on the fells will agree that, even allowing for temporary despondencies forgotten in retrospect and for the astonishing resilience of youngsters, a proportion of the boys is disenchanted forever with these pastimes. What proportion this may be it would be very difficult to determine but (of the "conscripts" from industry, at any rate) some estimates put it at a majority. And if you believe that the activities are good in themselves and not simply as a means there is an unanswerable failure here. Secondly, for normal adolescents even these neutral pastimes may be given distasteful and

irrelevant associations by the clumsily overt emphasis on "character" and example. Youngsters tend to judge a sport by its practition-
ers and the way they talk. In mitigation of these criticisms it is
important to add that when one is in unspoiled country a sense of
freedom is often conspicuously present and a resistance to authority
and its precepts may be encouraged by contrast; if the trainees are
sent out unchaperoned, Nature subverts the intentions of the character builders at every step. Nonetheless, it seems certain that the
basic merits of the activities are in many cases, if not negated, at
least severely limited by this general approach.

Whilst none of the other experiments has been based on profes-
sedly libertarian principles, some of them do stand at a noticeable
remove from the authoritarianism of Outward Bound. The Derbyshire Education Committee's centre at Buxton, which has been
running for more than ten years now, is amongst these. Its establishment was to the credit of the Director of Education for Derbyshire,
Jack Longland, whose influence in this field has been very considerable and entirely to the good. He has, it is true, inevitably become
involved in Outward Bound affairs but has, at the same time, firmly
rejected facile theories of character-transference – the playing fields
of Eton stuff. he has drawn attention to the loose identification of
"character" and "morals". And he has exercised a nice restraint,
suggesting gently that the whole concept of character is a more
elusive and complex subject than the more exuberant of the out-
door educationists seem to assume. The following notes, however,
don't pretend to represent official policy but simply a few aspects of
the working rules evolved at White Hall.

The consideration which underlies all others is safety. It might
not seem necessary to state this but it's worth mentioning since
some of the ends and means we criticise operate against it. Where
others' lives are concerned no-one has the right even to think about
so-called "calculated" risks. This said, the obvious first principle is
that the youngsters and adults who visit the centre should enjoy
themselves. The obvious test is whether they want to come again or
not. The aim is the stimulation of a permanent interest in any of the
activities. We are persuaded that we have been very successful with
this approach and this success must largely result from the general
absence of pressure. In detail, there is almost always complete freedom of choice as to which of the specialised activities – rock-
climbing, canoeing, caving, and so on – are taken and if anyone
wishes he can just go fell-walking instead. We do not assume that
everyone *must* like these pastimes. No-one is pressed to do anything
he finds difficult or alarming. There is no element of competition

and, accordingly, there is no obstacle to the co-educational course which is common. Potential leaders are not sought and relations between instructors and pupils are nearly informal. Indeed, the atmosphere at the centre has always been so friendly that there has been no difficulty in securing the assistance of as many unpaid volunteer instructors as has been thought useful every weekend since the centre was opened. Some of these instructors first came to the centre as novices. The cost of running this kind of service is not exorbitant in comparison with the sums spent on large playing fields for formal games and athletics. Many of us feel that such centres present the ideal forms of physical education and that where geographically possible – almost everywhere – whatever sorts of natural facilities are available ought to be used.

In conclusion, we must revert to the question of character and morals. It would require a long essay to separate and define these concepts adequately enough for useful discussion. Briefly, however, of this whole complex of attitudes some aspects we might dismiss as comparatively trivial affairs of habit or manners. Some of the religious and sexual content, as propounded in this context, we might wish to reject entirely. Some abstract qualities such as loyalty and self-confidence we might feel disinclined to class as virtues. But some sort of nucleus is left behind and towards the development of this we can offer certain non-verbal lessons related to the benefits mentioned earlier, which assuredly are a part of the experiential basis of any higher qualities. In particular, it may reasonably be claimed that such slight tastes of loneliness, hunger, or apparent hazard as may occur incidentally in these activities serve to make evident the primary values of company, food, security. And, above all, if it is possible for the youngster to visit the same centre at different seasons there is the nourishment of release and continuity and certainty that the natural world can give; with, in completion, the very inportant sense of process and impermanence that underlies it, a tragic sense, perhaps, but one of the foundations of humanism and real education.

*Anarchy 11*                                                   *January 1962*

# 3. Bombed site and comprehensive school

## Winifred Hindley

IN 1948 I took over a 14- to 15-year-old group of boys and girls with IQs ranging from 70 to 115, in a horsa hut built on a bombed site adjacent to the school. It was in the heart of industrial Salford at a time when the back-to-back houses and dark alleys were being replaced by blocks of flats; bookies' corners, fried fish shops, rag and bone depots, pawnshops and the Flat Iron market gradually disappeared and hot water and sophistication crept in. The old village was replaced by a rootless well-housed community.

We had none of the amenities now accepted for the education of children... no laboratories, gymnasiums or Art blocks, and yet in my hut I had everything to hand to satisfy the immediate needs of the child, to help him to grow. The pre-fab was a second home, where the adolescent often grew through a second chance. There were curtains, flowers, children's writing, painting, modelling and over a thousand books to satisfy a variety of needs and purposes. And because the Hut belonged to them, because the boys and girls created the environment, they shared in the care of it, writing and drawing were done on paper, not on walls and desks. The environment was permissive, sanctioning, and supportive; text books disappeared and, with them, arid exercises and lecturettes and because I taught them for most subjects relationships could grow. It was possible to create an atmosphere of poetry, literature and music.

English was my civilising agent. But the tiny hut was the place which made so much possible, which make these girls and boys safe enough to "feed" and sure enough to retain the childlikeness (*not* childishness), the naïveté Lawrence writes of... "It is only from his core of innocence and naïveté that the human being is ultimately a responsible and dependable being... It is one of the terrible qualities of reason that it has no life of its own, and unless continually kept nourished or modified by the naïve life in man or woman it becomes purely a parasitic and destructive force". It was while I was experimenting in this ideal and yet condemned situation that I began really to know that education is concerned with far more than the trading of facts to unwilling customers. "The soul of education is not subject matter but a blend of value, assumption, a certain moral love, a special quality of imagination and a peculiar flavour of sensibility".

Eventually reorganisation brought my satisfying and happy experiment among the ruins to an end. With a very sure knowledge of the truth of Wordsworth's:

> ...day by day
> Subjected to the discipline of love
> His organs and recipient faculties
> Are quickened, and made vigorous, his mind spreads
> Tenacious of the forms which it receives.

I went to teach English to less able (not backward) boys in a Comprehensive school. Naturally this presented me with problems of personal adjustment, but I feel that I can at this stage write objectively of the advantages and disadvantages of this kind of school. There were countless advantages in the shape of laboratories, experts in many fields of learning, a large organ, a stage, gymnasiums, a choice of 17 types of sports, a library, Art and workshop blocks. There was the stimulation of meeting daily a variety of people from all walks of life... the excitement which comes from belonging to a large, brilliantly organised community. There was the satisfaction of parents who had feared the 11-plus and saw their sons wearing the same uniform as the boy who had passed. Courses were provided to suit the developing needs of the boys of all ranges of ability; responsibility for the social and emotional needs of the boys was shared by set masters, tutors and teachers.

But I have come to believe very strongly during these months that all the amenities in the world are of little use if the child cannot "feed". I worked in the Secondary Modern Department with boys very similar in ability to those with whom I worked in the North. These boys will never join the ranks of the academics, unless it is to join the "paper chase" for one or maybe two bits of paper, and yet there they were sitting in rows in classrooms with the time-table so structured that they were in theory to receive eight daily injections of learning. Worse, there was no supporting environment. All that wealth of amenity and not the environmental support to satisfy immediate needs. All those walls... and not one of them mine... or theirs. All those people officially responsible... but too many. All those boys and men... and so few women!

In fairness I should state that those who structure the education of the less able boy are as aware as I am of its inadequacy in its present form. And also in fairness I should state that restructuring is made difficult by lack of rooms. The architects and planners of Comprehensive schools must have believed that you could grow children by innoculating them in "boxes". They seem to have planned with only a view to physical and intellectual development. They disregard the fact that the education of the Secondary Modern child needs a far different setting from that of the old type Grammar School. In the Comprehensive school I found myself once again in the kind of setting I had discarded in a condemned slum classroom 12 years ago.

All the planned opportunities and amenities are of little worth, however brilliant the planning, if education of the less able does not always give the boys and girls a purpose which they immediately recognise, in a safe environment with materials and books to supply immediate needs, and with an enduring safe relationship.

The boys I taught showed their needs very obviously. They were attention seeking. They met me before lessons and trailed after me after lessons to tell about pigeons or mice... or sick rabbits and tortoises, to bring scraps of crumpled poetry... Miss Hourd's "love offerings". The younger ones fought to carry my bags.

I knew from my Salford experience the need to create, to colour and cut and paste and I was ever rewarded for the trouble of carrying around my bags loaded with coloured crayons, paste, paper and scissors and watching the boys delve with satisfaction into the assortment. Gripfix has a wonderful therapeutic value; it appeals to the senses of touch and smell. When given the opportunity to make class, group, or individual books the boys did so freely, with a will. They were constantly asking for paper and books in order to go on making at home. But it was difficult and often impossible to give each boy the attention and interest and help he needed at a particular moment of his development. I had no room I could call my own. Often when they sought me in between periods I sent them away; I had to in order to survive myself. *I found myself censuring the demands which were essential parts of growth.* I had to compromise, and I found myself drawing on my early "regimental" experiences with a sense of guilt and inadequacy.

There was a considerable output of creative writing. London boys like Salford boys and girls often delight in illustrating their writing and the work I began to draw from the boys resembled that of earlier days except that it had not the meticulous care the Salford adolescents showed. It could not have – sugar paper books grow battered when constantly carried around.

Often when I have lectured on children's writing and taken the Salford children's work, the immediate response of teachers has been, "Surely this is Primary School work?" It had all the life and colour and care of the work of the Primary School child. And why not? Do we put away childish things at eleven? I contend that if we do, in many many cases we fail to grow children. The second year form I worked with in the Comprehensive School had strong primary needs which could not be satisfied in the prevailing structure. The boys were very demanding. It was as if they were saying in countless ways, "Look at me! I'm here". I changed my dress daily, having learnt the dramatic and social value of this in Salford; our modern pre-adolescent is very aware of dress. One day I broke the leaden ornamental horse shoe in my chain belt. Every form noted this. But my second year boys whose needs were starkly obvious, were very concerned. I wore the belt the following day, with the broken ornament dangling at my waist. They attached a veritable sporran of ornaments, key rings and charms to the belt. I taught these boys for eight 35-minute periods, but I am certain that I could have done so much more for them had I had them for longer stretches, and had I in some way shared the other Art subjects, and so made more easily possible communication "at depth". They brought a medley of mice, lizards and frogs which they kept concealed. They brought bulbs and cacti in a pathetic collection of old tins. But I was frustrated... I could not make a room which was used by so many attractive. I could not display work. And when Christmas came (a time I had loved and used in Salford for music and poetry and Art and games) the boys told me that I must realise that I was in a boy's school. *Yet* they surprised me with a home-made manger, crude and glorious and gay with holly and sparkle – a glimpse of that which I have ever believed is the most vital thing to preserve in any being... joy in making, delight in tiny things. But that gesture, like so many countless ones, could not be used; so, many vital teachable moments were lost. Signals, announcing the end of periods had to be obeyed instantly or the organisation broke down.

With the less able you can never forecast the growing moment, the moment for a poem, some music. If you have taught this type of child for a quarter of a century you are vibrantly aware of the right moment. In the pre-fab hut the record-player, the tape recorder, the music and poetry records were immediately available. In the Comprehensive school this was not so easy. I could not cope with the organisation of the mechanical equipment as well as all the materials needed for creative work.

The Comprehensive School is a comparatively new experiment. The one in which I worked will probably be in the forefront of the

revolution in the structuring of the education of those boys whose
ability is just above that of those needing and having remedial
education. But no change can really take place until new rooms (not
classrooms) are built. I could not have a room. There was not one
for me. Until this happens the necessity for smooth running of the
vast combine will have to be regarded as being more important than
the immediate needs of the child. Ruthless demands of the God
"Organisation" will impinge on creative moments; broadcast
announcements will blast across a poem, ends of periods will come
all too soon, and inmates will, as the day wears on become more
frustrated and tired. Defences will be less and less constructive.
Survival will be all important.

I cannot write about the able child, or the truly backward, their
needs are apparently catered for in the Comprehensive School, but
for the less able I cry aloud for a revolution in structuring. I conclude with the somewhat astounding realisation that the condemned horsa hut in Salford had more to satisfy the needs of many
children than the vast London Comprehensive School with its host
of amenities. There is a place for horsa huts in the Comprehensive
School.

*Anarchy 18*                                                    *August 1962*

# 4.   About Risinghill
## Martin Small

IT IS in the comprehensive school – in the contrast and disparity
between its theory and its practice – that the democratic nature of
the culture which we inhabit in England today is tried, tested and
found wanting. This is the conflict Leila Berg has endeavoured to
describe in her *Risinghill: Death of a Comprehensive School* (Penguin Books, 6s), but which she has unfortunately mixed up with an
attack upon the officials of the Inner London Education Authority
and an unnecessarily melodramatic picture of Michael Duane as a
prince of light against a legion of darkness. Darkness and light are
not in two separate and easily distinguishable sets of men, but all
around us – our whole culture displays the conflict between the

principles of mutual aid and of hostility which is the conflict within all of us, perhaps more clearly than any previous culture: to identify this conflict within ourselves and others, and to endeavour to transcend it and to help others to do so, is the task before him who would reform society – not to identify the conflict as between ourselves and others: for that there is such a conflict is the myth which enslaves human society. "A story of a courageous headmaster, Michael Duane, and the story of the closure of his school, is a blistering indictment of educational bureaucracy and bureaucrats, of intolerance and stupidity". (Ronald Deadman in *The New Statesman*, 26th April, 1968.) By giving a licence to this sort of trite comment which ignores the real tragedy of Risinghill, Leila Berg has failed to take adequate precautions to prevent the subsequent controversy over her book from obscuring the issues which the story of Risinghill should bring into prominence and debate. Leila Berg's horror stories of her encounters with the officials of the ILEA do not add to our understanding of officials and officialdom: her patronising division of the teachers on the staff of Risinghill – "Some were very good, generous and imaginative... [Others] had long ago surrendered their personality, the wishes and beliefs of their own personal life... A third section had first been bewildered, and then, under the influence of Michael Duane's personality, decided of their own accord to do what *he* wanted..." – does not enable us to understand better the particular neuroses of the teaching profession. But they have encouraged the subsequent controversy around her book to concentrate on the rudeness and inconsiderateness (or the absence of it) in Duane's attitude to the ILEA or to his staff or on the obviously unresolvable dispute about whether Duane was or was not ordered to use corporal punishment by the ILEA. And the wider social context of what Duane tried to do – of what he did achieve – and of wherein he failed – has become lost in a trivial desert of mutual personal denigration.

The problem of understanding presented by Risinghill is two-edged. It is necessary to understand what Duane was setting out to do, and next what were the methods he used: and these separate but overlapping studies must be related to an appreciation of both what ought to have been done and what could be done. Perhaps the conclusion will be that it was necessary and desirable to do more or less what Duane does in fact seem to have done: honestly tried to implement what he thought was the official policy of the ILEA (the education department of the LCC it was, throughout most of the history of Risinghill) in its most logical and completest form – simply in order to demonstrate that such an uncompromising logicality could not succeed while the political system was what it was – and as it still remains. Whatever else he did – and however arrogant and hamfisted he may have been – there seems no doubt that the progress of Risinghill under Duane's headmastership exposed a very real gulf between the theory and practice, not merely of the local education authorities of London, but even more fundamentally, of the democracy of a whole society.

The object of education is order. Order is conceived and striven for in very different ways. There are two different main lines of approach. Order may be sought, as an already received truth or system, to be imposed upon a situation to the exclusion of all its irrelevant or inadmissable details: this is the object of the rigid school – the rigid teacher – the rigid child. (Vid. Penelope Leach, "The Rigid Child" in ANARCHY 64, June 1966.) This is the function and nature of authoritarianism. Alternatively, order may be sought as an organisation of the environment and co-ordination of one's reactions to it, which is continually changing even while using earlier observations and experiences: this is the mode of the flexible school – the flexible teacher – the flexible child. This is the function and nature of anarchism. This schematic division of attitudes does not of course – at least not usually – ever describe a real situation, which usually has a balance of the two components: as each individual is in a state of conflict and competition between the two tendencies in his attitudes. It is a question of which tendency predominates – both on a given occasion and over a longer period of time – and this will be determined by the individual's underlying world picture: whether he sees the world as, although strange and even dangerous, not actively hostile to his personal identity – or whether he sees it and himself as in a perpetual state of war in which each seeks domination and mastery, in which one must either destroy or be destroyed. It is again the adult stage of the conflict which Erikson describes as originating in childhood: the conflict between the desperate search for the false autonomy of an impossible "Independence", and the mature acceptance of the real autonomy of mutual regulation. The rigid, authoritarian school is the work camp which allows the adventure playground, if it does allow it at all, merely as a diversion or a distraction – perhaps even a useful, recreative distraction – from the main business of school: the flexible, anarchic school is both adventure playground and work camp – but in which the economic necessity of the work camp is clearly recognised as a function of the existential reality that life and learning are in themselves an adventure.

That the child may learn that order must be continually recreated

– that he may be able to find rest in the assurance that order will be recreated, and that it will be recreated not simply by the repetition of old reaction but by experimenting in freedom in himself and with others, not discarding old formulas but critically re-examining and refashioning them: this is the comprehensive education our children need. Towards the end of Risinghill's short career Michael Duane was once asked, "What are you really aiming at here?" and he replied: "To remove fear from children in schools". And on the evidence assembled in Leila Berg's book – which, although highly partisan, has not been disputed in its main showings – it seems clear that he was beginning to do it. "One thing Risinghill has done for these children, even those who have been here a short time. It has made it possible for them to think about what they are doing and what they are feeling, and what other people think and feel. This is no small piece of education. Risinghill children can express themselves". The very publicity the school received formed for the children an important part of the education they received. "If we really wanted schoolchildren to understand about history we would set them to find out the truth behind some contemporary event. I think by the time the school was closed, Risinghill children understood history more than any other children. I do not think for them history can ever be again an arbitrary string of events like a string of beads, or something inhuman and unchangeable like the seasons. They may be cynical – and some of them are – but they know that history has something to do with the planning of people, people with problems and power. That is why history is not normally taught in this way, in State schools".

In order to understand what Duane was trying to do – and the conflict which ensued between him and the authority which superficially shared his aims and intentions – it is perhaps useful to go back to consider the conflicting and divided purposes of the early reformers who first conceived the idea of "the education of the people". (Vid. the review of Harold Silver's *The Concept of Popular Education* in ANARCHY 73, March 1967.) The education of the people is not necessarily a democratic idea, either in concept or in execution. The great humanitarian educationalist Pestalozzi conceived of the education of the lower classes as an initiation into a fixed and inferior social role: and intitiation to be achieved, without cynicism, by emphasising the parity of esteem of all social roles before God. "The child of the soil and the whole class of landless agricultural labourers must learn in their language lessons to express themselves accurately about everything that has to do with their calling... But laborious toil is their lot in life, and their language lessons must not set up interests which would undermine the bases of their happiness and well being... Education should enable men to follow their particular calling with godliness and honour". At the same time, the method of the education which Pestalozzi recommended – if not so obviously the end – was in a truly revolutionary way child-centred: "Every philosophical investigator of human nature is compelled to admit that the sole aim of education is the harmonious development of faculties and dispositions which, under God's grace, make up a personality. It is not possible to think of making a human child what he ought to be by any other means than solicitude for the development in him of love and all round intellectual activity, and finally bringing the two into harmony. He is constitutionally perfectly adapted to the achievement of his lofty destiny and to the performance of his duty, because his manhood disposes him towards these high aims, coming as they do from love, based as they are on activity, and allied as they are with freedom". (J.H. Pestalozzi, *Swansong*) And by the middle of the nineteenth century even the staid *Quarterly Review* was able to welcome without a qualm the prospect of a more enlightened lower class: "The clergy have, God be praised, preached down effectively that heresy of which I remember the prevalence, according to which even good men were induced to suppose that the all-wise God had given to men immortal minds, capable of great things, without the intention, with respect to a large portion of the human race, that it should be exercised. The ungodly selfishness is now exploded by which the upper classes of society were induced to suppose that mental pleasures were a luxury reserved for their exclusive enjoyment". (September 1846.)

It is only in our own day that we are beginning to understand that the education of the people is not necessarily the same thing as the democratic and comprehensive education of the people. I use the words "democratic" and "comprehensive" here and elsewhere in this critical and even mildly polemical way in order to suggest that there is a standard of education – democratic and comprehensive – which, although I do not expect to define completely, will I hope become progressively clearer as I suggest ways in which other theories and practice of education either approach to or are distant from it. The modern age seems to be increasingly one in which on the one hand norms of conformist behaviour become increasingly rigid and even paranoiac; and at the same time the sanctions and pressures which are devised to enforce these norms become ever more subtle, whilst on the other the attempts to escape and find ways out of this nonsolution of the human condition become ever more self-conscious, self-critical but above all hopeful as though such a determined absurdity – an innocence which is aware of its own innocence, conventional ineffectiveness – were the essential preliminary if not main element of a real solution. Do not confuse the escape of the prisoner with the flight of the deserter. The antimony of human existence speaks increasingly loud and bold: we must experiment – we must be free – or die. The story of education in America as well as in England is largely the story of experiments and miniature survivals. The work of such men as Homer Lane (vid. ANARCHY 39, April 1964) and David Wills (vid. ANARCHY 15, May 1962) and their helpers, followers and friends, has demonstrated the creative use and exploitation of humanity in the midst of a society obsessed by the need to dispose efficiently of its waste matter: where the system has seen only unusable material to be disposed with the minimum of fuss and as far as possible out of sight (vid. for example the article on "Sink Schools" in ANARCHY 53, July 1965) – such men have believed in and have discovered the ineluctable value and joy of the merely human: the value and joy which simply to believe in seems to be to discover. In our own day their work is continued by men like Neill at Summerhill and by Aitkenhead at Kilquhanity: and even within the state system there have been individuals who have done something – who have tried – Alex Bloom at St. George's-in-the-East, R.F. Mackenzie at Braehead (vid. ANARCHY 82, December 1967), and Duane at Risinghill. "Tom Paine's Commentary" (*Antiphon* volume 1 number 3, Winter 1964 – 1965) sums up a way of looking at such experiments which is superficially enlightened and sympathetic: but fundamentally defeatist if not exactly contemptuous. "For those of us who have taught at Summerhill it was always apparent that the theories of A.S. Neill would never work inside the present state system, and to convince any doubters on that score, we have before us the disastrous precedent of St. George's-in-the-East, where for a brief period the LCC did permit some experiment on the lines of Summerhill to occur in a day school... Duane must engage the sympathies of all of us who are genuinely interested in producing a wholesome system, but he was a bit of a donkey to expect that he could embark on the therapeutic work, in which lies his bent, within a competitive society in which educational competence is judged solely on the number of university entrants gained yearly".

To which Duane, and those who endorse his enthusiasm and energy and determination, even while retaining the right to be critical of his particular methods and of the reality or otherwise of his expectations – might reply: If not here, where? and if not now, when?

The school as an experimental and continually reorganised order of relationships is possible, even within the system which demands results in the shape of measurable academic achievement. In Holland the Children's Workshop Community at Bilthoven, which began with four small girls being taught by their father in one small room in January 1926, at least in 1954 had survived eight years of State patronage and inspection. "So you are going to Kees Boeke's?" said a friend to Wyatt Rawson when Rawson was about to visit the school and its famous headmaster on the eve of his retirement in 1954. "Do you know the sort of man he is? If you were walking with him in a desert, he'd make you see flowers growing on every side". (Rawson: *The Werkplaats Adventure*) "The institution Kees and his wife built up together – for she was always at his side, supporting and encouraging him – demonstrated one often forgotten fact, that just as children love the direct and spontaneous, so they love order and method; and indeed that, without the latter, spontaneity breeds only disagreement and strife, leading in the end to a rejection of freedom. Thus the problem of school life was how to preserve the spontaneity that gives rise to strong personalities without losing the order and friendly co-operation that are essential to a harmonious community. Order can be preserved, for a time at least, by the imposition or threat of force. But the fears and tensions due to such methods put an end to all naturalness and spontaneity. Some way must therefore be discovered of securing order with as little compulsion as possible, so that children may grow naturally, without their character being warped by fears or frustrations". The Werkplaats deliberately thrusts upon children the experience of freedom: it is strange that such a way of describing what is done at the school should seem appropriate – the growing experience of freedom, of the need himself to organise and be responsible for his relations with the world, is what every child naturally meets: until the school begins to manipulate, dilute and specialise that experience – and to cheat him into being an accomplice of his own enslavement under various pleas which however amount to only one: the dangerousness of freedom – ie the unmanageability of that which makes him distinctively human. There is distinctly something of the attitude of Froebel: the idea that the education we give our children is largely a matter, not of giving things to them, but of removing obstacles to their pursuit and attainment of their own goals: in Boeke's understanding of his own work. When Rawson asked him whether he thought the spirit of the Werkplaats would be diminished or altered when he retired Kees replied: "The spirit is not something in me. I am just like a catalyst, taking no part in the process but helping to make the right development possible. It is only that I try not to meddle with the children, not to hinder what is in them from growing. The spirit is not in any one kind of person: it is in all sorts of persons. And the spirit is contagious. We drink it in from wherever it is by direct assimilation, just as the plant draws water from wherever it finds it, not from any particular place. I remember, for instance, one child who was not long with us and died young. There was something in her that was beyond our limited life. She did not talk and yet her influence was felt by us all. It inspired a kind of reverence – a reverence that is in so many children already, so that they lead a pure, natural, and truly human life with all its spontaneous reactions. I would rather not call this spirit a divine spark; it is the real self that is in each of us, not in a single person or a special leader, but in every human being. Once it is not held back by moralising, once it is freed from false constraints, it will grow. There is no fear of that". At the centre of the Werkplaats' practice of collective and individual responsibility is the Bespreking (Talkover), a weekly forum at which all the members of the school – teachers and all pupils, both senior and junior – can discuss their particular grievances and problems as well as the general affairs of the school. According to Rawson, the only sanction against misbehaviour is the expression of disapproval of the community: and that this leads to the development of a healthy and mature sense of mutual responsibility between individuals and the school as a whole: all offices in the school are held in rotation. "For the great majority this background of a friendly group is a form of security. They are safeguarded against their own evil impulses, and, having the moral support of their school fellows, find they are able to live on a level they never thought possible. So strong is the moral pressure, however – and it must be strong if order is to be maintained – that there are from time to time children who feel it as oppressive and rebel. They would like to be in an ordinary school again, and be naughty and get punished for it. One or two have left because they didn't feel capable of the moral strength required. They wanted more external compulsion and fewer calls upon their own moral effort. But the vast majority of children are only too grateful to be helped to deal with their own moral difficulties, and to live in an atmosphere that supports their better inclinations. There seems to be at least the normal number of children with mental disturbances that really need psychological treatment, but they are carried along by the stream of the school's traditions and do not prevent its methods from achieving success. Indeed, its freedom very often enables them to work out their repressions and regain a normal balance after a term or two".

Freedom works. The Werkplaats demonstrates that children will accept responsiblity for their own actions – do not need others to take on the responsibility and thus the ordering of their actions for them – do not need a precast order and community but will naturally in an environment of trust fashion their own. In such an environment co-operation and mutual aid are the natural growth of the child's understanding. Rawson says: "Self-centredness is eschewed, and instead of the stress being put, as in so many Kindergarten, on the child becoming independent as quickly as possible, it is laid on learning to help one another and getting the job done. This social training leads on naturally to the co-operative attitude so aparent in the Junior and Senior Schools". The sadness of it is that the descriptions Rawson gives of the practice of freedom and mutual aid, must strike the sophisticated understanding of even the most sensitive of us as descriptions of something which sounds slightly artificial – perhaps indeed, what is more unforgivable, as just a little ridiculous.

The story of Risinghill illustrates the awkwardness and unfamiliarity of our society's experience of freedom. "We are so flooded these days by the elaborate formulations of experts that we have lost sight of the underlying simplicity of things, such as, for instance, that school is not *primarily* the relation of teachers and students, but of adults and children, and of course children and children". (George Dennison, "The First Street School". In ANARCHY 73, March 1967.) But of course it is not only confusing conceptual formulations which obscure the simplicity of things, but the institutional superstructure which has been imposed upon it: thus the teacher is not merely an individual human being speaking to others – both he and his pupils are conditioned to think of teaching and learning not as experiences which are part of and reach out to a whole social relationship, but as the rigidly separated functions of individuals who have been authorised to participate in them, either as victims or as executioners. Teachers no less than others suffer from the neurosis of institutionalised man. They believe – and the institution which maintains them encourages them to believe – in the perfectly rational action of an unshakeable and immovable equilibrium: they are mesmerised by the golden mirage of a synthesis of thought and feeling moving with the smooth efficiency of a computer (never mind that computers are always breaking down: the ideal computer never would: and so the ideal man would never break down or be at a loss for a thought, a word, a deed...) In his dream world the good, responsible teacher is an heroic explorer making a perilous journey into hostile territory (not simply an unknown country, as the Newsom report recommends). "Almost every educational dictum," wrote Duane in his review of John Holt's *How Children Fail* (*Peace News*, July 30th, 1965), "is gently but ruthlessly exposed for what it is – a formula devised to make mass-teaching more tolerable for harassed teachers – by his simply recounting exactly what happened between child and teacher in a variety of typical classroom situations..." And of such teachers who are in love with the myth of their own objectivity and unselfishness he writes bitterly: "They see no connection between their prevailing anxieties about work, health, and career, or their obsessive concern with 'control', 'conformity' and 'neatness', and their widespread failure to achieve satisfying and lasting sex lives".

Whether enthusiastic or dissenting, the criticism of Leila Berg's book and of Duane seems to have agreed – without quite appreciating the irony of the contrast – that Duane was excellent at the job of teaching and interesting young children and adolescents, but not so good or even thoroughly incompetent as a schoolmaster... "He was a progressive in certain directions, but streamed his schools, and had prize days and prefects, conventionally enough. It appears to have been his amused, informal and compassionate enjoyment of children, his rejection of corporal punishment, and his frankness, that enabled him to take to Risinghill a remarkable record both of praise and dispraise. One cannot be sure – and with such a work of partisanship one has to say this – if he had less useful qualities, since Miss Berg paints him heroically throughout". (Edward Blishen in *The Listener*, April 25th, 1968.) But perhaps even "less useful qualities" – like intolerance, rudeness or even just simple plain refusal to accept and "understand" – may be of fundamental value when dealing with areas of behaviour heavily entrenched behind an army of received and protected prejudice. Duane was "an anti-authoritarian", Blishen continues, "who understood that many children in districts such as Islington rejected 'the standards accepted as fundamental by most teachers with middle-class or artisan backgrounds', and that much of their behaviour was an attack on those standards and a defence of others 'set by those most dear to them, their parents'. The words are Michael Duane's own; they come from a memorandum distributed to his staff, and they suggest, with much else Miss Berg quotes, that he brought an unusual and coherent imagination to the task of schooling in such a district. He acted, as Risinghill's head, boldly on the basis of his beliefs; he abandoned

corporal punishment and drew in the parents, countering their fear
of formality by making himself cheerfully accessible. He was certain
that if there was 'no anger, no contempt, no moral pressure', then
the school would move away – however difficult this might prove –
from its old burden of hatreds, resentments, violent reluctance to be
involved in the educational process. But many of his staff were
against him. They were lost without their normal authoritarian
resources... From my own experience of teaching in the district, I
am certain that nothing can be faulted in what she says about the
predicament of the children and the desperate need that they be
taught by people who delight in them and are on their side. Her
analysis of the deep cancer of authoritarianism with the teaching
profession is utterly accurate. It was time indeed that someone drew
attention as passionately as this to the limits on educational experiment that may be set by authorities fearful of scandal. The case
against corporal punishment could not be better put..."

The argument against Duane seems to have mixed up two levels
of a feeling of repugnance, if not of active resentment, what may be
called, distinguishing rather crudely, the personal and the more
general level. The two arguments which are apt to get confused are
– that he was uncompromising to the point of stupidity in his attitude towards the system, and – that he was rude and intolerant so
much as to be irritatingly self-righteous in his relations with individuals. But is it possible to be too uncompromising – possible that,
as Keith Pople seems to be arguing in his oddly sententious review
of *Risinghill* in *Peace News* (17th May, 1968), Duane was "too
steadfast – almost to the point of fanaticism": but what are the
criteria of fanaticism (his fanaticism is my firmness, so to speak),
and is it a bad thing anyway, or is it just disturbing – and surely what
we need is the sort of disturbance which Duane and Risinghill created: not a "chaos" which had not been there before, but the exposure of a chaos which has become the unconfessed normality of our
social and not least of our educational life... As Arthur Uloth comments (FREEDOM, July 27th, 1968): "It has become fashionable now
to blame Duane for being intolerant of his reactionary staff, but this
is equivalent to asking a man to be a saint. Where ideas about what
life means are in total opposition all that can be managed is agreement to differ, and this is impossible where the people involved are
engaged in a joint enterprise, which requires the utmost co-
operation. The only solution is separation". Revolution and its re-
conciling of men to one another and to themselves only becomes
possible when the disguised conflict in this way – by separation, by
taking up distinct positions – is brought out into the open. Distinct

positions are not opposed positions – not at least positions opposed in such a way that only the total destruction of one can solve the conflict: however radical the differences are between authoritarians and libertarians, revolutionaries and conservatives (and Paul Goodman has pointed out that in one very important way the revolutionary is the true conservative who wants to conserve, use and maintain, light and laughter and green grass...), they are at last only differences of interpretation of a common human need – the need to be at one, at home, in the world.

Was Duane saint-like? – or have things got so bad that it is possible to be as offensive as the most unperturbed saint merely by trying to do one's best and by expecting others to try as well? From what Keith Pople says about Michael Duane's "folly" it would appear that it is. "What in the name of Humanity does Mr. Duane – and Leila Berg who writes about these things – expect the reaction of a teacher to be when 'shown up to be a liar' in front of children? I know of few mature personalities outside the world of education, who can stand up to this sort of thing. To do this to almost any person is tantamount to driving him mad... Carried to extremes, 'contempt for the System' can be made an excuse for anything and everything – for we all live within some sort of System and every System has its faults. This is the irony of the actuality: that people who want to transform almost any System (but especially in education) rather than withdraw from it or destroy it, must operate practically and live humanely within it. What we have to do when difficulties arise is *not* crucify each other for the sake of some principle or other but act *intelligently*". But perhaps it may be acting intelligently to act stupidly and inconsiderately: to take people at their word: to show them up publicly as liars and hypocrites (publicly, for a lie is not simply an insult in a relationship between two human beings, but a sin against the goodwill which is necessary to society as a whole): for how else are liars to learn the obnoxiousness of their lying and their obligation to tell the truth? Not to attempt to conceal from an individual your knowledge that he is a liar – not to attempt to conceal it either from the people with whom he or she associates – is to treat that individual as someone whose lack of honesty both should and can be reformed: but to make allowances for his or her not being a mature personality who can stand up to this sort of thing – well this is part of the mess we are in already.

The problem of our schools is that to the teacher ordinariness has become an embarrassing unfamiliarity: and that further (what is perhaps part of the same syndrome of the disintegration of our concept of humanity) saintliness is equally embarrassing, a superfluous and irrelevant gesture. But saintliness – as any orthodox theologian or common sense revolutionary knows – is neither irrelevant nor superfluous, but the natural and necessary development of our ordinary humanity. Saintliness in teaching perhaps more than in almost any other occupation is the standard of ordinary humane behaviour which must be striven for: to try to achieve it and to fail, is more useful and enlightening both to the teacher and to his pupils and to whatever larger public happens to notice, than any miserable substitute of expert technique helped out by the artificial limb of the "special responsibility allowance" which – as Duane himself recently argued in *The Times Educational Supplement* ("Good Relationships", July 19th, 1968) – encourages an evasion of the total reality of teaching, producing "an inevitable erosion of the feeling of all pervasive responsibility towards the child". The trouble with the controversy that has surrounded Duane and Risinghill, particularly since the publication of Leila Berg's book – is that it has tended to ignore the most important fact which is that Michael Duane was merely trying to do his job: indignation at his outrageous subversive literalness and obstinacy has been matched by a tendency to make of it a heroic and inimitable superpower: and one myth has fed the other. What we must try and see in Duane is not a saviour whom we have lost: as Brecht said, "no man is indispensable, and if he is he's up to no good" – our society suffers from the myth of the indispensable individual as much as from that of the useless one: but a man who was self-consciously and deliberately not a teacher, much less a head, a man helping children to develop their powers to the best of his ability and as far as – and if possible further than – the total social environment allowed. To think of him as a hero in the traditional sense: Brecht again – "Unhappy the land that has no heroes" – "Unhappy the land that needs a hero!": is as stultifying as to think of him as the villain who is rocking the boat of social adjustment and compromise. What we can do – and what his failure as much as his success can help us to do perhaps more than any other single public experience Britain has had for many years – is to see and learn from his actions and reactions: perhaps we might even call them his good and bad vibrations: where we as a society are falling down and what we must do to set ourselves right.

"The Headmaster", ran a highly confidential report upon a visit to Risinghill early in 1962 by twenty of Her Majesty's Inspectors, "has pursued a policy eschewing corporal punishment... [He] esteems cordiality among the major virtues... His approach to staff and pupils is informal... It is difficult to say that he carries the aura of the Headmaster around with him and though he inspires some liking, he fails to inculcate respect. Indeed, he may well regard this respect as basically unnecessary in human relations... The children do not hold authority in any awe... There is an atmosphere of indiscipline which is difficult to describe... Its effect in the Art Department is almost catastrophic. As far as can be seen it appears that only some of the children work at all and then for only some of the time. The loss of productive hours of work because the children are so uninterested and to put it simply, quite unruly, is enormous. Added to this is of course the frustration of the teaching staff who have so much to give, and also the tiredness of the staff which is very evident... There have been too many signs of strain among staff, among good staff, too great a feeling that there is neither unity of purpose nor strength of leadership. Even in the matter of discipline, on which the Headmaster holds lofty and inflexible views, there is no uniformity from house to house. The only thing of which children can be sure is that punishment will normally be benign and the staff hesitate to take upon themselves responsibilities which properly lie elsewhere. It may well be that friendliness too frequently degenerates into undignified informality; the regular clutter of children outside the Headmaster's door is perhaps not the symbol of comradeship but the revelation of confusion... In spite of the heroic efforts of some senior staff, the school's personality remains amorphous, fugitive and ambiguous". When we have the full text of this document (I have quoted extracts from among the longer but still incomplete text which Leila Berg prints) we will have an extraordinary self-revelation of the fearful unimaginativeness and incompetence of the authoritarian mentality: Duane's crime was not that he created chaos but that he made no effort to suppress it – he was a man who, perhaps not always successfully but at least honestly, started "from the ground up" with the individual children as they actually were in that time and place: and in so doing he "disorganized everything"... "The school had children of nineteen nationalities, more than most of the children, or even some of the teachers, had realized existed. Since the school had many Greek, Turkish and African children, Mr. Duane took on Greek, Turkish and African teachers. Having teachers of their own nationality, speaking their own language, mean that the non-English children knew they were granted as much respect as the English children. Their teachers were their prestige symbols. Messages were sent to their parents in their own language, and they too could be drawn into the life of the school; now they no longer need face the conflict of feeling the school as an enemy who drew their children away from them and yet an enemy to whom they had to submit both for their children's sake and their own. It meant that the particular extra problems of these children could be explained and understood. It meant that these children if they got into trouble could be helped to give a statement in court and would therefore have some possibility of justice. It meant that ideas and conventions could be examined, re-examined, compared, and pondered over. It meant many more things; but these few are enough to show that the authoritarian idea of conforming never builds on the possibilities within a situation, does not even solve the problems of a situation, but merely gets by, by pretending no problems are there. This is why the authoritarians said – which puzzled me when I first heard it – 'Mr. Duane disorganizes everything'."

All men are aware of the depth of the unknown which is in themselves – in their fellow men – and in the world in which they live: but for some this experience remains fixed in fear, whilst in others by some mysterious alchemy this fear has become transmuted into wonder: they do not endeavour to build an existence upon a miserable pretence of its completeness and compact invulnerable boundaries – they accept the boundless ocean and ride out onto it, not with their eyes closed, nor unprepared, but knowing that whatever knowledge they may have, whatever techniques of management they may learn, are but as tangents which describe the area of their insatiable ignorance. Of course these two distinct forms of experience are not divided between two distinct groups of men, but are varying qualities and conflicting tendencies in every human experience: perhaps indeed there can be no wonder without an element of fear, nor any fear which is without the touch of wonder: it is again a question of the balance of things and of the prevailing tendency: it is a question of whether we really believe in the rightness of wonder, or are obsessed by the inevitability of fear. *Risinghill* should help us to see where we stand. Leila Berg has made it clear where she stands: she believes in the natural order of symmetry, balance and harmony which Duane was seeking to discover and recreate in the shattered or at least disordered lives of his kids (and the inspectors were worried that the personality of the *school* was "amorphous, fugitive and ambiguous"!) – not in the conventional order of his situation and profession which he was expected to maintain. The best case for such maintenance of order that I have seen was made by Terence Constable, once head of the French department at Risinghill, in his article "The Risinghill Myth" (*New Society*, 13th June, 1968). "In rejecting the concept of external authority and by alienating many of his teachers in other ways, Duane, I consider, deprived himself of most of the normal mechanisms of communication and control". (A similar but less unselfish and thus perhaps more truthful objection was made by another ex-Risinghill teacher, Patricia Tuckman, in a letter to *The Times Educational Supplement*: "Had one-tenth of the time and energy spent to gain the co-operation and understanding of the staff and welding them together, so very much more could have been done. – May 17th, 1968.) "A Headmaster of a state school is not captain of his ship to the extent that he can pick and choose his entire crew. He must make do, like every other state head [and surely also, like every captain of every ship that has ever been], with a cross-section of ordinary people, the old with the young, the narrow-minded with the broad-minded, the altruistic with the selfish, the clever with the semi-competent. The essence of his job is to weld these people into a cohesive group dedicated to common purposes. If he fails in this, then he surely fails in everything... In dealing with individual children he certainly possessed unusual insight. In this, as in other respects, he was not unlike Homer Lane, the non-authoritarian educator active in the early years of this century. But Duane was not chosen as a clinical psychologist or as an assistant probation officer: he was appointed the professional and administrative head of a school of some 1,400 places.

"Although an instinct for handling children is a necessary qualification for a headmaster, it is far from being a sufficient one. Of equal importance are a capacity to get the best out of such teachers as he can recruit, and an ability to represent effectively the interests and needs of his school to the local authority". Constable goes on to question whether even Duane's handling of children was as much beyond criticism as Leila Berg suggests. "Duane's humanitarian concern for the minority distracted him from the rest of the school. Some of his children had terrible lives, it is true. But, rough-and-ready as life might be at the back of King's Cross, not all the children suffered the acute emotional and social deprivation which Mrs. Berg's book suggests. Many of the children in the school became more and more distracted, and then bored, as a result of the unproductive turmoil which prevailed in many classes". Duane went too far "in allowing children to feel that there was no place for authority at all. Without it, how could the gulf between two generations, between two classes, between half a dozen ethnic groups, ever be bridged? Certainly not by simply allowing children to do the things they *want* to do, for this would be to ignore how very transient these desires are, how they differ from child to child, and how they are influenced by powerful forces outside the school and the home. Authority does not exist to subjugate children but to give them a provisional means through people they have the chance to love or admire, of discovering the enjoyment and intrinsic value of learning. On my experience at Risinghill – except for a minority of children and teachers, and this in limited situations – no such means existed: the peer group reigned supreme". The charge of total abandonment of authority is followed up by citing particular examples of the chaos that ensued. "The intensity of the disorder reached a peak when, at about 2pm on 15th January, 1965, many children were to attempt a mass 'break-out'. Duane ran white-faced from exit to exit, then tried to calm them by appeals over the public address system (Mrs. Berg's 'mind-spattering' tool of authoritarian power). This subsided; but little over a week later, the school was again at fever pitch, in spite of the brave efforts of the exhausted young senior mistress to maintain some framework of order. In the room next to mine, children set fire to heaps of litter which filled the desks in the presence of a terrified supply teacher who found himself powerless to stop them". But perhaps this is an acceptable price to pay for what Duane was trying to achieve: was it perhaps even a necessary and healthy stage through which the emergent democracy of the school must pass? "Duane tried to adopt similar techniques in his school to those Lane used in his 'Little Republic'. The aim of these was to achieve self-reliance and social responsibility, mainly through tactfully engineered peer-group processes and by demonstrating that self-reliance and consideration for others paid off in terms of personal happiness and social cordiality. Duane was also much impressed by the analysis of social character made by Riesman in *The Lonely Crowd*. At Risinghill, Duane tried to avoid, for his children, the latent danger of isolation in adult life induced by competitive striving. This he abhorred equally with the hollow pseudo-cohesion of 'togetherness' and unthinking conformity". This is an honest tribute; but "Duane, in my belief, overlooked the technical difficulties in his way. I think he not only underestimated the tremendous power of the peer group, but also effectively disregarded the close bond between schooling and the world of work". Earlier in his article he has discounted the evidence of Risinghill's improved academic results (the number taking GCE "O" levels rose from 18 in 1960 to 80 in 1964, and the number passing – in from one to six subjects – from five to forty-two): the reason was "not any novelty in teaching or organisation but the extremely generous staff-to-pupil ratio among children already well enough supported by their parents to be able to stop on beyond the legal minimum leaving age"; and now he argues that even this development was peripheral to the real history of the school – a breakdown of academic standards and incentives: "neither Duane nor his staff could urge children to work or to behave tolerably with the promise (or threat) of examinations and what they might lead to. The organisational 'tension' which external examinations provide was almost totally lacking in his school. Before hastening to assert that this might be a good thing, one would do well to consider the price paid by its young people in terms of social and occupational non-advancement. Although utilitarian education(for white collar or for blue overall) might not be the most desirable feature of the secondary curriculum, when a single school drops out it makes the gesture at the expense of its pupils. In this respect the children of Islington were the 'waste clay' of the experiment".

Some form of authority, discipline and order must be provided by the adult world for the child, who needs a usable environment to grow up into – an environment that he can rely upon. But the authority which does not subjugate the child (cf. Erich Fromm's distinction between "overt authority and anonymous authority" in his preface to A.S. Neill's *Summerhill*, and Dachine Rainer's comments upon it in ANARCHY 15, May 1962; also Jeremy Westall's "Reflections on Authority" in ANARCHY 21, November 1962) must be functional and not institutional: it must grow out of the perception of what is immediately required by the situation – it will be naturally assumed usually by the more experienced and the adult, but the more it is in virtue of a demonstrable superior knowledge rather than of any official institution the more helpful the child will find it: authority, the authority which reassures and encourages, resides not in the individual but in the action. Is this the kind of authority we want and are working for? If we are, what Duane was trying to do at Risinghill is a step forward and our task must not be to retreat from it but to go on and beyond it: Duane's "anarchism" abandoned the old system of authority based upon fear, and surely Terence Constable and Duane's other liberal critics would not want to return to that even if the first consequences of abandonment of such shoddy authority must unhappily result in "liberties" being taken by those who have never known any other. (cf. the description of the working of the Werkplaats principle, quoted above.) We know now too well the cost exacted by the old authority of fear, the observations of such as John Holt and Michael Duane in our own day have made more irrefutable the arguments of earlier reformers like Lane and Neill: surely it cannot be maintained that the cost in emotional inhibition is to be balanced against "the price paid in terms of social and occupational non-advancement" by those who have been deprived (! – Constable does not use this term, but he implies it) of the traditional motives of fear and failure. If academic success, and the social and occupational advancement that go with it, cannot find other motives to inspire children to seek it then surely it is time to re-examine the value – and the price – of these things. "Examinations," said Duane himself on the school's prizegiving day in 1962, "are necessary in a highly technical society like ours, but to measure a school by exam results is like estimating the quality of a man's life by the number of calories he burns, or the number of footpounds of energy he expends. They bear no relation to the real purposes of living. Real life is bound up with other people, with personal relations, with love and man's need to serve." It is surely good that we have learnt and that our children should learn the use of intellectual and of mechanical tools: but are we so poor in spirit that we can only conceive of "social and occupational advancement" (for one person to advance it is necessary that someone else be left behind) as motives for such proficiency: what is at last the use of such tools where there is no simple joy in the use of them: if we have been educated to the slavery of position and status, is that any reason why we should resign our children to the same slavery? Examinations are necessary: in order that those who need to may test, and those who want to may prove, particular specialist abilities; but if we are to be a living and active democratic society, the obligation is equally upon the society to discover the particular ability of every man as it is upon the individual to demonstrate that ability. An elitist, hierarchical society may be able to afford to believe that not all men have value; but a democracy and a democrat must believe that, however unequal men may be in important ways, there is in every man a capacity to organise for himself an individually and socially meaningful and harmonious existence. A democracy is a statement of faith and an expression of determination: of faith in this universal capacity and of determination to find it: and it is above all in its schools, in the way it educates its children, that a society which pretends to be democratic demonstrates the truth or falsity of that pretence.

"Just occasionally something happens which pierces the fog of generalisation, and shows what's really going on in our schools. Risinghill was one of those happenings, and Leila Berg, telling its story, has written a book which anyone who wants to understand the educational debate in this country should read". (Virginia Makins in the *Observer*, April 28th, 1968.) "...The Risinghill battle stood out as a rallying cry: were comprehensives about a new deal for children, dismantling repressive forms of teacher authority in class, bringing a new sense of democracy and fulfilment to the most deprived as well as to the sons of Ministers in Holland Park, or was it just an administrative juggle?" (Richard Bourne in the *Guardian*, April 25th , 1968.) "Western civilisation," wrote Robin Pedley in his contribution to a collection of essays published in 1955, "has pinned its faith to 'democracy': more exactly, to government by representatives elected by and from the whole adult community. Most of us are well aware of the deficiencies of this system – of the frequently poor calibre of the men and women so chosen, and the superficial ideas which often sway the vote of electors. Are we then – with most head teachers today – fearfully to renounce this system within our own school community [he is writing with reference to the idea of school councils], to say that children, too, will be improperly swayed by popularity (a libel on those I have taught), or will simply be 'too inexperienced'? And to save them (and ourselves) from unwise decisions, are we to fall back on government by staff oligarchy, or even our own benevolent despotisms? Or should we take the view that part of our job is to prepare children to become responsible citizens in a democratic community, and give them the opportunity to learn by personal experience the pitfalls and paths of democratic government?" At Risinghill, says Leila Berg, we looked at ourselves and saw that our democracy was a fraud. "One day, at a [School] Council meeting, the head boy said that some members of the staff were not turning up for their playground duty, as arranged, and the prefects were having to do it for them, in addition to their own. Mr. Duane stopped him from mentioning the actual names of the teachers, by promising to deal with it. Immediately after the meeting closed, a deputation from the staff arrived to say they strongly objected to being discussed and criticized. Mr. Duane pointed out that no names had been mentioned, but this did not mollify them; 'the staff', in the abstract, had been criticized. They went to Inspector Macgowan, and he made it one of the items in his report (which County Hall was later to describe as 'the blackest report they had ever seen'). Later on in 1965, the same destruction of democracy was to happen on a larger scale. The School Council affair was the pupils' first introduction to a democracy that offers rights as long as the rights aren't used". And at the end: "All the deputations to the government of both children and parents, all the clauses of the Education Act hopefully intoned, all the meetings and the letters and signatures collected in the pouring rain had been just something that filled in the time, while authority got on with what it intended to do in the first place. A headmaster at another school had said to a Risinghill mother, 'You surely don't think these deputations will get you anywhere? The decision has

already been taken. This three months for the appeal to be considered, these kind invitations to state your case, that's just papering
over the cracks in the wall of democracy'. No one had wanted to
listen to him. Of course he was right".

One man can do so much and no more. When society itself is
mainly given over to "happy mutual robbery" (as Marat calls it in
Peter Weiss' play), it cannot be expected that the schools will be
secure havens of democratic practice: when push and pull are the
order of the day almost everywhere the young and thoughtless will
hardly react with immediate understanding to a real attempt at
democratic mutuality. At its worst the simplicity of a Duane who
takes democracy as an actually working proposition (and that he
was not as naive as all that would seem to be clear from the speech
he made at the 1963 prize-giving, quoted by Leila Berg on page 148
of her book: but he may have thought it good tactics to behave as
though he did) terrifies the teachers and sends wild with uncompre-
hending delight the children who have lived with and kept their
distance from each other by an entirely different set of rules hitherto. But real democracy: a real attempt to take it seriously and make
it work: is bound to be an exhilarating and somewhat frightening
experience at first: but to temper and channel that exuberance – to
exorcise that fear – what is needed is not less but more democracy.
Duane's reintroduction of basic simplicity into the scene of our
public education was like a douche of cold water in the face of the
English public. We can find his rudeness and his folly repugnant: at
the same time there was perhaps a trace of honest artifice in the
simplicity with which he accepted the logical conclusions of the
LCC's statements on comprehensive schooling and of his staff's
decision to abandon corporal punishment ("If the children don't
know that you've decided to abolish it," he said, "then the threat of
it remains – and so it is still there"): but we cannot evade the choice.
It is indeed hardly a moral choice we have to make: rather is it an
existential imperative we must obey or die – not tomorrow, when
the bomb falls, but today when we diminish our common humanity
by discriminating degrees of social usefulness. A man lives in an
expanding or a contracting universe: he cannot stand still: his world
and his society is moving outwards, to adapt to, and to utilise and to
enjoy, all men – or it is closing upon the dead centre of his fear. That
is the meaning of Risinghill.

*Anarchy 92*                                                    *October 1968*

# V. DEVIANCE

## 1. Towards a libertarian criminology
### Tony Gibson

MANY PEOPLE regard criminology as essentially an "Establish-ment" field of study. To a great extent such a view is indeed correct. The types of people engaged in this rather loosely-defined field include lawyers, psychiatrists, psychologists, sociologists and associated specialists, all studying the forms of social behaviour which are designated as criminal. In practice, there is a general assumption that the law, and the social customs which are main-tained by it, are wholly desirable, and the criminal, the person who breaks the law, is a morbid specimen – he is a "deviant", in some way bad or mad. Criminology, therefore, becomes on the one hand a study of these morbid creatures – what are their physical, psycho-logical and social characteristics? – and on the other hand, a study of how best to forestall, deter, punish and maybe cure them. Let us face it, it is very difficult for anyone reared in this society, no matter what his social class, to have a view very different from this conven-tional one. Revolutionary anarchists tend to talk a lot of hot air about the police force, but I have noticed that in their private lives they will, if driven to it, have recourse to the power of the police should their normal rights of citizenship, in the way of liberty of the person or ownership of property, be grossly attacked in an unlawful manner. The man who would permit himself or his dependants to be flagrantly robbed, assaulted or raped when recourse to police in-tervention could prevent it, does not command respect. We cannot use the police against those who rob us and abuse us by *legal* means, but that does not mean that we should be high-principled victims when the means are *unlawful*.

Forced as we are, then, to live behind the shelter of actual or potential violence, even if to a small degree, our assumptions about criminality in society are necessarily coloured by our day-to-day experience. It does not seem quite unacceptable that violent young hooligans should be sent to borstal, blackmailers should serve stiff sentences, and housebreakers should be repeatedly lagged, as an occupational hazard. Such acceptance implies that we have working stereotypes of "the violent young hooligan", "the blackmailer" and "the housebreaker", and their role as social deviants. We may be adamantly opposed to the *existence* of borstals and prisons – and quite definitely refuse to operate such horrible engines ourselves – but in practice we accept them along with so much else. They are part of the landscape as we have always known it. "Come the re-volution" we intend that things shall be different, but at the moment it is somewhat convenient that we believe ourselves to be partly, if not wholly, protected from casual violence, blackmail and having our telly pinched while we are out at work.

In order to get outside our own day-to-day assumptions, it is necessary to think of societies geographically or historically rather different from our own. If we consider London in the late eighteenth century, it does strike us a monstrous that mere children were hanged for petty thieving. If we think of the rich and powerful men who framed and upheld such laws, they appear to us as inhuman monsters, fit for extermination themselves. Knowing what they did of the privations of the poor, of the want and real hunger that wretched children suffered, how could they use the gallows as a fitting penalty for pilfering, we wonder? By an effort of imagination I wonder, while attending certain conferences, will Dr. X. there, and Professor Y. and Mrs. Z., all of them decent professional people who uphold our present-day penal code, be regarded as grotesque and unhuman monsters in some future age? I know that these three people are not monsters, that they are reasonably humane in their own lives, but nevertheless they are working within a framework of assumptions which may very well make them appear as monsters in some future age.

The assumptions of conventional criminology are that the law and all the apparatus which supports it can be taken for granted as a given fact. It could be, should be, improved this way or that as time goes on, but nevertheless it represents a norm which all right-thinking people support. Criminals are deviants, and it is the duty of criminologists to work towards the end of suppressing crime even if the ideal of abolishing it may never be reached.

A view alternative to this which is growing among social scientists, is that criminal activity is not a "morbid" social phenomenon. Basic assumptions such as that the role of the police force is the repression of crime are questioned. It is arguable, for instance, that one of the roles of the police force is the *generation* of crime. The police force is a well-established body with its niche in society, just as are the army, church, stock exchange, judiciary, etc. None of these bodies is going to operate towards its own dissolution; rather they will act to increase the range and power of their spheres of operation. It is in the interests of the police force, then, that the volume of crime should not decrease but rather increase, and that they should preserve a fertile breeding ground for the criminal activity of future generations. This preservation and generation of criminal activity is not, of course, a deliberate and cynical policy directed by police chiefs and corrupt officers, but the sum total of the operation of the police force.

The idea that the police actually increase rather than reduce the level of criminal activity may seem strange at first sight. The consideration of an analogous mechanism may help towards understanding just what is envisaged. If I suggest that the role of the medical profession is to promote disease, such a contention appears manifestly absurd, for we all know that doctors cure diseases and prevent their occurrence through measures of public health. Yet the medical profession never works itself out of a job. There are always just as many people suffering from diseases queueing up for treatment as there ever were, in spite of the vast advances in public health. There are just as many people demanding treatment because, in a sense, the medical profession is always "creating" new diseases. New diseases are "created" in several ways; first by improvements in diagnosis, so that some people who would previously have been regarded as not too unhealthy are now regarded as definitely sick and requiring treatment; second, the general rising standards of public health make people less tolerant of ailments which would previously have been regarded as within the range of normality; third, by prolonging the general expectation of life, the medical profession has created an enormous problem in terms of the multitude of degenerative diseases of old age which hardly existed in former times. In a very real sense therefore, the medical profession does keep on increasing the bulk and variety of what are recognised as diseases in the community, and there is no prospect of disease being abolished, however efficient the public health services are.

The creation and maintenance of crime by the police force follows a very similar pattern. It may be pointed out that the police have two fairly distinct functions, peace-keeping and the detection and arrest of offenders. The former function is analogous to the public health measures of the medical profession, and the latter to

the diagnosis and treatment of disease. Recent criminological researches into self-reported delinquency have highlighted the fact
that an enormous amount of criminal activity is carried on by people
who are in no way abnormal. It is, in fact, the norm of behaviour in
our society to break the law by overt acts which, if detected, would
lead to the usual penal sanctions on criminal behaviour. The police
have enough, and far more than enough by way of a pool of unlawful behaviour as the raw material out of which to manufacture the
criminal statistics of arrest and prosecution. Indeed raising standards of orderly behaviour and honesty (as, indeed, such standards
may well be rising) make no difference to the criminal statistics. An
act of public disorder which would have passed unnoticed in former
times may now be stigmatized by criminal prosecution, just as a
minor skin complaint, which would have passed without notice fifty
years ago, may now be the subject of elaborate National Health
procedures.

The volume of ill-health may be regarded as not quite infinite in
its potential for expansion, as theoretically, people will not bother
to consult their doctors about every minor ailment. The range of
human behaviour which can be designated as "criminal" is certainly
infinite, however, for it merely needs legislation to make it so. In
practice, legislation designates a far wider area of normal human
behaviour "criminal" than the police can hope to cope with. If one
type of crime goes out of fashion – for instance proceedings against
adult male homosexuals have been discontinued – it is likely that
another will take its place. The persecution of homosexuals has now
been replaced in great measure by the persecution of people using
certain drugs. The stereotype of the drug-taker is partly the creation
of the police force, because they press home charges against the
type of person selected for that role. It is interesting to reflect on the
fact that cannabis used to be obtainable by the pennyworth at chemists' shops, and anyone who was so inclined could use it to drug
themselves with impunity.

The police force is just an example of a social institution which
can be analysed in this way by a social science not committed to
buttressing the status quo. Such a social science can be truly scientific in that no issues are prejudged by it. Marxist social science is by
no means untrammelled by conclusions which the theorist is committed to demonstrate, and indeed it differs little from conventional
capitalist social science. The problems of official criminology in the
countries of the modern Russian Empire are very like those of the
West, except that more emphasis is put upon crimes against the
State. Indeed, Marxists are rendered incapable of providing an

adequate analysis of the social institutions of capitalist society because of the pre-assumptions of their own credo which are in many ways closely similar to those of the modern capitalist ideology. The State is seen as the necessary force restraining the social deviance of the individual or of individual groups. A view alternative to this is that behaviour stigmatized as deviant may be the manifestation of something that is basically socially healthy. The waste, repression and cruelties commonly associated with such deviancy may be seen as the by-product of the inertia of older institutions.

Sociology, like psychology, is a self-reflective study, and many people have felt the need of a social theory to explain social science. Perhaps the nearest we can come to this is in the consideration of how the so-called natural sciences led to the study of the phenomenon of man by man himself. Just as the biological sciences gave rise to a discipline now known as psychology, so sociology has arisen by the application of the scientific method to the behaviour of groups. In so far as the social sciences are used to buttress the status quo, or indeed to justify any revolutionary programme such as that of the Marxists, they fail to provide an adequate analysis, just like the individual psychologist who fails adequately to analyse his own personal motivation. The extent, then, to which we may be capable of adequately analysing social institutions in which we partake, must depend upon the rigour of our methods. There is nothing to be gained by considering whether a conclusion is good or bad "propaganda" for whatever we believe in and give our loyalty to. It is natural and right that we should have our personal loyalties, but if we wish to free social science of the encumbrance of attitudes which prejudge every issue, we must lay our own value judgements on one side. Will this produce a "libertarian" criminology? At least it will be free of the need to bolster this or that social system.

*Anarchy 98*                                                        *April 1969*

# 2. The zoo-keepers of deviancy

## Jock Young

WE LIVE in a world which is characterised by the extreme segregation of one social group from another. The modern city is divided up into different ideas, and this residential segregation is reinforced by divisions that occur at school, at work and in leisure activities. As Frank Musgrove put it

> The suburban bureaucrat may live year in and year out without any but the most fleeting contact with anyone of a different level of occupation, education or civilisation from himself. His work is at the administrative headquarters remote from the factory operatives whose destiny he helps to shape; there he associates with others of like kind; he travels home, insulated by his motor car from contact with any other order of being, to an area of social equals; his leisure is spent in the club with others of the same social standing. We have unthinkingly evolved or deliberately fashioned social concentration camps: places in which one social class is concentrated to the exclusion of others.

Thus class is segregated from class, young people from old, rich people from poor, criminals from non-criminals, coloured people from whites. Moreover even where there is actual physical propinquity social distances maintain segregation of a very real sort. This is precisely what Michael Harrington was referring to when he called the massive hidden poverty of America: "the invisible land".

Our society is characterised by exclusion, as one class moves into an area the "better" class retreats out, the young create a consiracy of silence to shield them from the middle-aged, the middle-aged in turn incarcerate their aged, the white man fears the coloured as a neighbour: we create vast leprosariums in which we put the criminal, the insane, the crippled, and the old, and we leave all these social outcasts to the ministration of experts in deviancy; the psychiatrist, the social worker, the priest, and the criminologist. Now this process of segregation has very real consequences in terms of society's reaction to its so-called deviants. For it limits drastically the quality of the information we receive as to the motivations, attitudes, behaviour and humanity of these individuals. And it is because of the distorted information that we are bombarded with, because of the demented caricatures that are presented to us, that we – like the 1940's German inundated by anti-Semitic propaganda – lash out blindly at these scapegoats, support organised violence against them in our name, lament the passing of the hangman.

If we take a boy who is caught stealing in a small community, his social group has a rich multi-dimensional knowledge of the lad which is derived from an actual face to face contact with him. They would know him not just as a thief but also in terms of a whole series of human attributes: the cheerful lad who delivers the papers. Stan – the publican's nephew, the boy who worked in his spare time in the village store, etc. In place of this, we have in large urban societies, one piece of information only as regards the boy, namely that he is a delinquent and around this label we perceive a hazy aura concocted of prejudice and fantasy. Now there are two major interconnected sources of this information: the mass media and the expert; and an examination of the content of this information, I suggest, will tell us more about the desires and stereotypes of middle-class journalists and experts in deviancy than it does of the life style of the delinquent or the meaning of his crime. For deviant groups are, so to speak, living Rorschach Blots onto which are projected the prejudices and class interests of these men. The notions put forward by the experts differ from those put forward by journalists in one important respect only: they are more conceptually sophisticated. They are, on the face of it, more scientific, more elaborate, more tolerant, and more "progressive" but beneath this patina they contain the same prejudices, for within the velvet glove of therapy and treatment is concealed the same iron fist of punishment.

The experts are the personnel which society selects to man the social barricades between the deviant and the hypothesised "normal" citizen. Their task is to evolve theories which explain deviant actions to the rest of society and to derive from these theories notions of means of curing, training or treating the deviant. That is these personnel perceive themselves as having primarily the therapeutic role of assimilating "the poor", "the maladjusted", "the immature personality", "the undersocialised", "the sick", "the adolescent gone wrong" into the ranks of a posited consensus of decent well-integrated people to whom they perceive themselves as belonging. That their clients, the deviants, often interpret their attempts at therapy as being punitive and coercive is regarded as lack of self-insight, that a few renegade experts attack them as being professional ideologues of middle-class values, is regarded as a sad loss of objectivity.

The hallmark of these theories is that they tend to deny the legitimacy, or in fact, the very existence of norms and values which are different from those of the theorist. They evolve a series of theoretical ploys the end result of which is a total mystification of the relationship between society and the deviant. The following principles would seem to operate:

**1. Denial of Authenticity.** The meaning that individual delinquents ascribe to their crime, political "extremists" ascribe to their activities or the reasons junkies give for why they take heroin, is ignored. Instead "real" causes are discovered in terms of "personality disorders", genetic defects or lack of social control, thus, for instance a person stole a car *really* because he was separated from his mother in early childhood, because he has XYY sex chromosomes or because he has a weak superego. The action itsef becomes denuded of meaning and any conflict over the ownership of material possessions is somehow forgotten.

**2. Denial of Existence.** Alternative values and norms are perceived as being in fact an absence of values, that is if doesn't uphold your particular sexual, economic or political values then the deviant has no values at all. For example:

"they are acting like animals";

"the drugtaker is impulsive, thrill-seeking and amoral".

Hedonisitic norms are the main contenders for this treatment.

**3. Denial of Personal Integrity.** Political, sexual and criminal deviancy is ascribed not to the emergence of alternative standards but to personality failings on the part of the individuals concerned. Thus the communist in the West is seen as undersocialised and the liberal in Russia as mentally ill. The imputation of "weak" personalities to deviants is often extended to the working class and negroes in general. As this is where, according to the statistics, criminals originate from, this theoretical insight is seen as fitting the evidence splendidly. Thus Eysenck writes: "there are very good reasons for assuming considerable differences between the classes with respect to the degree of socialisation to which they are subjected." Now people with a very low degree of socialisation are, according to Eysenck, psychopaths, so one would be able to construct a continuum with well-balanced middle-class people at one end, psychologically inadequate psychopaths at the other and the working class as a whole tending towards the latter. Working-class people are, then, not properly socialised and Eysenck clinches the argument by citing their well-known predilections for aggressiveness and premarital sexual intercourse!

**4. Denial of Freedom.** The deviant is impelled by forces beyond his control which are only properly comprehended by experts. The activities of normal people on the other hand are rational and based on free choice. We must pity the deviant, not punish him because he is unable – like us – to help what he is doing.

**5. Denial of Cognisance.** The deviant is unable to realise the real reasons why he acts the way he does. He needs the superior cognisance of the expert to delve out the hidden factors which motivate him.

**6. Denial of Aims.** The aims of deviant groups and the attitudes and behaviour of its members are systematically misperceived and misinterpreted. Onto the real aims of such groups are projected the obsessions and fantasies of the experts.

**7. Denial of Numbers.** Deviant activities are thought to occur only in small minorities which are either psychologically maladjusted or live in socially disorganised areas. Now where the numbers of the individuals observed to be manifesting deviant behaviour is *obviously* large, an extra twist to the theory is added, namely the notion of the corruptors and the corrupted. Thus deviant activity is the result of a small clique of maladjusted individuals (the corrupted). A strike then is doubtlessly engineered by a small group of Trotskyites, the occupation of LSE by six or seven foreign militants, and every marihuana smoker is turned by a Machiavellian pusher!

**8. Affirmation of Objectivity.** The study of social phenomena, it is insisted, should be value free and should utilise objective concepts such as those used in the natural sciences. Thus Robin Blackburn describes this position as suggesting that: "once theories are thoroughly cleansed of all 'value judgements' it is believed that they will be governed by the wholesome discipline of objective facts. The predictable consequence of this attempted purge of values is to orient theory and research towards certain crude over abstracted value notions masquerading as scientific concepts". An "ideology of objectivity" emerges but the moral yardstick of this objectivity is middle-class values. "Psychopathy", "Anomie", "social disorganisation", "under socialisation", "maturity", "weak superego", are all value-laden concepts despite the ongoing pretence of objectivity.

It is amusing to note how these principles are generally only applied to *lower working-class* criminals: thus if one takes the "Ferranti Affair" of 1963 where the company overcharged the Ministry of Aviation to such an extent that they eventually agreed, after a wrangle, to return £4,250,000, still leaving themselves with 21% profit; this near-criminal coup would seem to make the activities of

the Great Train Robbers a little amateurish. Yet only one criminologist, to my knowledge, Dennis Chapman (and he with his tongue
in his cheek) has suggested that the Board of Directors should be
psychiatrically examined to see if they exhibited signs of weak su-
peregos, undersocialisation, immature personality or evidence of
broken homes, etc. Nor has any subcultural theorist up till now
produced any account of the activities of the notorious Ferranti
Gang.

Now these experts are not cynical men, they are sincere dedicated people who see their role in a progressive light. They seek to
*treat* the criminal and the deviant, not to *punish* him. But this
ideology of therapy is immensely more insidious and allows dimensions of coercion and punishment which even the most "unenlight-
ened" and vindictive supporter of the moral order would never have
the tenacity to pursue. As Ronald Laing puts it:

> To work smoothly, it is necessary that those who use this stratagem do
> not themselves know that it is a stratagem. They should not be cynical or
> ruthless: they sould be sincere and concerned. Indeed, the more "treat-
> ment" is escalated – through negotiation (psychotherapy), pacification
> (tranquillization), physical struggle (cold-packs and straitjackets),
> through at one and the same time more and more *humane* and *effective*
> forms of destruction (electro-shocks and insulin comas), to the final
> solution of cutting a person's brain in two or more slices by psycho-
> surgery – the more the human beings who do these things to other
> people tend to feel sincere concern, dedication, pity; and they can hard-
> ly help but feel more and more indignant, sorrowful, horrified and
> scandalized by their actions. As for the patients, the more they protest,
> the less insight they display; the more they fight back, clearly the more
> they need to be pacified; the more persecuted they feel at being des-
> troyed, the more necessary to destroy them. And at the end of it all, they
> may indeed be "cured", they may even express gratitude for no longer
> having the brains left to protest against persecution. But many do not.
> This only goes to show, as one leading psychiatrist said to me: "It's the
> white man's burden, Ronald. We can't expect any thanks, but we must
> go on."

Moreover the expert, because of his position of power vis-à-vis
the deviant, will tend to maintain his theoretical "insight" by a
process which has been called negotiating reality (T. Scheff), that is,
he elicits from the deviant precisely those reponses which tend to
verify his theories and that this is a negotiated situation based on the
notion that if you – the deviant – are co-operative and helpful and
show insight into your problem, we will be co-operative with you
insofar as we will obtain material help for you, obtain you an early

release, not give you shock therapy, give you warmth and sympathy or protect you from the law. In short, successful therapy involves convincing the deviant of the stupidity of his own idea of what he is doing and a translation of these ideas into those of the therapist's. This is called self-insight.

But the expert has not only the power to negotiate reality, to determine the sort of information which he is willing to see and hear, he has also the power to change reality. W.I. Thomas's famous dictum that a situation defined as real in a society will be real in its consequences has immediate relevance here. For one would expect the stereotypes that the expert holds of the deviants to have very real consequences for their future behaviour and the way they perceive themselves. Thus Goffman in *Asylums* charts what he calls the moral career of the mental patient outlining the manner in which the particular images the hospital holds of the mentally ill are internalised and acted out by the patient. Thus, particularly in those cases where individuals are incarcerated in total institutions for therapeutic reasons, the deviant begins through a self-fulfilling process to begin to look, to act, and to feel like the anomic, undersocialised, psychotic, amoral individual which the therapeutic personnel portray in their theories of deviancy. This position of power has an effect on the expert himself. Thus Lindesmith in a critique of research conducted on drug addicts writes:

> In addition to considering the effects of institutionalization upon addicts, one must also consider its effects upon investigators. The institutionalized researcher or observer who is accustomed to handling inmates in an authoritarian setting tends to assign certain types of traits to those over whom he exercises power. He is in a unique position to note the recalcitrance of inmates who do not respond as it is thought they should to the benevolent and well-intentioned programs imposed upon them. By long familiarity with institutional life he sometimes comes to attach little significance to the loss of liberty by others, and he may have difficulty in understanding why addicts seem not to understand or appreciate that they are being locked up for their own good.

Within the total institution; the prison, the mental hospital, the Borstal, the individual is stripped of his autonomy, his privacy and identity are violated, his entire life is bureaucratically organised, regulated down to the minutest detail and often over a period of years the inmate is reduced to an almost childlike dependency on his captors. As the White Paper on the Adult Offender candidly notes:

> Some offenders are so handicapped, mentally or physically, that the

chances of their successful establishment in society are necessarily small. They will need continuous and intensive support for a very long time, and there is room for further voluntary effort here. The personality of some is so eroded by long years of imprisonment that it may well prove desirable to promote the provision of hostels, possibly with a sheltered workshop, which for the rest of their lives will give them the same sense of security that they have experienced in prison. If these unfortunates can be contained in this way it will be better than sending them back to prison and their potential victims will benefit.

Not all violence is necessarily physical: the prolonged assault of society on the dignity and sense of individuality of the deviant, the attempts to mortify him, distort him and manipulate him, are more reprehensible than the casual physical blow as the wounds that are produced can sometimes never be healed. Violence on this scale: organised, "rational", tenacious and, above all, sincere makes the sporadic violence of the criminal look half-hearted and innocuous.

Now within the field of criminology has grown up a body of sociologists, the Chicago school, who have to some extent rebelled against the type of expertise and value position implied in the theories referred to above. Chief amongst these are Becker, Goffman, Lindesmith, Matza, Erikson and Kitsuse. They have what Alvin Gouldner, in a singularly perceptive article, called: "A kind of underdog identification". They tend therefore to identify with the deviant rather than with respectable society. Now it is this school which has in my view quite justifiably the largest following amongst younger criminologists both in this country and in the States. Is it to these people then that we should turn in order to find libertarian criminology? I think not; for this school is caught in a dilemma between self-interest and identification with the underdog. As Gouldner puts it:

There are other more practical costs that would have to be paid were Becker (or anyone else) to announce his position in a direct manner. A straightforward affirmation of sympathy with the underdog would create practical difficulties for Becker as a researcher. For he might one day wish access to information held by rule-enforcers and rule-makers who, in turn, might be dismayed to hear that Becker was disposed to view them from the standpoint of those whom they feel to be threats to society. Again it might create a certain uneasiness among those who, either directly or indirectly, provide the resources which Becker like any other research entrepreneur requires. An outright expression of concern for or sympathy with the underdog thus conflicts with the sociologist's practical and professional interests.

Or as Dennis Chapman succinctly puts it:

The social sciences accept the stereotype of the criminal for to challenge it would involve heavy penalties. The penalties are: to be isolated from the mainstream of professional activity, to be denied resources for research and to be denied official patronage with its rewards in material status.

Self-interest then leads the liberal criminologist into a position of playing it cool, of maintaining his "unbiased" position of scholarship, of sympathising with the prisoner but only in terms of an amelioration of his condition, of making the odd pot shot at the establishment but always in terms of gradual reform, of the odd change here and there, meat twice a week and television for the inmates, nothing that smacks too much of radicalism. He is moreover dismayed at the philistine attitudes of the Press and the Public; he embodies a stance which, as Gouldner argues:

> expresses the satisfaction of the Great White Hunter who has bravely risked the perils of the urban jungle to bring back an exotic specimen. It expresses the Romanticism of the zoo curator who preeningly displays his rare specimens. And like the zookeeper, he wishes to protect his collection; he does not want spectators to throw rocks at the animals behind the bars. But neither is he eager to tear down the bars and let the animals go. The attitude of these zookeepers of deviance is to create a comfortable and humane Indian Reservation, a protected social space, within which these colourful specimens may be exhibited, unmolested and unchanged.

Has the criminologist no other role then than that of either being a paid ideologue of the establishment or a collector of strange specimens of humanity, a connoisseur of deviant behaviour? There is I believe a pressing need for an anti-criminology, somewhat like Cooper's anti-psychiatry, the stated aim of which is to demystify the current notions of the position of the criminal in our society and to expose the ideology of establishment criminology. For criminology is political: its whole subject matter is that of relationships of power, of conflict over desired resources, of the mode of repression of the weak and of the guardianship of property.

In 1968 Rainer Langhans and Fritz Teufel of the Berlin Kommune were tried on the absurd charge of inciting arson. They had passed a questionnaire around Berlin with a list of buildings asking people to tick those which they would most like to see burnt, there was additional space for people to write in buildings not mentioned. After a lengthy trial in which the prosecutors attempted to prove the psychological, sexual, and social abnormalities of members of the Kommune, the court decided as follows:

On the basis of their essentially abnormal character-structure, especially in their behaviour, their concepts and their way of life, as exemplified in the accused during trial on July 6 and 7, 1967, the accused will be examined both psychiatrically and neurologically by Dr. Spengler, head of the Board of Health of the National Institute for Forensic and Social Medicine in Berlin. The expert has to present to the Court an extensive, written and scientifically based verdict.

Langhans and Teufel in response, turned on the court and proposed that all its members, including the public prosecutor, should be psychiatrically examined. They might also undergo an intelligence test the results of which should be published extensively!

Now and then the tables are turned, when madmen question the sanity of psychiatrists, criminals the honesty of judges, perverts the sexuality of the decent and it is against the ideology of normality, the hypocrisy of the wealthy, that we must work, exposing the real conflict issues that lie just beneath the surface of the mystification and jargon of the experts.

*Anarchy 98*                                                    *April 1969*


# 3.   To be or not to be a female delinquent
## Sally Anne

THE PROSPECT of becoming a female delinquent is open to most women. The process of being classified as delinquent is easily comprehensible to those who undergo this experience. Unfortunately the "delinquent state" is not viewed in such simple terms by most theoreticians. Since the nineteenth century the characteristics of delinquents have aroused the interest and curiosity of a whole host of writers, anthropologists, psychologists, sociologists, etc. The kaleidoscopic image which emerges may have the unfortunate effect of confusing the delinquent girl or woman who may have a genuine desire to relate her own image of herself to this complicated theoretical framework. An additional complication facing the delinquent girl lies in the fact that certain theories, e.g. that of Lombroso, are notorious for being in and out of fashion at regular intervals. The only consistent point in this kaleidoscope is the implicit value-judgement that delinquency is an inferior status and hence most explanations of delinquency are based firmly on the assumption that "delinquency" is *ipso facto* a disease or stigma which must be explained away. There is no attempt to think of delinquency as a very useful concept and powerful weapon in the political and social sphere. Therefore, in attempting to describe the theories on the delinquency of women, one is forced to play the role of devil's advocate and accept temporarily the uncomplimentary value-judgement.

This value-judgement, judged by traditionalist standards, is particularly uncomplimentary so far as women are concerned. Most women are notorious for their dull, conformist and law-abiding tendencies. This is the natural result of their social conditioning. Hence any deviant behaviour is likely to incur a greater stigma. The nature and characteristics of a female delinquent have always intrigued and baffled most writers. This bewilderment is the natural outcome of considering a human being solely in terms of an abstraction, and a tendency among some writers to think of the female delinquent in terms of the feminine myth.

There are basically four general theories which explain the criminality of women: the anthropological, mystical, physiological and sociological explanations. The anthropologists, led by Lombroso, tried to define the "true" criminal. Influenced by Darwin, they were convinced that such a species of human beings existed, and armed with atavistic arguments they set out in search of it. Lombroso believed that the true criminal was a throw-back to a primitive species and could be physiologically defined. This regression was far more likely to occur in the case of men, since they were more intimately bound up with the "struggle for existence". Women, being of a "maternal and gentle disposition", were therefore less likely to fall into the paths of evil. But the "born female delinquent" was, by Lombrosian standards, a very special specimen. She was more destructive than her male counterpart. The prostitute and the murderess were the closest approximations to Lombroso's prototype of the born criminal. They were singled out because they broke the two behaviour taboos for women: that of sexuality and that of aggression. Those "delinquent" women who didn't conform to the idea of the born criminal were labelled the "occasional criminal" and were in fact "moral women" (in the strait-laced Victorian sense) who were being led into crime through the strong but perverted influence of their male friends.

Inmates of Holloway may be interested in some of Lombroso's descriptions. He noticed that, in general, prostitutes, thieves and murderesses weighed more than moral women. Prostitutes had larger hands and smaller feet, the palms of their hands were more developed than their fingers. Criminals tended to have dark eyes and dark virile hair. This virility of face and general physique was attributed by Lombroso to the atavistic origins of the women. Having defined the physical characteristics of the female delinquent, Lombroso tried to give his species a definite personality. "In general the moral physionomy of the born criminal approximates closely to that of the male. The atavistic diminution of the subject shows itself once again in the psychology of the female criminal, who is excessively erotic, weak in maternal feeling, inclined to dissipation, astute and audacious, and dominates weaker beings, sometimes by suggestion, at others by muscular force, her vices and even her dress increase her resemblance to the sterner sex. Added to those virile qualities are often the worst characteristics of women; namely an excessive desire for revenge, cunning, cruelty, love of dress, and an untruthfulness forming a combination of evil tendencies, which often result in a type of extraordinary wickedness". Lombroso's theory has subsequently been much criticised.[1] His analysis proved to be a source of embarrassment in so far as his description of the "born criminal" fitted some of the most respectable citizens of his time. His concept of the born criminal is primarily a romantic one, and is inappropriate when we think of some of the prostitutes who keep returning time and time again to prison. Most murderesses either kill members of their family, or friends. They are frequently victim-precipitated homicides, in so far as the woman was first attacked and subsequently killed her attacker in order to defend herself. In other instances, where the victim is a child, the woman is overcome with remorse and frequently attempts suicide.

Although Lombroso has been criticised and ridiculed, his theory has had a profound influence on criminologists.[2] The Lombrosian analysis assumes a macabre aspect for women both inside and outside prison, when we remember that one of the purposes of the anthropological school was to define the criminal type with sufficient accuracy so that those human beings who fell into this category could be segregated from the rest of the community by imprisonment and by capital punishment if necessary. This analytical aspiration is still maintained by some modern criminologists, e.g.

Sheldon and Eleanor Glueck, although they have tended to concentrate most of their attention on predicting delinquency among boys.

While Lombroso approached the "female delinquent" with a pseudo-scientific disdain, Pollak's approach or analysis can only be described as mystical. Like Lombroso, he maintained that the worst type of female criminality could only be described in bestial terms. However, unlike Lombroso, he maintained that the proportion of female offenders had been vastly underestimated. The statement "woman is less criminal than man" was therefore false. Her criminality was mainly of a hidden kind. As the weaker member of the human species she was compelled to rely upon her ability to deceive people. This highly developed capacity for deception could have slightly unfortunate consequences. She was better able, by virtue of her status as general housekeeper, to obtain poison from the chemist, which could be used to kill members of her family. In addition to straightforward poisoning, she frequently indulged in infanticide. She was able to conceal her pregnancy, the birth of her child and its subsequent murder. The picture which Pollak paints could have been derived from Victorian melodrama, but not from reality.

If the kaleidoscopic image was confined to Lombroso's and Pollak's theories, the individual female delinquent may find the result both amusing and perhaps alarming. However the delinquent is regarded as a many-splendoured thing by most criminologists, and our "delinquent" has to wade through a number of perhaps slightly less esoteric theories in order to get a comprehensive view of herself. Women have been defined sociologically in a secondary role, which has strong sexual undertones, and most of the theories which explain delinquency among women can be fitted within this general theoretical framework.

The physiologists claim that while sexual crises do not automatically lead to law-breaking, they can nevertheless be a powerful contributing factor. Thus Ann D. Smith, the author of *Women in Prison*, states that "Variations in female criminality in the different age-groups are certainly to some extent due to physical causes. Although stresses at the climacteric may be experienced by both men and women, there is no male counterpart to the series of psychological crises which women undergo." Thus a female delinquent, according to the physiologists can largely attribute her condition to a lapse during a sexual crisis. There are basically four periods in a woman's life in which sexual crises do occur. These are puberty, menstruation, pregnancy and menopause. "With the onset of puberty, however protected young girls may be in their home, impulses to rebellion and general dissatisfaction and frustration with the limitations of childhood encourages them towards anti-social behaviour, especially if sexual precocity is accompanied by intellectual immaturity."[3]

However, this picture of revolution against the domestic hearth is far too simple and cannot be accepted as it stands. It is fairly common for girls in borstals to have spent some time in approved schools, prior to which they probably underwent another period of institutionalisation in an orphanage or other institution. Even if they have been fortunate enough not to have experienced institutionalisation, their home backgrounds are not entirely "satisfactory" and have generally failed to provide the necessary emotional security. The basic insecurity and the need for adventure is prevalent prior to puberty, and the act of rebellion, which in itself can be a very constructive thing, is probably the result of other factors. The act of rebellion generally consists in running away and having sexual intercourse, sometimes prematurely and sometimes over and above the prescribed sociological limit. The majority of girls in approved schools and borstals haven't committed a specific crime, but are deemed to be in need of care and control.[4]

Icard (1890), Healy (1915), and Pollak (1950) maintained that there is a definite connection between menstruation and delinquency. Healy quoted Gudden's research in 1907 in which he found that practically all the shoplifters whom he examined were either at or near the time of menstruation. Burt (1930) also supported this argument. Unfortunately for the physiologists, his analysis also contained a small but significant grain of commonsense. He maintained that it would be incautious to presume that offences were committed by women only during periods of menstruation. It was quite conceivable that women carry out their thefts with less skill and greater carelessness on these occasions, and so are more likely to be detected.

The third period – that of pregnancy – has, surprisingly, received little attention. Pregnancy tends towards a temporary lack of balance and self-control in women, and some writers have maintained that there is a tendency amongst women to commit theft during this period. Most writers have concentrated on the effects of the natural termination of pregnancy, i.e. childbirth. Puerperal and lactational insanity are frequently found in cases of infanticide and child destruction.

Whilst the effect of pregnancy has received very little attention from writers, the influence of menopause has been the subject of much sociological comment and controversy. Most writers maintain that menopause has a more disturbing effect upon women as contrasted with the earlier sexual crises, insofar as the change of life leads to a certain biological imbalance which is accompanied by such psychological states as severe depression, anxiety and emotional instability. In addition, the loss of physical attraction, which has a tremendous commercial value in present-day society, acts as a further complication. Pollak (1950) maintained that the peak age for many crimes committed by women was between the ages of forty and fifty, particularly for such offences as shoplifting, receiving stolen goods, offences connected with irritability and lack of control, such as insulting behaviour, perjury and breach of the peace. Menopause has a worse effect upon the single and separated woman as the unsettling effects are aggravated by the lack of the security afforded by a home life.

The physiologists' explanation of female delinquency is not limited to the purely biological aspect of the different sexual crises but also extends to the psychological aspects. The female delinquent is supposed to possess to an exaggerated degree such "feminine" characteristics as excitability, hysteria, depression. These characteristics are not peculiar to female delinquents, and can be found in the rest of the population. Such states as manic depression are quite common in contemporary society. There are primarily two courses open to the female delinquent. She can either dismiss these characteristics as completely inapplicable or inappropriate to her own character, or she could accept the physiologists' argument.

The theoreticians have paid most attention to hysteria amongst female delinquents. Serious interest in the subject began in the 19th century. Sexual repression was supposed to be the main cause of hysteria, which sooner or later manifested itself in false accusations and other bizarre forms of behaviour. The decline of Victorian sexual morality has to some extent considerably modified the argument favouring sexual repression as the main cause of hysteria. Yet Healy (1915)and Pollak (1950) maintained that sexual frustration and hysteria are to be found in practically all cases of false accusations made by women. Palthorpe (1932) extended the same argument to cases of kleptomania. A recent publication *Delinquent Girls in Approved Schools* drew the reader's attention to a number of cases of hysteria found among young girls in approved schools. Some of these descriptions were similar to the Victorian descriptions of hysterical behaviour. But these girls were known for their "sexual promiscuity". It follows that the old explanation of hysteria is untenable, and that the penal institutions hold a number of seriously disturbed girls who shouldn't be there in the first place.

One must also not forget that the penal institutions are particularly conducive to hysterical behaviour.

Depression, like hysteria, has frequently been regarded as an emotional outlet for women. Cameron (1944) and McNiven (1944) maintained that melancholia in extreme cases may cause women to take their own lives or the lives of others, usually in their own families.[3] In general a conscious realisation of being peculiar can create a sense of being rejected by society, which may lead to anti-social behaviour as a compensation. This general feeling of inadequacy is particularly prevalent among girls and women who have at some time lived in institutions.

The two alternative choices open to the female delinquent, i.e. the acceptance or the rejection of the physiologists' argument is surely a very difficult one. If the physiologists' claim is based on the assumption that female delinquents are the only people who are susceptible to these severe psychological states, then that claim is untenable. These characteristics are common to the rest of the population and become "publicly visible" in mental hospital language. It is absurd to presuppose that there is such a thing as a delinquent character. The two alternative choices open to the female delinquent are therefore grounded on an individual's self-analysis, as is indeed the case for the rest of the population. The self-analysis could be carried out at two specific points in time, before and after imprisonment. Any differences, both in degree and kind, would act as an interesting reflection on penal correction.

While the female delinquent can easily understand the immediate relevance of depression and anxiety, it seems highly unlikely that she would appreciate the Freudian part of the kaleidoscopic image. The Freudian analysis of female delinquency is simply based on the penis-envy theory. It would surely be rather absurd to expect a woman who had defrauded the national Assistance Board or failed to keep up with HP payments, to agree that the principal motive for her actions was her desire to possess a penis.

The Freudians, like the physiologists, saw a direct link between women's sexuality and her delinquency. Their spectrum of analysis didn't have a wider sociological framework of reference. This wider framework of reference can be broken down into two inter-related parts: firstly a woman's reaction to unfavourable factors (e.g. loss of physical attraction, lack of marital status) which affect the woman *vis-a-vis* her role as a woman; secondly her reaction to other unfavourable factors which arise primarily from her position in the social strata. The largest age-group in penal institutions consists of girls in their teens. The teenager deemed to be in need of care and control, and the girl convicted of shoplifting are fairly common examples. Therefore if there is any correlation between youth and contact with the law, it would be fairly logical to assume that the second largest age-group would consist of women in their twenties. The second largest age-group, however, consists of women in their forties and fifties. (I have already alluded to the effect of menopause.) Generally, most women depend very heavily upon physical attraction. The loss of this attraction has a detrimental effect upon the woman, as less attention is paid to her and her own evaluation of herself is considerably decreased. It is frequently at this stage that marital problems, in the case of married women, and general isolation, in the case of single or separated women, may appear overwhelming. The importance of the marital status as a stabilising factor has been the subject of some controversy. Criminologists like Radzinowicz claim that marriage has a positive effect upon women. They are less likely to break the law since this would have a detrimental effect upon their family. On the other hand, marriage brings its own problems, and the pressure to keep up with the Joneses may be such as to lead the woman to commit fraud or to fall behind with the HP payments. Most of the women in Holloway have children, although not all of them are married, and it may therefore be more plausible to re-define the "marital status" as a relationship status, which is centred round the idea of a nuclear family.

The secondary role according to women does not only place a heavy emphasis on physicality and marital status, it also conditions women to underrate the importance of intelligence. It is a fairly common assumption among sociologists that women in prison are, on the whole, not very intelligent; their lack of intelligence being a contributory factor in their incarceration. The intelligence of women in prison is considered to be below that of the general population, and even below that of men in prison. Dr. Charity Taylor noticed that the women who were sentenced for child cruelty and neglect had a very low level of intelligence. In a society in which a certain level of intelligence is necessary for survival, the female delinquent who fits this description may be regarded as a "social failure".

The most contemporary aspect of the kaleidoscopic image draws a direct comparison between delinquency on the one hand and failure or inadequacy on the other. Delinquents are regarded either as failures as people, or as failures as members of society, or both. There is no satisfactory definition of personal failure, and any attempt to arrive at a definition involves a high degree of conceit.

However, using very narrow criteria, one can attempt to define social failure. Thus in a materialist society, poverty would be regarded as tantamount to social failure. Frances Heidensohn, in attempting to arrive at a general theory on the criminality of women, considers that most of the women in Holloway are (a) women who have been sentenced for crimes against property, some of which are of a petty and apparently motiveless nature, and (b) women who come from the poorer or less influential sections of the community. Her theory is based upon sound common sense, and were it not for the fact that it ignores the psychological aspect, it could be acceptable (as a partial and not a general theory). Most of the crimes committed by both men and women are crimes against property. This is a natural reflection of the values of society. In addition to a large proportion of the pressures of consumer society, directed through advertising, the mass media, etc., are aimed specifically at women. So it is reasonable to assume that sooner or later a fair proportion of women are bound to get into trouble over, for example, failure to pay HP instalments. Membership of the poorer or less influential section of the community is an immediate disadvantage since it fails to give one the contacts, the scepticism, cynicism or straightforward "know-how" to avoid arrest and imprisonment. These women are at a double disadvantage. Apart from belonging to a less influential section of the community, many of them are likely to be entirely dependent, economically, on their men. It is not unusual to come across an instance of a woman with a large family who is given a very small sum of money on which to manage. She has left school at 15, is totally unequipped to lead a reasonably independent economic life, and finds herself literally bound to the home and the children, living on a pittance, and forced to find some illegal means of coping. Add to this ignorance of some of the basic facts of the commercial and legal world – and the picture becomes very grim.

The kaleidoscopic image has therefore moved from the bizarre atavistic arguments of Lombroso to the more mundane but commonsense theory of Frances Heidensohn. The poverty-hypothesis has been of general interest to criminologists, although it has never been specifically applied to women. Its restatement in this form is important since it relates the prospect of becoming delinquent to social status. A recruitment of future delinquents from the top elites of society is always highly unlikely.

At the beginning of this article I stated that delinquency was a very useful weapon in the social and political sphere, and this, to my mind, appears to be one of the few constructive ways of viewing female delinquency. Lombroso's and Pollak's theories are bizarre, Freud's is laughable, and most of the physiologists and sociologists see only certain aspects. A female delinquent is very much part and parcel of society – at times she *reflects* its sick values, at other times her action is a positive rebellion *against* the values of society. The question of who is, or what constitutes a female delinquent, is (outside the strictly legal sphere) a ridiculous one, and should not have been the subject of so much thought and effort.

# Footnotes

1　Most of the criticisms of Lombroso's theory have been directed at his unscientific approach (eg Charles Goring in *The English Convict*). The plausibility of the born-criminal hypothesis has not yet been sufficiently criticised.

2　The modern followers of Lombroso include the Crimino-Biological School, the Neo-Lombrosians and the Endocrinologists. The Crimino-Biological School is mainly concerned with the allegations of certain inborn tendencies and predispositions towards criminal attitudes. Bodily features are significant only as far as they are connected with corresponding mental traits, and social factors are not entirely ignored. Thus Ernest Kretschmer, who belonged to this school, attempted to combine psychological and pathological characteristics with certain bodily types and thereby to determine the type of crime which is likely to be committed. The Neo-Lombrosians, in defining the criminal type, replaced the physical type with the psycho-pathological type. The Endocrinologists found a direct connection between both criminality and disturbances of the ductless glands.

3　Ann D. Smith: *Women in Prison*.

4　*Delinquent Girls in Approved Schools*.

5　In the United Kingdom, one in three murders is followed by the suicide, or attempted suicide, of the murderer. In a number of these cases of murder followed by suicide the latter is a woman.

# 4. Notes on detention centres

## Stan Cohen

IT IS ABSURD – some might say – to expound at any length on the subject of detention centres. The libertarian anarchist's position should be quite clear: they are destructive of the human soul, they were conceived in the spirit of military discipline and they are run with the full weight of authoritarianism and repression: so tear them down and don't waste words. As one of Salinger's characters says of the Gettysburg address: Lincoln should just have stood in front of the crowd, shook his fist at them and walked away.

At times I am in sympathy with this way of approaching some of our institutions. But as a libertarian who is also in the unfortunate position of earning a living by being a sociologist who studies and teaches around the subjects of crime, delinquency and other forms of deviance, I am also conscious of having to fight this form of thinking. There is an anti-intellectualism rampant both among one's students (where it takes the form of demanding easy ways to answer exam questions) and, alas, among one's political comrades (where it takes the form of demanding easy slogans or programmes for action). Anarchists, whose intellectual roots go deeper back than any other group fighting the horrors of today's society should be the first to see that a committed and passionate position is not incompatible with an orderly argument. In conventional criminology of course – as the contributors to ANARCHY No. 98 made clear – we find under the facade of an orderly, "neutral" argument a whole range of assumptions which make it quite clear who is putting whom up against the wall. I don't want to set up any such facade of neutrality; my antagonism to detention centres is undisguised. But antagonism needs to be documented as much as acceptance.

## How they started the short, sharp, shock

Detention Centres were first formerly proposed in the Criminal Justice Act, 1948, their immediate inspiration being the military detention centres of the Second World War. The idea, in the words of the Home Secretary introducing the Bill, was to provide something for "... the young offender for whom a fine or probation order would be inadequate but who does not require the prolonged period of training which is given by an approved school or borstal institution". What better to fill this gap than to give the offender "... a short but sharp reminder that he is getting into ways that will inevitably lead him into disaster"? There was very little questioning of this initial conception – it fitted in well with the times.

The first centre was set up four years later, in 1952, and others followed at fairly regular intervals, achieving high rankings on the sentencing chart for Teddy Boys, a fashion maintained more recently for the Mods and Rockers. By the end of 1966 there were four Junior (14-16) and 14 Senior (17-20) Centre for boys and one Centre for girls. The sentence is for a minimum period of three months and a maximum of six months. The move from short (three-six months) prison sentences for young offenders following the implementation in 1963 of certain sections in the Criminal Justice Act, 1961, resulted in large shifts from prison to Detention Centre. In 1955, 586 boys were sent to Detention Centres, in 1961 the number was 2,311 and in 1966, 7,154.

From the beginning it was made quite clear that the function of the Detention Centres was purely deterrent. The idea was to provide, in the oft-quoted phrase, a "short, sharp, shock". John Conrad, in what is for the most part an enlightened and sensitive analysis of penal policy and practice, blandly comments that to him, Detention Centres are "the most interesting innovation in the English correctional system". He sadly notes that the "short, sharp, shock" phrase has haunted Detention Centre staffs (implying perhaps that the staff would prefer some other conception of their function) and goes on to quote an experienced Detention Centre Warden who says that the phrase "... disturbingly suggests that somewhere in a dim background there is carried on a system of semi-legalized physical torment. Nothing, it need scarcely be said, is further from the truth." No one, it need scarcely be added, can indict a system more thoroughly than its adherents.

But Conrad reminds us as well of the origins of the phrase:

To set in solemn silence in a dull dark dock,
In a pestilential prison with a life long lock
Awaiting the sensation of a short sharp shock
From a chippy, chippy chopper on a big black block.

In the seventeen years since which Detention Centres have been run something like 45,000 boys have been, to use the fashionable euphemism, "admitted" through their gates and awaited the sensations arranged for them by the dutiful staff. To these boys, the sensations have not been seen as particularly short – when you're 15 or 16, three or four months in such a place can seem a long time; nor particularly sharp – a phrase which implies a sudden chop rather than a series of dull thuds; nor much of a shock – for very few boys is this their first experience of the legal system: many have been through the courts and received probation, approved school and other forms of "treatment". One can understand why Neal Pharoah in one of the few articulate such accounts which exists, described his experiences in a Detention Centre as a "Long, Blunt, Shock". Perhaps a "long, blunt, thud" would be more accurate. For many boys, some of whom have grown up in families and neighbourhoods where violence is frequent and all of whom have been subjected to the brutalities of our school system – the Detention Centre atmosphere is not altogether discontinued from previous experience.

In terms of the official conceptions of what the Detention Centres are all about, there has always been a remarkable consistency. One gets a feeling of timelessness reading through the original outlines in 1948, the Detention Centre Rules in 1952, the annual reports of the Prison Commissioners (later the Prison Department) since 1952, various Home Office circulars and other publications such as the *Justice of the Peace and Local Government Review*. In fact, as early as 1942, the well-known juvenile court magistrate John Watson justified the use of "punitive detention" for juvenile offenders in terms almost identical to those used in regard to Detention Centres nearly thirty years later:

> ... the provision meets the case where no long period of training is called for and all that is necessary is a short, sharp punishment to bring the offender to his senses and act as a deterrent. There is a very definite demand for some form of treatment of this kind which would be of short duration but thoroughly unpleasant and available as a penalty for minor offences, including minor breaches of probation. What is needed is a small local establishment in which the discipline is of the sternest, the food of the plainest, where everything is done "at the double" and where there is a maximum of hard work and the minimum of amusement; the kind of establishment a young offender would not want to visit twice and of which he would paint a vivid picture on his return home.

The least that can be said for these principles is that they were clear and unambiguous. There was also – in the official mind at least – a clear picture of the type of offenders for whom the regime was to be designed: those who had not yet developed an anti-social attitude (perhaps the Centres would give them the opportunity to do this?) and needed an early warning. The Detention Centres were to become the standard way of dealing with the young offender for whom, to quote the Home Office handbook *The Sentence of the Court* (1964):

> ... a long period of residential training is not yet necessary or justified for their offence but who also cannot be taught respect for the law by such non-custodial measures as fines or probation.

The regime which derived from these principles was to be based on hard work, physical exercise and training, little recreation, paramilitary discipline and a lot of time marching around, lining up and changing clothes. These features were based on what is again a clear but on closer examination wholly unfounded set of justifications, derived from a combination of army, public school and Hitler Youth ideologies. At various times, the following elements were emphasized: rigid discipline combined with wholesome influences; the inculcation of personal standards of cleanliness, obedience and good manners; the direction of energy into constructive sources; the long-term deterrent effect of unpleasant experiences; self-pride in physical powers; the beneficial effects of exercise for the mind and body; the sheer consumption of time in useless activity. These and similar elements of thinking have been accepted with little questioning, their relevance to the basic causes and outcomes of delinquency never demonstrated. The few attempts which have been made by the spokesmen of the system at any creative thought about these links have been too pathetic to quote at any length. According to an editorial in the *Justice of Peace* (1/4/61) for example, Detention Centres are successful "...in restoring some semblance of discipline and personal pride to the young men whose neglect of these qualities was frequently at the root of their delinquent behaviour". Such thinking defies comment.

## It's all like Butlin's now

Hasn't all of this changed? Aren't there now social workers in some Detention Centres and after-care arrangements? And don't the Home Office circulars talk about the introduction of more "positive" elements into the regime?

Detention Centre Wardens and other apologists for the system want things both ways. On the one hand they still propound the original philosophy and on the other, they claim that those who condemn the system for being harsh and unconstructive are wrong – things have changed, there is reform and positive training, the military aspects have been played down. Some outsiders, of course, are really worried by this latter rhetoric and think that the system has been watered down too far. A magistrate I interviewed two years ago told me that he didn't see much use in sending a boy to a Detention Centre any more, "it's all like Butlins now".

In practice, there has been very little change at all; this is not the way of such institutions. As Conrad says about the penal system as a whole: "Inertia, the law and the inherent bureaucratic resistance to change, preserve not only the physical structure but also the ideas, the organization and the expectations of the system". Certainly there have been some modifications to the original regime and one cannot deny that social workers have appeared on the staff of Detention Centres. There has also been some research. But the modifications have not involved any basic change in the conception of the Centres' purposes nor have they been due to any feedback from research about the effectiveness of the regime. The changes have been part of a general window dressing in which it is felt that one has to apologise for anything nasty and introduce, for the public's consumption, phrases such as "positive", "beneficial effect", "constructive", "for their own good" and even "rehabilitative".

The recent rather jaundiced looks at psychiatry by people such as Szasz, Laing and Cooper have warned us about the potential risks of despotism appearing under such new disguises. Anarchists have quite rightly taken an interest in this argument (see ANARCHY 70 on *Libertarian Psychiatry*), although the anti-psychiatry line has been (characteristically) overstated in its recent adoption by the trendy New Left. From a somewhat different political position, C.S. Lewis's warning is the same:

> Of all tyrannies, tyranny sincerely exercised for the good of its victims may be the most oppressive. It may be better to live under robber barons than under omnipotent moral busybodies. The robber baron's cruelty may sometimes sleep, his cupidity may at some point be satiated; but those who torment us for our own good will torment us without end, for they do so with approval of their conscience.

Of course we want neither robber barons nor omnipotent moral busybodies – at the moment we've got both. It is not just a question though of being sceptical about new methods of control which are exercised for their recipients' "own good" but also of being careful of not exaggerating the amount of change which has taken place in institutions like Detention Centres. Even organizations such as the Quakers who have recently published criticisms of Detention Centres seem to have been taken in by the rhetoric of change. They quote official reports as early as 1956 and 1959 which mention modifications of the regime and a shift of emphasis from deterrence "to stimulation and towards a positive form of training". They mention that in 1963 Wardens agreed that activities such as shoulder-high arm-swinging and marching in Indian file were "unnecessary" and there were suggestions that boys should be given opportunities to discuss the reasons for their commital and the obligations they have to face on release. The Quaker report also mentions the effects of compulsory after care, introduced in 1964 and in 1965 an official report describes the use of discussion groups to help inmates become aware of their own problems. The Quaker study group finally quotes the report of a staff conference in 1966 to the effect that emphasis was now being placed "not only on proper discipline and fast tempo but also on the establishment of relationships between individual members of staff and boys".

Now what lies behind this rhetoric of change? We need not be driven to conspiracy theories about the Home Office and well meaning critics deliberately distorting the truth. We know from other areas of life that public statements are made about policies which are not really practised or which are only given lip service to. There has not really been a move away from a system based on deterrence and rigid discipline. The atmosphere in a Detention Centre is still para-military, there is still the 6.30am limbering up in the open-air, the compulsory P.T. periods, the parades and all the rest. What we have seen is the uneasy grafting onto the system of concepts which are alien to it and the appearance in official statements of a new apologetic tone: discipline is not enough, there must also be rehabilitation. The system is becoming unsure of itself. Let me give some examples of this (and also of cases where the original principles are being unapologetically re-affirmed), again drawing upon official sources.

In 1959 there appeared in an important White Paper (*Penal Practice in a Changing Society*) not only the announcement that more Centres were to be built without any change but an attempt to retrospectively alter the original concept of the Centres: "In the first detention centre...emphasis was placed on the elements of hard work, brisk tempo and strict discipline. From the outset, however, it was understood that these stricter elements should be used as part of a constructive reformative system in which the staff would make a real effort to find out what was wrong with a boy and put it right". Two years later in 1961, a change not at first sight very consistent with these sentiments was announced: a switch for senior Detention Centre staff from civilian clothing to uniform. (The Quaker Report, to do it credit, also found this change "difficult to understand...at a time when more liberal ideas were being introduced into the regime".) In the same year a Centre was opened at New Hall and its function described in a journal for magistrates: "From the start the boy is taught that he must do as he is told and that he lives in a community where second best is not accepted". Two years later, a note attached to a Home Office circular (192/1963) for justices proclaimed the news that Detention Centres were "intended to provide a sharp sanction by means of a short but strict lesson" (where have we heard those phrases before?). But there was an explanation and apology to come:

> The insistence that every boy should give of his best in all activities is the real element of shock. Throughout training a boy is strained to the limit of (though never beyond) his ability and this unflagging element is far more taxing and salutary than mere conformity with rigid discipline.

Rather pathetically then, we are reassured that no boy is being strained beyond his ability and that no-one *really* believes in trying to change people by ensuring "mere" conformity: what nonsense in this enlightened age!

In 1964 the handbook *The Sentence of the Court* was published, reaffirming that the Detention Centres' regime was "brisk and firm", etc, that its intention was "primarily deterrent" but that "without reducing the emphasis on high standards of discipline and behaviour, much positive training can be given". A White Paper in 1965 stated that no changes in the organization or methods of Detention Centres were proposed. In June 1967 a review of the system, however, was announced (partly prompted by publicity given to allegations of violent treatment of some inmates) and the report of the Home Office appointed Sub-Committee of the Advisory Council on the Penal System is expected shortly.

## The liberal wolves

What I have been suggesting – a little unfairly and unsympathetically – is that the spokesmen of the system have been caught in a dilemma imposed on them by the diffusion of the liberal rhetoric. They are trapped in the system, because they genuinely believe its basic assumptions but they are increasingly being called upon to justify the system in ways that erode some of these assumptions. The sophistry this dilemma calls for, results in making contradictory claims, or repeating old slogans but adding new words (such as "constructive", "positive" or "beneficial") which have the effect of

annihilating the intention of the original message. Or else euphem-
isms are used: a recent Home Office Booklet describes the Detention Centre regime as "brisk and deterrent without being harsh or
repressive...more stimulating than punitive". This is surely nonsense: if the regime is meant to be punitive, why call it stimulating?
The liberal reformers will all too happily join in this sort of game:
Proposal 9 in the Howard League of Penal Reform's memorandum
of evidence to the Advisory Council is to change the name of the
Detention Centres. They feel that the name has become allied in the
public's mind with the short sharp shock idea and it should be
abandoned in favour of simply using the institution's individual
name.

An example of this sophistry can be seen in an article by *The
Times* Home Correspondent a few months ago. He concedes that
critics have a point in singling out the military features of the regime
but then says "...this hardly establishes a charge that the Centres are
pursuing discipline for its own sake". The reason he gives for this is
that the boys are involved in training. But how can training be
achieved in two–three months? But, ah huh, says Mr. Fowler, "the
aim is not" (thank God, one might add) "to completely reshape the
boy". The aim is more modest and is summed up by a Warden,
whom he quotes as follows:

> What the lad wants to see most is that authority is strict; that it is fair; and
> that the people administering the authority are human.

This is a marvellous quote for anarchists to savour. The poor old
Warden, driven into a corner by the wolves of liberalism and permissiveness, has to save himself by re-asserting a conception of
authority which they all share. Why is he so touchy? Who says that
authority is not strict, unfair and inhuman? (We might quarrel about the fairness of authority but we do not doubt that it is strict and
human.) Many of the "changes" have been bones thrown to keep
the wolves of liberalism at bay. The Centres have also been opened
up and shown to people like magistrates and even (reluctantly) to
researchers. The visitors haven't always been impressed but at least
they've been convinced that the barons are quite nice guys and after
all, they really mean well.

Even the sternest critics of Detention Centres equivocate when it
comes to taking up a position in regard to the basic nature and
objectives of the system. In reply to a critical letter which made this
point about the British Psychological Society's memorandum to the
Advisory Council, Dr. Cockett, the convenor of the working party
responsible for the memo writes:

> Perhaps we may...add a more general comment, lest Dr. Norton retain

the impression that we were attempting to defend or justify the existence of Detention Centres. Neither defence nor attack was, or could be, any part of our aim – which was to consider what we know and what we think professionally and to present it with a view to improvements and modifications where necessary. This appears to us (and, we imagine, to the British Psychological Society) to be a worthwhile aim which is not promoted by any kind of overstatement.

Now, in terms of my unease about anti-intellectualism, I would agree with Dr. Cockett's defence of his working party's aims. Clearly, overstatements are not enough. But there comes a point – and anyone who has read Paul Goodman cannot doubt this – where professional integrity demands much more than the presentation of knowledge.

# Who gets sent

One of the most frequent reasons given for any failures in the Detention Centre system is that the wrong sort of offender is being given this sentence by the court; indeed *The Times* article quoted earlier implied that the only factor making Detention Centres less successful than they might be, was that the wrong sort of boy was being sent. In the memoranda to the Advisory Council from the Howard League, the British Psychological Society and other bodies, the question "for whom is the Detention Centre suitable?" is given much attention.

Originally, Detention Centres were designed to fill the gap between long term custodial measures and measures such as fines and probation. It was thought – and this conception still remains – that the highest success would be achieved "with offenders of little criminal sophistication and without previous experience of long periods in institutions (such as Approved Schools)... The regime is unsuitable to those who are seriously handicapped physically or mentally" (*The Sentence of the Court*). Another Home Office circular elaborates on these criteria:

> It is not possible to define in precise terms on the basis of theory or experience, the type of boy who is likely to benefit by treatment at a Detention Centre but it is clear that careful selection is the key to success. Detention Centre treatment is generally found to be unsuitable for certain classes of boy, notably those who have already undergone long-term institutional training, have appeared many times in the courts, show symptoms of maladjustment or more serious mental disturbance, are dull and backward, or are physically unfit for strenuous exercise. The most hopeful category is perhaps that of the well-

developed, undisciplined young offender, who has hitherto come off best in his conflicts with authority though without having developed a bent from crime and who requires to be taught, through the unpleasant experience of enforced discipline in detention, that interference with other people and their property will be dealt with firmly and inescapably by society.

Are these official criteria met? As early as 1957 there was mention in official reports of an increase of boys "who were unable to receive the full benefit of their period of detention due to physical disabilities". In 1959 the unfortunate presence of boys with emotional disturbance was mentioned. The 1965 report was uneasy about the increased proportion of "the criminally sophisticated, the feckless, the inadequate and the emotionally disturbed". Research by Charlotte Banks showed that "unsuitable" boys were being sent, despite improved medical and psychological screening. Out of her sample of 302 boys, 78 (ie 26%) were "not suitable" for detention: these included 10 who were innocent of the offence for which they were convicted (one wonders what sentence *they* were "suitable" for), 11 for whom the sentence was too severe, 19 who were suffering from physical handicaps which would make the regime too tough for them and 38 who were judged to have "severe psychological handicaps". In case anyone should think that one is being too refined and soft-hearted about who is fit for the regime, an interesting case dating from August 1967 may be quoted. A boy was found guilty by the Gloucester City Magistrates and spent six weeks in a Detention Centre before his appeal was heard. The court was then told of the painful and difficult time the boy had in participating fully in the regime because of his club feet. The sentence was kindly replaced by a £30 fine.

What are the characteristics of the bulk of boys sent? Elizabeth Field has recently summarized five studies of Detention Centres which go into this question. The first point is that the boys are by no means first offenders, who are being stopped short in the early days of the delinquent careers. In the five studies quoted by Field, the number of boys with *no* previous court appearance ranged from five to eighteen per cent.

In one sample of boys over 1965/66 the proportion with no previous conviction was six per cent, with one to two convictions, 37% and three or more convictions, 58%. Not only have most of those sent already had some experience of the legal system but a much larger proportion than was originally intended to have been in one or other institution, such as a children's home or approved school. As early as 1957, 44 out of 498 boys released had previous approved school experience. Although there have been changes of fashion over the years in sentencing policies, the type of offence for which boys are sent to detention centres has remained fairly constant: about fifty per cent for offences against property, twenty per cent for taking and driving away and ten per cent for violence.

There is no doubt some truth in the belief that failures in the Detention Centres (as measured by re-convictions) are based to some extent on mistakes in sentencing. For example, over eighty per cent of the 44 boys with previous institutional experience I quoted earlier, were re-convicted within a couple of years. The Detention Centre perhaps does succeed better with some boys than others (leaving aside the wholly barbarous way in which boys are exposed to a regime which even by the most superficial standards was not intended for them). But how do we know that the same boys for whom the Detention Centre "worked", would not have responded equally well to some other measure? And who precisely is this group for whom the Detention Centre is such a perfect answer? Clearly all those who defend the system as it is or else want to tinker with it, have some image of the ideal offender who is going to shoot up the success rates.

But looking at the Home Office document quoted earlier, it is not too clear just who this group is. And when bodies such as the Howard League and the British Psychological Society get round to defining who shouldn't be sent to Detention Centres, the list gets rather long. Here, for example, is the Howard League's list of "negative criteria":

1 The severely disturbed, including the grossly neurotic, those with major character abnormalities, sexual difficulties and the psychotic.
2 The educationally subnormal and very backward.
3 The brain-damaged, the epileptic.
4 The very passive and inadequate.
5 The grossly deprived.
6 Those with previous experience of institutions such as children's homes or approved schools.
7 The seriously drug dependent.

New "diagnostic centres" are being called for to assess these categories. They should have enough work on their hands. Perhaps we'll be seeing above the gates of Detention Centres, "There, But For The Grace Of A Highly Skilled Medico-Psychological Diagnostic Staff, Go I".

# The utilitarian argument

Although it raises complex methodological and other issues which I don't have the space to go into, there is a superficially simple argument which claims that detention centres work. Their success is measured by the straightforward utilitarian criterion of non-conviction after a certain period of release. On the basis of this criterion for example, studies have shown that factors such as number of previous convictions, previous institutional treatment and certain psychological characteristics are associated with failure. What, though, is the overall success rate using the official criterion, which of course is not the only relevant one?

Elizabeth Field's summary of six research projects on this question, carried out mainly over the last eight years, shows a fairly consistent picture. Re-conviction rates six months after release vary from 17%–20%, after a year they go up to 29%–48% and after two years from 36%–55%. The general picture is that on the average, more than half are re-convicted after two to three years. A few years ago, the Home Office calculated that for the under 17 group, the re-conviction rates after five years was 75% and for the over 17's group 79%.

The naive outsider might be excused for not being particularly impressed by these figures. Yet the spokesmen for the system are always proudly pointing to its success rates and reminding you that they would be even better if those nasty "unsuitable" boys don't get sent. Even critics of the system concede that its success rates are impressive: the British Psychological Society's memo describes the 50% non re-conviction rate after two years as a "significant contribution".

Who is being conned? Until we are given a satisfactory definition of just what constitutes a "significant" or a "high" success rate, we cannot really be expected to be convinced by the utilitarian argument. The argument is sometimes refined by noting that the Detention Centre success rate is better than Borstal and much better than Prisons. But these differences obviously arise out of different types at the receiving end – boys in prison, for example, are more likely to have longer records and to have already been through Borstals and/or approved schools. Banks has shown that when a group of prisoners with three–four months sentences were matched with a group of detention centre boys in terms of previous convictions, age and type of offence, there was no significant statistical difference in the two groups' success rates.

Donald West's rather sad conclusion to his discussion on Detention Centres (in *The Young Offender*) is perhaps worth quoting:

> Judged by the re-conviction rates of those passing through detention centres (more than a half re-convicted in the three years following release) the system is not particularly successful in deterring future criminality but then neither are the approved schools and borstals, which give more prominence to reform by education, social training and individual attention.

In the light of this sort of conclusion about the Detention Centre's success and the generally rather dismal picture that the statistics have shown for so long, what is really bizarre is to find people insisting that the system is still at a development stage and we have to give it time to show its worth. To quote from an editorial in the *Justice of Peace*, etc, (25th March, 1967): "Detention Centres are still an experimental form of custodial sentence. It is too early yet to say whether they have a permanent place in our penal system". This, after fifteen years – with thousands of boys passing through, substantial research which, to say the least, has not shown that the system is very successful and (if this is relevant) an annual cost of nearly £900 per boy. Just imagine someone in industry or commerce keeping a system going for seventeen years (as the Detention Centres have now run) and calling it "at the experimental stage".

# From the inside

No account of an institution can be complete without an account of what it looks like to those inside, in this case, both the boys and the staff. My only information on this derives from reading other people's research, descriptions by ex-Detention Centre boys like Neal Pharoah and discussions with a few other ex-inmates. This information must therefore be necessarily incomplete.

The only full study that exists on the attitudes of boys in Detention Centres is that by Anne Dunlop and Sarah McCabe. They interviewed a sample of 107 boys from two detention centres at the beginning and towards the end of their sentences. In terms of their background, the boys showed "a high degree of illegitimacy, of absence from the family home, of unsatisfactory family relationships, of poor educational attainment and of employment that was sporadic, aimless and sometimes dull". Their attitude at the beginning was subdued and apprehensive although some were resentful and aggrieved. They expressed dislike of specific deprivations such as early rising, physical hardship, no-smoking and other deprivations. They recalled with particular distaste their reception at the centre. Towards the end of the sentence, these deprivations and the various disciplinary measures, tended to be looked upon as minor irritants: the main burden of the sentence was the fact of detention itself and the loss of liberty. Any punitive and deterrent effect that the sentence might have, resides in the enforced deprivation of liberty itself and not in the elaborate regime devised for the boys. The staff tend to evaluate performance according to conformity to the regime, but as the Quaker Report on Detention Centres says:

> The statement "All Wardens comment on the excellence of the discipline" (Report of the Work of the Prison department, 1965) may mean nothing more than "all boys have learnt that it pays to conform".

And the point is – as the Dunlop and McCabe follow-up study showed – that there is no evidence of any connection between what is seen as satisfactory behaviour inside the detention centres and the likelihood of further convictions after release. In the same way as conformity to enforced routine may have little relevance to the situation outside, it is unlikely that the so-called positive aspects of the regime, such as the work programme, is in any way related to the employment situation outside – particularly when work (such as scrubbing floors which are clean already) is used as a punishment. As Neal Pharoah rhetorically asks:

> Is it true to say that three months of blind obedience in digging holes, endless P.T. and continual unreasoning deprivation provides the emotive suggestion needed to serve as a deterrent when once more the offender is returned to his environment?

I have not paid any attention to the extent of violence and brutality against the boys. To do so might be to fall into the trap of attributing this behaviour to the idiosyncratic personalities of a few members of the staff, instead of directing attention to the intrinsic features of the system. Very few people who have any experience of Detention Centre life will deny that the occasional beating up and the more frequent kicking or knocking around occurs. It would be odd if we found otherwise.

There has been no really satisfactory account from the inside to base a full picture on. As a sociologist, one expresses the ritualistic hope that future researchers will provide such an account – although proposals I have seen for research on Detention Centres don't look very promising. They are still expressed in the depersonalized sociologese of "functions" or the reductionist psychologese of "personality traits". In another role, one might express the hope that no research will be necessary, because there will be nothing there to do research on.

*Anarchy 101*                                                        *July 1969*

# Main references

John Conrad: *Crime and Its Correction* (1965)
Anne Dunlop and Sarah McCabe: *Young Men in Detention Centres* (1965)
Elizabeth Field: "Research into Detention Centres", *British Journal of Criminology*, January, 1969
Neal Pharoah: "The Long Blunt Shock", *New Society*, 26th September, 1963
Howard League for Penal Reform: *Memorandum of Evidence of Detention Centres* (1968)
British Psychological Society: *Memorandum of Evidence of Detention Centres* (1968)

# VI. EN-VIRONMENTS

## 1. Direct action and the urban environment

### Robert Swann

SINCE THE Cuban crisis the international tensions, which in the past few years, made every demonstration of the Committee of 100 or CNVA, of immediate urgency to try to prevent a nuclear holocaust, have to a considerable degree relaxed. In the international game of "chicken" with the chips down, neither side was willing to push the button. As a political consequence, it is probable that we are seeing a major change in Europe, possibly including (acc ording to Joseph Harsh in the *Christian Science Monitor*) disengagement, denuclearisation, and eventual unification of Germany, an easing to controls in East Germany, Poland, Hungary, and Czechoslovakia, as well as continuation of the process of destalinisation in Russia itself. As Harsh puts it, "as a result of England's exclusion from the common market, we may see an end to the iron curtain in Europe, and this is all to the good". Basically, however, the danger of war remains, even though it doesn't appear so threatening. But in the coming period it may not be as easy to enlist people in demonstrations partly because there will not seem to be an immediate threat of impending crisis. Partly, however, it will because there has been a tendency of the C of 100 and CNVA demonstrations towards repetition or "ritualism" as *Peace News* puts it. These factors are causing a reappraisal of peace force strategy on both sides of the Atlantic. Also, as a result of the decisive defeat of most "peace candidates" there is a growing realisation of the enormous task which faces us in order to lay the groundwork for any real political changes in the US if not in England and elsewhere. It is true that we have made a beginning in the World Peace Brigade to forge an instrument to help break down international barriers and create in embryo the

243

alternative to armed international conflict. But we have a long, long road before us, and none of our efforts will be successful until we have found the keys with which to unite the needs and problems of the "ordinary citizen" at the local level to the national and international problems of peace. It is in the hope of trying to find some of these "keys" that I am making these suggestions for a strategy of action. We must, eventually, begin to face more forthrightly the social and economic problems that surround us and find ways of utilising our knowledge of non-violence to apply directly to these problems. Our preoccupation with crisis-oriented projects will only lead to our defeat in the long run if not in the short run.

A few years ago (1958) Aldous Huxley wrote in *Brave New World Revisited* about what he considers, aside from war itself (but directly related to it), to be the central problem of our time. "We know that for most people life in a large modern city is anonymous, atomic, less than fully human. Nevertheless, the huge cities grow huger and the pattern of urban-industrial living remains unchanged. We know that in a very large and complex society, democracy is almost meaningless except in relation to autonomous groups of manageable size; nevertheless more and more of every nation's affairs are managed by the bureaucrats of Big Government and Big Business. It is only too evident that, in practice the problem of over-organisation is almost as hard to solve as the problem of over-population. In both cases we know what ought to be done, but in neither cases have we been able, as yet, to act effectively upon our knowledge".

Big cities, big governments, centralisation, over-organisation, over population, alienation, mass paranoia, mass schizophrenia, dictatorship based on mass psychology run like a refrain through Huxley, Fromm, Mumford, and many another critic describing modern man and his diseases, of which war may be said to be only the final result; lacking ability to solve his problems in any other way, man tries to end it all in an orgy of self-extermination.

In Mumford's most recent book on the city (*The City in History*) he develops the thesis that war as an institution, essentially war as we know it, is a product of city culture, and was not known to man before city culture in Mesopotamia, approximately 3,000 years ago (in the perspective of evolution this is very recently). Mumford tries to show that the ritualistic "war", or hunting of neolithic man and primitive tribes, bears little or no relationship to war as developed in city culture. City culture, especially in its decadent phases, was closely related to a priesthood or "authority" with its accompanying magical power and divine rights ("They know better than we do") which alone possessed the power and the control over its citizens to make mass participation in war and slaughter possible. This has remained down to this day. Mumford's main point seems to be that until we can understand and control the city, to make it liveable, vital, and free from the fears which create insecurity and paranoia, we cannot expect to free ourselves from the institution of war, and the control it has over us.

Centralisation of power, and the accompanying loss (if he ever had it) of decision-making power of the "ordinary citizen", is undoubtedly at the root of much of man's social and psychological ills. We may, however, question some of the "answers" made by men like Huxley about such things as big cities, or over-population. (L. Mumford points out that a rise in the birth rate may only be a direct, if irrational, biological response of the species to the threat of biological extermination itself. Almost all species react in this way under a similar threat. "The answers", which Huxley refers to in his last chapter under "What Can Be Done", may be generally summarised as "de-centralisation" meaning, in large part, physical decentralisation of large cities. While most critics of modern civilisation would agree in general with this diagnosis, they might disagree as to degrees (extreme decentralists like Borsodi and F.L. Wright on the one hand, or "regional city" decentralists like Mumford and Catherine Bauer on the other). But it has remained for Jane Jacobs (in *Death and Life of Great American Cities*) to dispel some of the myths and attack some of the assumptions which have associated freedom, and individual decision making power (democracy) with physical decentralisation on the one hand and dictatorship, arbitrary power, mass control with centralisation in big cities on the other hand. Some of this drive, of course, to decentralisation has resulted in the expansion of the suburbs – the pseudo-life of the city – and is the result of over-sentimentalism of nature in the eighteenth and nineteenth century. ("Even Thomas Jefferson's intellectual rejection of cities of free artisans and merchants and his dream of an ideal republic of self-reliant yeomen – a pathetic dream for a good and great man whose land was tilled by slaves".) "City air makes free" was the medieval saying when city air literally made free the runaway serf, and, says Mrs. Jacobs, "City air still makes free the runaway from the country towns, from plantations, from factory farms, from subsistence farms, from migrant picker routes, from mining villages, from *one class suburbs*".

But it is on the central assumptions most de-centralists make where Mrs. Jacobs makes her heaviest attack. It is, she argues, not over concentration which causes the ills of the city, but rather under-concentration and under-diversification. Where cities are functioning best (as in Greenwich Village in NYC and in the North-end of Boston) we find not only a heavy concentration of population (as high as 900 per acre – most de-centralists recommend maximum around 80–100 per acre), but also a maximum of diversification of small business and industry, and a lively population participating in local government. It is, in fact, where cities are not working proper-ly (where "erosion" sets in early) as in the dull, grey and monoto-nous suburbs, or pseudo-city, that the major malfunctioning dis-eases – high crime rate, paranoia, alienation, decay, etc – develop. It is, then, not cities in themselves which are causing our problems, but what is wrong with cities and what we are trying to do about it that should concern us. Perhaps especially if we are concerned ab-out the threat to ourselves, our children and the cities in particular which the bomb poses. It is illogical to fight against war itself and not against the crimes perpetrated against the peoples in cities.

"The will to order", says Huxley, "can make tyrants out of those who merely aspire to clean up a mess. The beauty of tidiness is used as a justification for despotism". In discussing city planning and rebuilding, Mrs. Jacobs says, "There is a wistful myth that if only we had enough money to spend – the figure is usually put at a hundred billion dollars – we would wipe out all our slums in ten years, reverse decay in the great, dull, grey belts that were yesterday's and the day before yesterday's suburbs; anchor the wandering middle class and its wandering tax money, and perhaps even solve the tax problem.

"But look what we have built with the first billions: Low-income projects that become worse centres of delinquency, vandalism and general social hopelessness worse than the slums they were sup-posed to replace. Middle-income housing projects which are truly marvels of dullness and regimentation, sealed against any buoyancy or vitality of city life, luxury housing projects that mitigate their insanity, or try to, with a rapid vulgarity. Cultural centres that are unable to support a good looking bookstore. Civic centres that are avoided by everyone but bums, who have fewer choices of a loiter-ing place than others. Commercial centres that are lack luster imita-tions of standardised suburban chain store shopping. Promenades that go from no place to nowhere and have no promenades. Ex-pressways that eviscerate great cities. This is not the rebuilding of cities. This is the sacking of cities".

What is most significant about Mrs. Jacobs' book is that through her insights, her diagnosis of what is wrong with cities, she clears the way for a practical attack on the problem on which every citizen has a role to play if he wants to. This is especially true when we see the possibilities of applying the techniques and understandings of non-violence to this task. Moreover, it is probable that only if the ordinary citizen does play a vital role can the necessary changes take place. In fact, "ordinary citizens ... have the advantage over planners" in understanding what needs to be done, because "planners have been trained and disciplined in deductive thinking" while what is needed is "inductive thinking", based on every day observations which is what most citizens are accustomed to doing. This is why, as Mrs. Jacobs points out, often at board of estimate sessions in New York (and other cities) ordinary citizens "very plain people, including the poor, including the discriminated against, including the uneducated, reveal themselves momentarily as people with grains of greatness in them, and I do not speak sardonically. They tell with wisdom and often eloquence about things they know first hand from life. They speak with passion about concerns that are local but far from narrow". The planners, officials, traffic commissioner "... know all about such protesters (who often come to meetings with signs and petitions): well meaning people, but in the nature of things, 'untrained' in these problems, concerned with 'parochial interests', unable to see the 'big picture'". But it is these people who by their "very earnestness and directness of their reasoning about concrete and specific local effects is the key, I think, to rescuing cities from destruction by traffic" (as well as many other problems which plague cities).

For it is often these very people who are also the helpless victims of planned paternalism (whether in democratic USA or communist Russia) who are pushed aside and made to pay involuntary subsidies for "slum clearance" or "urban renewal", etc. or forced to live in one of those monolithic slabs of homogeneous planning, where life becomes increasingly endangered as the crime rate increases, or to move to another slum, which in turn becomes increasingly worse with each depredation and added human increment. "Meantime, all the art and science of city planning are helpless to stem decay – and the spiritlessness which precedes decay – in ever more massive swatches of cities".

We can no longer ignore the fact that even if we are successful in preventing the bomb from blowing up the cities, our own policies will surely destroy the cities themselves. But what is more likely, if this process continues, is that the cities, like Samson, will pull down all of Western (if not Eastern) civilisation with them in a final orgy of extermination, Yet there is a way out if we can, as L. Mumford said recently, "Put the needs of human beings ahead of General

Motors", or the sterile dreams of planners (Russian, American or other).

It is disappointing that neither Huxley, Mumford, nor Mrs. Jacobs takes into account the potential of nonviolent action to effect the changes, and transformations they all speak of as being so crucially important. It is, however, perhaps understandable that intellectuals who see and analyse the problems most acutely do not always see the means needed to bring the transformation. It is most disappointing in the case of Huxley whose emphasis on the means and ends relationship should make him the most aware. For while all the methods and ideas mentioned by Huxley (in his chapter in "What Can Be Done", in *Brave New World Revisited*) are undoubtedly inadequate to cope with the extent of the problems he poses, by leaving out nonviolence – the Gandhian techniques and spirit – he leaves out the one idea capable of challenging and organising all the latent forces needed to cope with these problems. Yet it is Mrs. Jacobs' insights which have given us the tools, the concepts whereby we may apply the practical means of nonviolence.

It is obvious by this time that I am proposing that the peace movement in general and nonviolent action in particular should include in their agenda, in fact, make it a first priority, a constructive programme for *revitalisation of cities*. As I have tried to show it will not come about except through action by concerned citizens (planners and officials may be helpful but more often be opponents). And who is better equipped by the way of organisation, motivation, and understanding than members of the peace movement for the task of catalysing such a programme? If we will not, or cannot, who will? We have been searching for the vital links, the keys, where we can join our insights and understandings to the needs and problems of the ordinary man, at the point where he feels threatened in an immediate way, since the threat of nuclear holocaust seems remote, abstract, hard for most men to understand. Is this not such a place, here in the city, where the threat cuts across class and race boundaries, but where the new danger is to produce new forms of solidified class, and race segregation, whether in the suburb (as a by-product) or in the "slum clearance" and "renewal" projects?

In our search for peace, we must begin, as Abbé Pierre said last summer in London, "à la bas", with the poor, the helpless, the unprotected, not as social workers though they may be very helpful – but as peacemakers determined to right the wrongs, to redress the balance which gives Big Government, Big Business, Big Money, all the advantage over the individual, especially here in the city "slums" and blighted areas, where the automobile ("General Motors must come first") and ignorance or callousness of official policy wreaks havoc, almost as destructive (though more insidious because it is less immediately apparent) as the bomb, itself.

What, then, are the specific tasks that need to be accomplished, and what is the strategy of action, which may be undertaken to accomplish these tasks?

First, then, a brief outline of the tasks and objectives which we should be seeking (I am indebted to Mrs. Jacobs for most of these). On the political and planning level: (1) *Re-districting of cities* into viable political and social units and (2) *Analysis of districts and neighbourhoods*, for needs, in terms of diversity, traffic, money, etc.

On the level where direct action techniques may most fruitfully be applied: (1) *Defence Against Automobiles*, or attrition of Autos, as Mrs. Jacobs puts it. (2) *Defence of so-called "Slum Dwellers"* in danger of eviction for "slum Clearance". (3) *Fighting the Blacklist of Banks*. (4) *Defence Against Proposed Expressways*, which may threaten vital community tissue and create new erosion.

Each city would, of course, have to work out its own strategy in terms of its needs, size, problems, and available personnel, but a co-ordinated effort on a regional level would make maximum use of available resources of people and money, and would permit maximum flexibility for strategy as well as co-ordination of information and ideas. At the political and planning level it would seem natural and appropriate to develop committees through the structures of Turn Toward Peace and political groups such as PAX. Special interest groups, some with professional skills might undertake the tasks of re-districting cities along the lines suggested by Mrs. Jacobs. In this task they might very well enlist the aid of official planners and planning commissions. Such districts, would not likely coincide with present districts, and would remain unofficial (although the long range of objective might be to encourage them in political re-organisation on horizontal lines). A kind of local "parallel government", however, could be developed; community councils, and ad hoc committees to carry out specific functions. One such specific committee would work on *Analysis of Neighbourhoods* within the district, depending on local citizens for information and ideas to formulate proposals and underline needs. Such committees could be co-ordinated through local peace centres (Greenwich Village Peace Centre for instance, is an obvious and ideal location for this purpose, and undoubtedly is already performing this function to some degree). In large cities each district might eventually get its own peace centre. Such districts would, or should begin to have real political significance. The best illustration of this kind of development is the *Back-of-the yards* districts in Chicago, where essentially three men were responsible for developing a viable political unit out of the most depressed and hopeless district in Chicago. (See Saul Alinsky's *Revielle for Radicals*.) In Mrs. Jacobs' words "the district's power to get from city hall the municipal services, facilities, regulations, and exceptions to regulations it needs is regarded with considerable awe throughout Chicago. In short, the *Back-of-the yards* is no portion of the body politic to take on lightly or unthinkingly in a fight". Let no one think that such a district is not a potential factor of great political significance.

But it is on the level of the possiblities of direct action which I wish to pay special attention. While, hopefully, such action would be co-ordinated through a peace centre and directly related to the suggestions or recommendations of unofficial planning committees, it would not depend on such prior developments, and might very well precede over-all organising, helping to catalise such organisation as a result of action, itself, just as sit-ins in the South preceded the over-all organisation of the *Student Nonviolent Co-ordinating Committee*.

Let us examine, then, specific areas of action: Under *Defence Against Automobiles*, there is abundant opportunity for action. Here, as Mrs. Jacobs puts it, "The conflict is real. There is no need to invent tactics artificially". Pedestrian and car are in constant struggle. The general strategy is simple: reverse the present policy in most cities of improving traffic conditions (speed-up, one way streets, expressways, etc.). This policy is only creating a worse problem of erosion, more decay, etc. as more and more cars are dumped into the city.

In her chapter on this problem, Mrs. Jacobs argues persuasively for this reversal of present policies. She shows how it is, in fact, the continued increased invasion of the automobile which constantly worsens the cities' problems. As every new expressway, every new widened street, every "improved" one way street system, and speeded up traffic light control system, is put into play our problem intensifies, becomes worse. What actually happens is that a cycle is set in motion which creates new problems as rapidly as the old ones are solved. For instance, each "improvement" encourages more cars to enter the city, and as this happens simultaneously other things happen. More cars require more parking space, which creates demands to tear down more old buildings to make room for them. Tearing down old buildings in turn usurps space for either businesses, people, residences, or small parks, all of which are needed by the city if it is to function properly. Cars do not contribute to the city, but usurp space needed for other purposes which cities need for diversification and intensity. Secondly, as more cars are used public transportation systems are not used, and this in turn discourages and reduces the use of these systems. Thus, the systems become worse in competition with the motor car, schedules are reduced, and as a result more people are encouraged to use the motor car because of the poor service. Thus the cycle goes on, the traffic gets worse again, new measures are required to "improve" traffic conditions, etc. One other point should be noted here. As the centre city becomes more and more usurped by the automobile, the resulting congestion and noise discourages local residence and more and more people "flee" to the suburb to avoid the confusion. They in turn, however, become commuters adopting the motor car and adding their part to the problem. The best illustration of the extreme result of this cycle is Los Angeles, where the process has reached the point of such congestion that the traffic commission is considering the use of helicopters to remove stalled cars from the expressways during rush hours, in order to relieve the hopeless tieups created. Los Angeles with the best system of expressways in the country, and the highest percentage of transport by car (95 per cent) has the worst traffic problem in the country, not to mention the worst smog problem, a byproduct of the automobile exhaust.

What, then, is the policy and programme to reverse this process: On the political and planning level a campaign to "defend the city against erosion by automobiles" could be instituted. Such a campaign could utilise all the conventional techniques and methods of education through mass media and advertising. By enlisting groups with strong vested interests in preserving and vitalising the centre city, money and support could be raised. Such a campaign would advocate use of public transportation (working to improve it at the same time), walking instead of riding, within the city (possibly even tieing in with President Kennedy's physical fitness programme), and work to educate through discussion and public debate the reasons for such a programme. Co-ordinated with such a programme, but not necessarily dependent on it would be a programme group as those most vitally affected by traffic conditions. At first such action might be primarily symbolic, to dramatise and advertise the problem itself. This might take the form of sit-downs to prevent traffic from entering a certain district or street. (It is interesting to note how in C of 100's demonstrations and Ross Flanagan's action in Berkeley, where by sitting down in the street and stopping traffic this action was used to publicise opposition to nuclear war. Is it possible that we could combine the immediate practical needs of cities with publicising the dangers of nuclear war by instituting such action projects?) Later the campaign, after unsuccessful negotiation with the city officials would begin prolonged direct action Satyagraha to effect the changes where a reduction in traffic and greater freedom for pedestrians was vitally needed. A deliberate programme of blocking traffic would begin at strategic points with organised citizen groups setting up a self-appointed traffic corps. Mothers would be most likely for this job, especially where new children crossings are needed. We have already seen how often spontaneous demonstrations have developed, where due to speed of cars and other factors, mothers, often with baby carriages, have deliberately blocked traffic in order to get official traffic changes. This could be on a continuous organised basis. For instance, had the campaign to block Washington Square to traffic been unsuccessful at an official level, the community itself could have taken direct action to set up barricades manned by local people on a round the clock basis. Some might have been arrested, of course. (It is possible that in a campaign of this kind some of the young teenage people, including some of the "gangs" might be enlisted to protect their "turf" from the automobile, rather than the opposing gangs from the other "turfs".)

Mrs. Jacobs suggests that where too wide streets exist (and too narrow sidewalks) that the sidewalks should be enlarged and the street narrowed. Again, if the street were blocked off for pedestrian use, it would be virtually the same result, even if the city were slow or unwilling to widen the sidewalks (local neighbourhoods might even widen their own sidewalks).

Mrs. Jacobs issues a word of warning here about the cities need for trucks. Trucks are needed to carry on commerce and help build the primary and secondary generators of diversity without which cities cannot survive, or remain healthy. A selective policy favouring trucks over cars is needed. For instance, some entire streets might be blocked to all traffic except local and *trucks*. In general, though this is a city-wide problem, requiring measures such as permitting use of ramps off crosstown expressways to be used by trucks only, thus forcing local traffic off expressways and encouraging through traffic only, except for trucks.

Many possibilities for direct action would open once a campaign could begin. Each instance of direct action would help advertise through the publicity received the general campaign. Although I have separated out the traffic problems as the focus of the campaign, this is only because it tends to be the most dramatic, ubiquitous, and obvious, of all the cities' problems. In reality, the educational campaign would include an attack on all the many phases of city "unbuilding". Direct action, as it might be applied to proposals for expressways which "eviscerate the city", or slum clearance projects which only solidify all the factors (class segregation, single type dwellings, separation of residence and business, etc.) which created the slums in the first place, could include all the many techniques of nonviolence to dramatise the problem, and strengthen the spirit of resistance. Such techniques as: refusal to pay local taxes until a fair hearing has been held: mass sit-downs at city hall, or at the location and time of threatened evictions, etc. (Mothers have staged sit-downs in needed playground areas where contractors are supposed to begin demolition for city "renewal" or clearance projects.)

In this respect it is interesting to note the campaign in New York City which just ended in successfully preventing the *Lower Manhattan Expressway* from becoming a reality. This was reported by the *Catholic Worker* (February) which participated in the campaign. So far as I know, nonviolent techniques were not used in the campaign, but is it possible that a follow through on the campaign, as suggested in the article, might develop into an over-all approach to community, district, revitilisation, possibly using nonviolent techniques, if appropriate. The very success of this campaign is heartening and important. For in our struggle with the larger problem of war it is important to set out limited objectives, which are possible to attain, and which we see and understand as part of the long range objectives. Such successes help to build our ranks and give us courage to move ahead. For here, at least some of the people have learned the important lesson "that it is not wise or necessary to let public authority do for them that which they can do for themselves" in the words of Father La Mountain, author of the article. If enough people can learn this lesson of how to solve their own problems, of how to *defend themselves*, we may well be on the way to nonviolent revolution, the removal of paranoiac fears, and the casting off of the need for violent "defence" on the part of the paternal state. But it is up to the pacifist to understand and articulate this relationship between short range steps and long range goals.

In relation to the problem of "bank blacklists", which means the blacklisting of large areas of districts by banks so that mortgage money is uniformly prevented from entering these districts (a process which creates slums in itself) it would be most profitable to study the example of the Back-of-the-Yards district in Chicago.

Here, an effective threat of boycott of all the savings banks in the area, was successful in changing the minds of a number of local banks. As a result mortgage money became available and eventually the Back-of-the-Yards district was helped to pull themselves up by their own bootstraps. This single factor may be *the* most important one in preventing the creation of slums in the first place, and secondly in precipitating the forces which could begin to "unslum" many areas now rapidly decaying.

I wish to make myself very clear on one point. I am not suggesting that a drawn battle line should be set between planners, on the one hand, and local or district actionists on the other. Quite the contrary. This would be completely against the spirit of nonviolence. On the whole, the intentions of planning units and officials are good, and sincerely meant to be in the best interests of the local people. Their proposals must be carefully and sympathetically considered, even if rejected, and whenever possible a close working co-operation should be established between officials and non-official district groups. Strong co-operation and support on issues and planning proposals where agreement can be reached will increase the effectiveness of resistance when resistance is called for. A strong positive re-inforces a strong negative and lends power to the whole movement. This is certainly part of the power of nonviolence. In the same way many positive and constructive steps may be taken independently by the neighbourhood and district, once it has begun to "flex its muscles", and gain insight into its needs. For instance, local business and small manufacturing may be encouraged by the civic groups helping to obtain bank financing (where this is difficult), perhaps organising banks into pools, as insurance companies do, to underwrite risks, in the same way new housing or rehabilitation loans might be underwritten. Small neighbourhood public parks or "tot lots" might be planned by the districts and financed by raising money locally, after forming a corporation; not waiting on city action, and thereby using some small, unused and ugly piece of ground (Hyde Park neighbourhood in Chicago has been successful in this respect, especially before "urban renewal").

On the political level the overall long-range objective would be to persuade planners, officials and citizens of the need to make far-reaching changes in thinking and in political structure, along the lines of horizontal districts, rather than the confused vertical structure now almost universal (see Mrs. Jacobs' chapter on "Governing and Planning Districts"). At the same time that such changes are being made it should be axiomatic that having demonstrated its practicality the nonviolent method would gain immensely in currency, as it has gained in the south (and north) in relationship to race segregation. It would be up to the peace movement as to how clearly such methods would be related to the problems of War and Peace, whether or not a vital connection will be made and the public moved a few more inches towards a nonviolent foreign policy at national level. Several factors are in our favour here and argue for the adoption of this approach simply as a strategy for political peace action, if for no other reasons: (1) We would be speaking to the heart of vital issues, on the local and daily level of people's lives. It is these kind of issues which more often shape political issues and parties; (2) It is in the cities, especially in the north, where the peace movement is strongest and best organised for such a large undertaking; (3) few will be against us, except the patricians who want to "wipe up the mess" in the city from their suburban heights (where they plan an alternative – the Bomb – in case other plans are unsuccessful); (4) The city directly affects every man, woman, and child, especially through city centred mass culture and the struggle with the motor car which its sprawling suburbs spawn; (5) Further, an attack on revitalising centre cities is also an attack on segregation in all its forms: First, by *reversing the flight to the suburbs* with their class, race, and religious segregation (winning the legal battle of school desegregation isn't going to have much value as M.L. King pointed out recently, if at the same time suburb and housing segregation continues to reproduce school segregation in practice); and second *by preventing vast areas of the city itself from becoming solidified in class segregation (which tends towards race segregation)*, and third, by *unslumming the ghettoes themselves*, developing income and race diversity.

Simultaneously, as a by-product of successfully halting the suburban sprawl, it would succeed in preventing the further devastation of vast areas of vitally needed farmland, and wildlife preserves.

Human beings, and cities, in particular, vitally need wild life and farmland within close proximity, not only the farm products needed, but the sharply contrasting environment as a natural balance to the concentration and intensity of city life. In this fashion countryside and city form a polarity increasing the vitality and meaningfulness of each – a mutual symbiosis. What human beings do *not* need is the pseudo-city found in suburban life with its rather "sentimental desire to toy, rather patronisingly, with some insipid, suburbanised shadow of nature" (Jacobs). Suburban life with its sterilised segregated pattern, free from contact with the noise and smell of industry, means raising children in the atmosphere of a matriarchal society, which in turn breeds its own evils, perhaps out

of sheer boredom and ennui, in extremes of adult and teenage
sexual debauchery and delinquency (the city may have its brothels
but it was the suburb which created "wife swapping" parties). The
highest crime rate in cities are areas which were yesterday's suburbs. The dull, grey areas with their monotonous row, or single
family housing. These are the areas – neither genuinely city nor
country – which give the most problems, are the most difficult to
digest into the complex life of the city itself. Today's suburbs will be
tomorrow's headaches. "The suburbanised and semi-suburbanised
messes we create in this way become despised by their own inhabi-
tants tomorrow. These thin dispersions lack any reasonable degree
of innate vitality, staying power, or inherent usefulness as settle-
ments. Few of them, and these only the most expensive as a rule,
hold their attraction much longer than a generation; then they begin
to decay in the pattern of city grey areas. Thirty years from now we
shall have accumulated new problems of blight and decay over
acreages so immense that in comparison the present problems of the
great cities grey belts will look pidling. Nor, however destructive, is
this something which happens accidentally or without the use of
will. This is exactly what we as a society have willed to happen".
(Jacobs)

In the late eighteenth century, as Mumford points out, along
with the sentimentalist there was a healthy impulse to escape the
disease and congestion of the city ("women and children first"), but
in the motor car age it has become a route to avoid facing either the
complex problems of the city life or real rural life.

One final point while I am attacking suburbs: historically, cities,
centre cities, do not in general reproduce, biologically, as rapidly as
rural or suburban areas it may relate more to simple boredom. At
any rate, taken in combination with the tendency of all species to
reproduce under threat of extinction (Mumford), suburban life may
in large part account for the population explosion (at least in USA).

At the same time that the city as a social invention is probably
better adapted to our technological civilisation than it was to other
less technically developed civilisations, it is by virtue of the same
technology that cities have been able virtually to eliminate their
ancient enemy, disease. But most important for the first time in
history, thanks also to recent studies in the life sciences, we are
growing to a revolutionary understanding of the kind of problem a
city is: "organised complexity". With this new understanding we
can now begin to analyse and see how a city really functions. This is
essentially what Mrs. Jacobs's book is about. If at the same time we
can apply our new understanding of nonviolent techniques as a

means to bring new health for cities, real social and political transformations may take place, which, partly as a by-product, will eliminate the threat of war.

If for India with the vast majority of her population in villages,
the most pressing need was a constructive programme to revitalise
village life, for Western civilisation with the vast majority of its
people in cities of 30,000 or more, is not the most pressing need a
constructive programme to revitalise cities?

*Anarchy 41*                                              *July 1964*


# 2.   The new squatters
## Nicolas Walter

THE LONDON squatters campaign, now six months old, is an
interesting example of an extremist political movement with no
official support which therefore depends very much on the attention
of the mass media; and it has had plenty. Every stage in its development has been fully reported in the press and on radio and television, and there have been several attempts to fill in the background.
The most thorough have been two documentary programmes
broadcast in the BBC-2 *Man Alive* series in March and April [1969].

The present squatters movement has many affinities with the
great movement of 1946, and there are a few direct links; one person who took part in the old movement wrote an account of it for a
broadsheet produced by the new one. Obvious parallels are the
growing concern about housing, the emergence of the movement
under a Labour government which has proved unable to deal with
the situation, and the involvement in it of political activists. But the
divergences from 1946 are more significant. For one thing, the housing situation today – however bad it may be – is not as desperate as it
was just after the war, so there is not the same kind of spontaneous
mass action; no one expects to see forty thousand people squatting
this year as there were twenty-three years ago. And instead of
Communists taking over a large movement, this time there are
various kinds of anarchists, libertarian socialists and radicals starting a small one.

The movement has two natural sections – the homeless people, and the people who are trying to help them. The homeless belong to a recognisable type – what Aubrey Harvey called "casualties of the welfare state" in the title of her Fabian tract of 1960. They are working-class and under-educated, they have many children, and they cannot rely on help from friends or families in emergency – they are people without shock-absorbers. Often a single misfortune gives the push towards disintegration; a breadwinner falls ill or loses a job, bills become debts and rent runs into arrears, the family is evicted and driven from place to place, it loses its place on the council waiting-list and ends with the father in lodgings and the mother and children in a hostel (and frequently some children in care).

Very few can be properly described in that crushing phrase, "problem families". As Jim Radford put it on *Man Alive*, "There are families with problems, whose basic problem is that they haven't got a home. That's the problem from which most other problems stem, and we want to help them solve it". After all, when there are fewer homes than families, someone is bound to go without, and, whatever acceptable form of words expresses it, the basic reason for homelessness is lack of homes, which is not the fault of the homeless. It is cruelly ironical that so many of them are unemployed labourers – exactly the people who could solve the problem by building more houses if our society worked efficiently.

Television is an effective medium, but you really have to visit the accommodation provided for homeless people to appreciate the full extent of the humiliation they suffer. Add to this the attitude of those in authority, and no wonder some of them are taking a short way out. Asked if she was frightened of squatting in Ilford, Carol McNally replied: "No, not now. It's gone too far now, I'm fed up with waiting, I'm desperate". And asked about the child they were taking with them, Danny McNally said: "I've got four children in care, they won't get this one". Margaret Beresford put it another way. "We don't mind it being hard, it will be a change from here anyway". And Ben Beresford added: "The years I fought for this country, and to think I come back to this, and have to bring up my children in this state". A single conversation on *Man Alive* conveyed the bitter feeling behind the squatters movement.

"Excuse me, where have you come from?"
"Nowhere. I don't live nowhere, that's why I'm here."
"And how long have you been homeless?"
"Seven years."
"What made you decide to come and squat here?"

"No one else will help – they're the only people who's tried to help me -- no one, they don't want to know."

The political activists, who are mostly working-class as well, also belong to a recognisable type. Though they were for some reason described on *Man Alive* as "an odd mixture", they actually belong to what is known as the libertarian left, which has been a normal part of the political scene for several years. Most of the leading figures got to know one another in a similar movement – the Committee of 100 – and have been involved in such "groupuscules" as the East London Libertarian Group, Solidarity, Socialist Action, the North Kent Socialist League, the London Anarchists, and so on. The accusation that they are trying to exploit the growing concern about housing is refuted by the fact that they helped to create this concern; the libertarian left has a strong tradition of participation in the homeless struggle. Back in 1963, for example, there were a Solidarity pamphlet on the subject, a Committee of 100 demonstration at the Newington Lodge hostel in Southwark, and a violent struggle over an eviction in Notting Hill. But the crucial experience was the year-long campaign by and for the homeless people in the King Hill hostel at West Malling, which ended in 1966 with complete defeat for the Kent County Council and considerable discredit for the Labour government.

The point was that direct action had been shown to work, and if it worked once it could work again. The King Hill campaign was followed by similar campaigns at the Abridge hostel in Essex in 1966, at the Durham Buildings half-way accommodation in Battersea in 1967, and at the Coventry Cross council estate in Bromley-at-Bow in 1968. The activists in the homeless struggle built up a pretty big fund of experience and good will before the squatters campaign began. They are also committed enough to be prepared to break whatever laws they consider unjust, and to go to prison rather than back down when there is trouble. They are obviously an essential factor in the movement, but it would be wrong to infer that it has been created by outside agitators. The King Hill campaign began spontaneously among the hostel inmates, and when outsiders joined it a general principle was that decisions should be taken by the homeless people themselves and the activists should confine their part to giving advice, gathering information, getting publicity, and raising support; and this pattern has been repeated in every subsequent campaign. Anyway, as Jim Radford pointed out, for the activists "it's not a question of 'them' and 'us' – it's just us". When the activists decided last autumn that the time had come for a more radical form of direct action, they were already in touch with families in several homeless hostels and slum estates, and there were plenty of people who wanted to move from crowded into empty accommodation, whether they got outside help or not.

One should also look at the situation in a wider perspective. The King Hill campaign was also followed in 1966 by the first showing of *Cathy Come Home* and the establishment of Shelter. Jeremy Sandford, the author of *Cathy*, had been writing about homelessness since 1961, and has been involved in some of the campaigns. In the same way Audrey Harvey, the author of the Penguin Special *Tenants in Danger* as well as the Fabian tract, has been writing about the problem since 1957 and has also been involved in some of the campaigns; before that she took part in the Committee of 100, like so many of the activists. Nor should one forget, for example, Stanley Alderson's bitter Penguin Special on *Housing*. Political extremists are by no means the only people who feel strongly about homelessness and despair of orthodox methods of curing it. The squatters can count on widespread sympathy, if not outright support. A man watching a demonstration in Ilford, who was asked if he sympathised with the squatters, said simply: "My sympathy is with anyone who wants a house". There is a profound feeling that a home is not a commodity to be bought, or hired, or a concession to be granted, but a basic social right.

The London Squatters Campaign was formerly established in East London last November. Three stages were planned – first a symbolic demonstration to prepare the ground, and finally real takeovers. The organisation seemed rather chaotic to anyone who saw any of it, but it worked, and escalation was rapid. The opening demonstration was at a block of luxury flats in Wanstead on December 1, and several occupations followed in both East and West London that month. The first takeover came in Notting Hill in January, and the main takeovers began in Ilford in February. The West London squatters were eventually given tenancy by the Greater London Council. The East London squatters were at first involved in litigation with the Redbridge borough council; it then gave in and even offered to make its empty houses available to other London councils for their homeless; but it later resorted to brutal evictions, in some cases without court orders.

So there have been some setbacks – a few evictions, the usual business of people being arrested or sued on one pretext or another, and the usual business (shown on a *Twenty-Four Hours* programme in February) of empty houses being wrecked by council workmen to make them uninhabitable. But there have also been successes – several families enjoying a home life again, the security of tenure granted in West London, the formation of more squatters groups in North, South, and South-East London, and outside London in Harlow, Reading, Leeds, Edinburgh and Belfast, and the wide (and almost entirely favourable) publicity in all the media. So far so good, but what is the next step? As Jim Radford said, when Horace Cutler of the GLC promised the McNallys a home: "We're glad about that, but we're concerned with the millions of families who can't come on television programmes, and in many cases are afraid to squat". Nevertheless, the squatters are largely encouraged by their first six months. There are new takeovers in the London area nearly every week, most of them without any publicity, and many of them with little or no help. To quote Jim Radford again, "People are now going ahead and starting to do this in their own localities – that's the whole point of it".

Of course squatting provides only a short-term solution in most cases, simply because the houses taken over are due to be demolished soon. Even so, as Maggie O'Shannon, the pioneer Notting Hill squatter, emphasised, "They're only going to stand for two or three years, but two or three years in the life of a child at five or six years of age means a hell of a bloody lot". In the meantime, far from jumping the housing queue, as they are often accused, the squatters are actually stepping out of it. Ron Bailey pointed out that, if the London councils did decide to put homeless people into their derelict property, they could empty all their hostels. But what about long-term prospects? Jim Radford said rather hopefully: "I hope it's going to end in massive reform. If it doesn't, then it may lead to revolutionary change". But, whichever way it goes, he insisted: "This works – that's the main thing, squatting works. It worked in 1946, it's working again in 1969".

There is no ambition to build the campaign up into a mass movement under political control. The activists are trying to establish an example to follow rather than a leadership, and they are populist rather than elitist. Their attitude is expressed in Jim Radford's comment on a scene showing a child-care officer threatening to take the Beresfords' seven children into care: "We identify with the families. We don't go in like that patronising child-care officer, trying to find out how we can make this family fit into our pattern. We go in to see if we can help that family". More precisely, perhaps, to see how they can help the homeless help themselves. Helping themselves to an empty house may restore their self-respect and put them back on their feet. The first thing is to go to the people and show what can be done. Asked if he was an interfering trouble-maker, Ron Bailey replied: "I *am* an interferer, and I *am* going to make trouble. Isn't it about time that some trouble was made?" Similarly Maggie O'Shannon said: "They might call me a trouble-maker. OK, if they do, if I'm a trouble-maker by fighting for the rights of the people, then by all means I'll be only too glad to be called one".

The squatters have two simple aims – to do what they can in a few places, and to encourage other people to do what they can in other places. The first priority is direct action – to get some homeless people into empty houses by their own efforts; the second priority is propaganda by deed – to spread the idea of squatting by the news of what has been done rather than by talk of what might be done. As Ron Bailey put it, "If it catches on as we hope it will catch on, it will start to rehouse people. People will start taking over houses in their hundreds, thousands and, we hope, tens of thousands. We hope that people from slums and hostels will rise up in one united protest".

What the new squatters are saying is that, if you think something should be done, do it yourself. They are certainly reminding us that something should be done about homelessness in this country. Can we go on accepting a situation in which twice as much is spent on "defence" as on housing, in which millions of people are living in slums (nearly two million in places officially described as unfit for human habitation), and nearly twenty thousand people are in homeless accommodation (over half in London) – when half a million houses are empty, and it is worth keeping property empty to make a bigger profit later? This situation is actually worse now than when *Cathy Come Home* was first shown. Cathy has taken matters into her own hands, and more and more people are deciding that it is not stealing to squat in an empty house, but stealing to *own* an empty house – or even a full one. When property is seen as theft, squatting is seen as the beginning of justice.

*Anarchy 102*                                              *August 1969*

# 3. Freedom and environment

## Brian Richardson

1970 IS World Conservation Year, and unprecedented attention is being given to the relation of man to the environment. It has at last come to public attention that, with rising populations and the new technology, this effect is potentially, and in some areas actually, disastrous.

It is a good time for libertarians, sharing this general concern to look with special interest at the result of these environmental changes on man's freedom. In order to be able to discuss the possible effect on the civil liberty of the citizen of his physical surroundings, we have to reconsider what constitutes civil liberty – what are the rights of modern man in his setting, today and tomorrow? Civil liberty is being able to do what you want to do, so long as you do not harm anyone else. The degree of outside restraint on your freedom must be directly related to this need to respect the rights of others – any imposed restriction other than this is arbitrary, and an infringement of civil liberty.

Further, you should be able to do what you want to do up to the limit of your potentiality, and any arbitrary obstruction of the development of your potentialities (such as commonly happens at school, where only the privileged attend reasonably sized classes, for instance) infringes civil liberties.

The distinction between rights and liberties is academic in this context. If one proposes that it is man's right to benefit to the full from the achievements of art, science and technology, and to take a significant place in the natural order, than any unjustifiable denial of these rights is an infringement of his liberty to enjoy them.

Seen this way, civil liberties are constantly changing. With the advent of printing it became a civil liberties issue whether the presses should be available to the citizen to publish his opinions. The invention of radio and TV now raise the question of the freedom of the air and the accessibility of the media for the free expression of opinion.[1]

The physical framework of life largely determines one's opportunities to act freely. If a theatre, for instance, is built with only a proscenium stage, the dramatist is prevented from presenting his play in the round. A theatre such as the Nottingham Playhouse that gives the producer the choice of different stage and audience relationships, enhances everybody's freedom. Similarly, the whole physical environment as is developed, impinges on the citizen's life in both limiting and liberatory ways, and can enhance or restrict civil liberties.

Edward J. Mishan, in his essay on "the coming struggle for amenity rights"[2] puts it this way: man with his wonderful new technology invents a wealth of goods and services. These are costed, and so far as they can be accounted profitable, are produced. But he also produces (as "spillovers") bads and disservices. These are at present not accounted for either in terms of overall financial gain or even in simple equity. Just as modern man has a right of access to goods and services, so Mishan argues, he has an equal right to protection against spillovers that harm his interest. "...a typical example is air travel, which produces services for the passengers while simultaneously producing prodigious disservices, aircraft noise, for large numbers of the population...in a more accommodating universe, in which a person could somehow lock out these spillovers from the space surrounding him, he would be able to charge for admitting them into his private space just as the owner of private property charges for the use of it".

The main civil liberty areas that occur to me, in considering the physical environment are
(1)    The basic necessity for people to have good housing, in terms of hygiene, space structural soundness and beauty; the effect of the built environment on privacy and community in towns, suburbs, institutions and homes;
(2)    The threat to man's natural right to fresh air, silence, sunlight, clean water and unadulterated food, and to his right to experience beauty in nature and to enjoy our inheritance from the past;
(3)    The effect of the procedures and rules accumulating round home, workplace and public spaces, regulating man's behaviour in respect of safety, public health, traffic flow, town planning, trading, education, political assembly, entertainment, sport and so on.

It would be a lengthy work indeed that explored fully all these areas, and I can do no more than dodge about giving some examples that will at least indicate the connection between the environment and civil liberties.

## Shelter, privacy and community

The influence of good housing on civil liberties should hardly need elaborating. It has been accepted public policy for over a century, since local government in its modern form was established, that sanitary arrangements, water supply, street cleaning and maintenance, size of rooms, damp-proofing, ventilation, and space between buildings, should be provided in accordance with standards laid down in byelaws. The effect has been to transform public health from the squalor of the early industrial revolution, to today's general level of well-being. It is a remarkable achievement, detestable though we may think the rigidity and authoritarianism of the law-makers. Nevertheless, standards over the country are not uniformly high, and one missing element almost everywhere is that of delight.

"Byelaw" housing – the product of the literal interpretation of the minimum requirement of the building byelaws – produces a sickeningly dreary environment. So much was produced and endured by so many people as normal, that a blow was dealt against the traditional aesthetic values attached to town and village housing from which we have not yet recovered. I suggest that the time has come for us to claim our right to live in beautiful, and not merely hygienic surroundings.

Not only are standards too low, but the stock of housing still does not meet the needs in sheer numbers where they are wanted. Particularly in London the local authorities have waiting lists thousands long, and homelessness is a great and increasing problem. Audrey Harvey, writing in the *RIBA Journal*[3] points out that the real extent of housing need doesn't even have much relation to the size of the waiting lists, and among the reasons she gives are that many families have been in the district too short a time to qualify (two years is often stipulated), that people without children are often turned down, unmarried mothers are discouraged as they are unwelcome tenants to some authorities, that elderly people in poor conditions often do not apply because they assume their applications will be refused, that waiting lists are sometimes closed in areas of comprehensive redevelopment, and that council flats are often overcrowded, but this cannot be disclosed to the authority. She adds that Ministerial statements about a surplus of housing over households in some areas can mean that the early provincial housing estates lacking vital amenities are being deserted by families who have tried their luck in livelier places.

Nothing produces such a negation of civil liberty as homelessness. Although some successful campaigns have been (and are being) waged to improve facilities in, and management of, hostels for the homeless, it is still intolerable that the threat of homelessness should be a scourge to so many thousands of people. Only after the basic need for shelter has been met, is it possible to look at the opportunities for living a full and free private and social life.

Privacy is a well-known civil liberty issue, but the direct effect that the planning and construction of buildings has upon it has been given little weight by civil libertarians so far. The NCCL campaign for privacy concerns itself mainly with the deliberate and malevolent invasions of privacy rather than the unintended intrusion of noise through thin partitions and the overlooking of windows in congested and ill-considered housing layouts.

However, in terms of the degree of privacy postulated as desirable by Chermayeff and Alexander,[4] most modern housing is insufferable. The domain of privacy of individual, family, neighbourhood group and local community in relation to each other and to the city, are scarcely articulated, even in the best modern examples, in spite of the acknowledged stress of mass urban life, and the consequent need to establish an identity, and to be able to "get away from it all" from time to time.

How many people, for instance, have a sufficiently private garden or courtyard to be able to share my simple pleasure of running naked into the fresh air after my morning shower, without upsetting the neighbours? More serious, perhaps, is the lack of opportunities for lovers to be together, uninhibited by the fear of being overlooked or overheard, which affects almost everyone, particularly in the daylight hours.[5]

The loss of privacy is particularly acute in institutions, where insufficient regard has been paid to it in the original design, or where overcrowding has made privacy impossible. An organisation set up to look after the interests of hospital patients has pointed out that at the very time when the shy and modest Englishman most wants to be left alone to suffer his misery, when he is sick and weak, he is catapulted into a busy and public hospital ward and has to perform his most intimate functions in conditions of unfamiliar exposure. Lack of privacy in boarding schools, approved schools, prisons (with their disgusting "slopping out" procedure), mental hospitals, old people's homes and hostels, causes endless misery to the inmates.

There is an obverse to the coin of privacy, which is the need for community. Although much lip service has been paid to community by planners, it is still notorious that modern mass housing fails to provide facilities for it. How frequent the housing estate where the houses were built first, much later a shopping centre followed, possibly an apology for a church was added, and the community centre never materialised at all. Often there is not even a pub within miles.

Even more totally neglected is the consideration of suitable designs for an extension of the idea of community living now being contemplated with increasing interest by young people, and realised in the emerging Commune movement. This attractive and constructive attitude[6] to the challenge of modern life seems to me to require particular emphasis to be put on proper arrangements being made for privacy as well as for collective activity in the community house, yet most British communes are experimental and short of funds. They are consequently having to face the difficulties of shared housekeeping and the establishment of a secure and private personal base in improvised premises.

But our society desperately *needs* such experiments. It is encouraging that a community near here, composed of relatively well-to-do people, able to equip themselves really well,[7] has prospered for seventeen years to my knowledge. They are not bound by any strong ideological ties (nor religious ones – religious communities have always had a capacity for endurance) and are not, so far as I know, exceptionally enlightened people, except insofar as they obviously care about their surroundings and have comfortable and beautiful accommodation. This must have contributed largely to the success of the venture. I hope that the young communards can generate enough resources to be able to equip themselves adequately and stand an equal chance of success. The interesting structures produced by the so-called drop-outs in the American West show how much can be done with little, if the ideas are good.


# Pollution

We have no constitutional Bill of Rights in Britain, so we cannot conduct the same kind of campaign here as the American Civil Liberties Union is doing in the United States to establish the citizen's right to an unpolluted and whole environment, but their line of argument is worth our attention. The 5th and 14th Amendments of the Federal State Constitution provide that neither the

United States, nor any State, or their agencies, shall deprive any person of "life, liberty or property without due process of law". In American law the liberty guaranteed by the "due process" Amendments has been stated as "not merely freedom from bodily restraint but also the right of the individual to contract, to engage in any of the common occupations of life, to acquire useful knowledge, to marry, establish a home and bring up children, to worship God according to the dictates of his own conscience and generally to enjoy those privileges long recognised at common law as essential to the orderly pursuit of happiness by free men".

The position in America is discussed in an article in *Civil Liberties*[8] in which the author quotes a law case in which it was said that, "the personal right is the right to live in and enjoy an environment free from improvident invasion or impairment" and urges the courts to act decisively on this interpretation of the constitution, arguing that environmental rights are indeed basic to a free society. He emphasises that constitutional protection of these rights is particularly important because of the irrevocable nature of the environmental changes. "Let us assume that a youth's hair is wrongfully clipped, or a girl is required to wear a skirt, or a child is exposed to prayer in a public school. If the legislature or other authority which infringed the right changes its mind as a result of the ordinary political processes, no fair-minded person would say that the damage to mind or body was permanent or irreparable. The point applies to many other deprivations of liberty or property. If however there is a right to an unquarried mountain, to a river that is not buried with millions of yards of fill or to an urban neighbourhood not torn apart by an expressway, the denial of that right is substantially irrevocable. We are generally unable to restore what we have destroyed. We can more easily reform our own human institutions than we can reform a bulldozed landscape... We can have many haircuts. We have only one earth and according to many politicians, scientists and college students (whose rare unity may be some evidence that they are right) not much more than 14 years to save it."

We in Britain cannot, even if we wished, leave it to the due process of law to protect the environment, though one must acknowledge that parliamentary response to a pressure group can have results. The success of the Smoke Abatement Society in recent years in getting the Clean Air Act passed has produced a dramatic improvement in the city air. Mishan, arguing from the point of view of a liberal rather than a libertarian, sees an advantage in extending legislation, analogous to the laws prohibiting slave labour and the unrestricted sale of firearms, to protect men's rights to such basic amenities as quiet, privacy, clean air and unpolluted water. Speaking to those who have accepted that the Market, when constrained by wise legislation can serve desirable though limited social ends, he says, "...the arguments for extending existing legislation to cover men's rights to basic natural amenities are no different in kind from those used in defence of men's rights to private property... With respect to equity, it is a cardinal liberal tenet that every man should be allowed the freedom to pursue his own interest *provided* that in so doing he inflicts no harm on others. The post-war eruption of environmental spillovers forms a crucial proviso; an instance that is, of severe and growing damage to the welfare of innocent people as a by-product of the pursuit by others of profit or pleasure, for which damage there is at present no legal redress of any value".

But public education is the key factor, and we must welcome the wave of books now being published that open people's eyes to the changes, good and bad, that we are capable of making to the environment.[9] ANARCHY has carried much crusading material relevant to the subject, on ecology, agriculture, liberatory technology, and housing.[10] The movement towards food reform must regain its momentum, and not only to ensure that foods available in the shops are free from adulteration, a job manfully tackled by the local authorities' public analysts, but also that the whole diet is sound and in tune with a sensibly manipulated natural order. The case for vegetarianism is very strong in the context of world food shortage, since to create meat food for man used seven times as much land as vegetable food of the same nutritional value.

The aesthetic case for an undamaged and wholesome environment is inextricably linked with the social and practical aspects, but deserves special attention on its own account. Again, an enlightened public opinion is an essential prerequisite for success. Iain Nairn with his *Architectural Review* "Outrage" campaign, and the Civic Trust, have done much. Some local "preservation" groups have entered into the spirit of do-it-yourself politics in a commendable way (like the Dublin squatters reported in FREEDOM recently). But a glance round at new buildings anywhere, and the lack of any indication that architects have become collectively concerned about the results of their work, fills me with gloom.

Our towns are becoming more and more sordid and anonymous, and when we leave them we desecrate the countryside. Particularly at the sea's edge aesthetic sensibility leaves us altogether. I am writing this on holiday near the Welsh coast, and my old-fashioned green tent nestles under a hedge against the gale and will leave no trace of its presence there next week. But a mile towards the coast there are vast caravan parks, gimcrack holiday bungalows, Cheam-style semi-detached houses and a general appalling scatter of rubbish. Fortunately the landscape is magnificently rugged, the indigenous architectural style is strong, and much of the shore too rocky for human exploitation, and this outweighs the damage, but it is a near thing and many other places are not so lucky.

The situation could be redeemed. The crowds of holiday-makers and their cars and boats are a jolly sight, and an economic necessity for the local people. If only the style of buildings and equipment were good of their kind, comparable with the standards that seemed to obtain in the past, all could be well.

I mention this example because it is on holiday that people particularly aspire to freedom, and it seems that our freedom to enjoy a holiday by the sea is threatened by the built environment in a more obvious way than elsewhere.

## Authority and the environment

Apart from privacy, the area of environmental civil liberties that has received most attention from libertarians has been the legal restrictions placed on the use of public places. Of these the main concerns have been to preserve the rights of political assembly, procession and demonstration. Often the Queen's Highway, as it is legally known, provides the only public space available for political activity. The law allows no right to do this, the only recognised lawful use of the highway being for citizens to pass and re-pass along it. Any other use causes an obstruction to other people doing this, and whether actual or potential, this obstruction is an offence against the Highways Act. To stop and do up your shoe, talk to a friend, look in a shop window, fart, make a speech, sit down, play games, sell goods, all are theoretically punishable offences if, for however short a period, you obstruct free passage. Nor does it have to be proved that anyone was in fact obstructed. Of course in this situation the police are constantly using their discretion and their power is used on infrequent occasions, lulling us into a sense of comparative freedom.

However, Pat Arrowsmith, Jim Radford, and many others less famous, know very well that you are *not* free to stand up at a street corner, or on a wide pavement, or even when other people are already speechmaking, and to voice radical opinions, because the police can and will stop you.

Strange then, that it is not an obligation on local authorities to provide public spaces aside from the highway, where people *can* gather and hold meetings without obstructing. Many such "Trafalgar Squares" do exist, and have been vigorously fought for, but often it is found that every bit of land in a neighbourhood is either privately owned and governed by laws of trespass, or is highway. If a local authority does administer a public open space, it often imposes byelaws with all kinds of weird prohibitions – the notice boards in London parks often make hilarious reading. I recollect not being amused though, when I was prevented from hearing Bertrand Russell speak in Hyde Park because the police prevented him from using a microphone.

Practically all our surviving commons have fallen to the local byelaw, and it is in large part due to this that the so-called Gypsy problem has arisen. The Gypsies have been with us for several centuries and are not a problem, but they have suffered a crisis in recent years that has caused them great misery and the settled population some annoyance because they have been unable to find space to put their trailer caravans without finding themselves unwitting law-breakers. Before the days of official planning, their small requirements were easily catered for on commons and lanes and waste ground, but being travellers they never claimed any serious entitlement to be in any particular place. Now they find that the whole territory has been buttoned up with them left outside.[11]

Their opportunities for making a living have changed, but they are adaptable people and have coped with this, what they cannot do anything about is the physical denial to them of any place to stop, so they are hounded wherever they go. This is as clear a case as any that could be found of the interaction between the environment and civil liberties. It stems from the negligence of the planners to allow for their way of life, and the mistake can be rectified by the provision of sites and the repeal of repressive legislation (though not without a hard fight).

It is more difficult to see the answer to some other situations where the community (through its elected representatives and all that) puts restrictions on the private individual for the supposed benefit of the majority, and these restrictions lead to hardship. Intelligent plans for the use of the community's resources in land and buildings are essential, and we must acknowledge that control needs to be exercised to ensure that individuals conform to the plan. So how can the liberty of the individual be reconciled with the community interest?

The trouble is that controls and limitations multiply, and the original purpose behind them is lost. Arbitrary bureaucracy rears its ugly head, and one is tempted to advocate clearing the lot away and abandoning control altogether. But our society is at present run on the capitalist principle of buy cheap, sell dear; private profit is success and exploitation of the community interest for private gain is thought to be all right unless specifically unlawful. The necessary self-control that could replace public control does not yet exist. Libertarians strive to make it so, but meanwhile must try to see that sensible public policy, authoritarian though it may be in the making, is at least administered fairly and humanely.

The organised action of the citizens of Kensington where the new motorway makes conditions intolerable for the local residents is an admirable example of the struggle for civil liberty. But there are not enough George Clarkes to go round, and there should be courses open to ordinary men in less extreme situations to challenge harsh official decisions.

It would be an advance, for instance, if free legal aid were available for people appearing before tribunals. Our village was recently represented at a tribunal at which we succeeded in opting out of Greater London, but I was staggered at the legal fees we had to pay to stand a chance against the QC retained by the London Borough that wanted to keep us in. We could not have raised enough money without wealthy anonymous benefactors chipping in, a circumstance which split the village because of the suspicion that there was a political advantage for the Conservatives in our success.

Most distressing for the people involved, especially if they are elderly and not adaptable to change, is the powerlessness of the individual to resist compulsory purchase. The official method of monetary compensation may reflect the market accurately, but does little to ensure that anxiety is dispelled or disruption minimised. Even if the purpose behind the compulsory purchase is laudable (and it is not always so) and is good policy for the majority, it is not good enough to shrug one's shoulders at the "inevitable" cases of hardship and let the local officials sort it out according to the book (which only has to do with legal nicety).

Surely society is wealthy enough to expend money and care generously on minimising the suffering caused in cases where the rights of the majority conflict with those of the individual. Why shouldn't it be like winning the pools to find that your carefully tended garden is in the line of a road improvement?

Mishan, again, has a proposal to provide machinery for this to happen.[12] He says that the cost associated with adverse spillover effects should be a charge on the production costs of the perpetrators of the spillover. If they cannot reach agreement (through the courts or otherwise) with the affected groups they would have to desist entirely from producing the spillover-generated goods. Thus an airline company would have the option of continuing all its services provided that completely effective anti-noise devices were installed, or, to the extent that they were not completely effective, of paying full compensation for all the residual noise thrown at the public. "Under such a dispensation the costs of operating the Concorde over Britain would have to include compensation for inflicting on us a plague of sonic booms. As an economic proposition it would be a dead duck."

Often the restrictions placed on people's liberty is manifested in the form of rules which spring from the nature of a building or its management rather than from social necessity. There are rules preventing council tenants from keeping pigs, not because it would be a bad thing for this country to import less Danish bacon, but because there is no room for a pigsty, and pigs are *infra dig* anyway. Frivolous? But what about car ownership when there is no space to put a car?

To take the Gypsy example again: how can the Gypsy way of life fit into a standard council house without upsetting the rule book and annoying the neighbours? A London borough did prepare a scheme for houses to be built mews-fashion over yards big enough for loaded scrap lorries, but for some reason this desirable environment was not realised, and this contribution to the Gypsies' freedom to live the life they want to live was thwarted.

Sometimes the building is all right but the management is restrictive. I know a county town where the best hall is unused for most of the time because it is in the technical college, and the education authority exercises proprietorship, allowing only occasional public musical performances. The architect had contrived to satisfy all technical requirements for public use of the hall, and the college caretaker is beseiged with requests to hire it, which would be profitable for the college and an extension of the freedom of the townspeople, and it seems to me as much a scandal to waste a part of the built environment in this way, as to fail to provide it.

A teacher's account[13] of a different case corroborates my experience: "We build new (school) buildings and then use them only five days a week. We staff and maintain them mainly on a part-time basis. All community projects, both young and adult, must have their beginnings in accommodation. Authority must set up the machinery for full-time use, including Saturdays and Sundays, the most useful days, and 52 weeks a year. Railway stations, airports, hospitals, and the like could not operate only five days a week; they are staffed to be available all the year round. When education for leisure is becoming such a priority it is essential that a new basic framework of administration be set up to give real and lasting continuity of use. It is a criminal waste of specialist amenities to build swimming pools, tennis courts, gymnasia, floodlit play spaces of every description, and then allow them to be used for only a fraction of the year. In our own case we have a detached and self-contained theatre, specifically designed as such – and yet it cannot take on a life of its own in the community because of the administrative restrictions imposed upon it". *

In school design, new patterns of education are gradually affecting the buildings. In primary schools particularly, the shift from teacher-centred to child-centred activity has brought about a more fluid, open form of planning, and tables nest together in groups rather than in the serried rows of our young days. Groups of children can be large or small depending on the work (or play) being done. But what of secondary schools, still being built with rows of identical classrooms for 35 segregated boys or girls each? Or the wastefulness of my daughter's secondary school, separated from its neighbouring "twin" boys' school by a desert of grass out-of-bounds to children, and with absolutely no "comprehensive" use of the facilities of the combined premises?

And what of the new monster hospitals being built to centralise specialist medical services, and feed hapless patients (who must be clearly labelled or they may be wrongly processed) into a great medical machine? How can these giant buildings fail to influence the way the Illness Service is administered? (They can have nothing to do with a "health" service which needs to be embedded in the community.)

I have tried to draw attention to the civil liberties implications of some elements that are too often thought of as a neutral background to life. But it would be wrong to think that the character of the built environment is of absolutely overriding importance, and that putting it right will of itself create the good life. We do not want to create beautiful prisons, we want to do without them altogether. It is the decision about the kind of life to be lived that is fundamental, and the creation of the environment to accommodate that life style is supplementary.

*The recent tendency for hospitals to operate a 5-day week because of staff shortages shows dramatically how disastrous this is for the civil liberty of the citizen unlucky enough to be injured at the week-end!

There is, however, much interplay between the environment that is constructed and the life that is lived in it. The built environment that we create for ourselves, and the natural one which we conserve or destroy are a faithful reflection of our values and priorities as a community.

*Anarchy 117*                                              *November 1970*


# Footnotes

1    ANARCHY 93 discusses radio freedom.
2    Edward J Mishan: "The Spillover Enemy, the coming struggle for amenity rights" (*Encounter*, December 1969).
3    *RIBA Journal*, August 1970. Audrey Harvey was writing as housing advisor to the Child Poverty Action Groups.
4    Chermayeff and Alexander: *Community and Privacy, towards a new humanism in architecture* (Pelican).
5    Some research is being done. The *Architect's Journal* has featured articles on privacy and has illustrated housing schemes where special attention has been paid to it through courtyard planning. The *Municipal Review* has referred to work going on in this field by T.A. Markus, Professor of Building Science at Strathclyde University, and has commented on the delicate balance of privacy and isolation, commending further research.
6    A model for such a community, briefly mentioning the requirements of the accommodation desired, stressing community and privacy, appears in *Communes*, journal of the commune movement, June 1970.
7    St. Julians, near Sevenoaks, Kent.
8    *Civil Liberties*, journal of the American Civil Liberties Union, April 1970.
9    A host of books, from Rachel Carson's *Silent Spring* and Lewis Herber's *Our Synthetic Environment*, to Nan Fairbrother's *New Lives, New Landscapes* (Architectural Press, 1970).
10   ANARCHY 23, 35, 41, 69, 78 and 97.
11   Grattan Puxon: *On the Road* (NCCL).
12   *Op. cit.*
13   *Official Architecture and Planning*, July 1970.

# VII. RETROSPECTS

## 1.  After a hundred issues
### C. W.

THE editors of FREEDOM have kindly asked me to comment on the lessons to be learnt from bringing out a hundred issues of ANARCHY, and I cannot do so without thanking my colleagues in the Freedom Press Group for the complete editorial autonomy which I have had, as well as for undertaking the monthly donkey-work of stamping and despatching, and dealing with orders and subscriptions in addition to the normal load of such tasks for FREEDOM. I should also thank the hundreds of people who have written for the journal, and Rufus Segar who has designed almost all the hundred covers, and has done them so well that some people prefer the cover to the contents.

ANARCHY, like FREEDOM, is a propagandist journal. Its purpose is to convince people of the validity of the anarchist point of view, and to persuade them to initiate some kind of anarchist action. This is the aim against which its success or failure should be judged. So perhaps the first thing to say about it is that from the acid test of sales, it has not been a success. The two dozen or so issues which have completely sold out have sold 2,800 copies. Every other issue has sold less than this. In an early issue, suggesting that it would be a useful exercise in mental self-discipline if we anarchists, instead of aiming at infinity, were to calculate what we might expect to achieve by 1970, I said that I aimed at a circulation for ANARCHY of 4,000 by that date. How wildly optimistic was that modest ambition! Most anarchist publications have suffered from the fact that, with their limited human and material resources, the effort to produce the goods absorbs all their efforts, and nothing is left for marketing. Obviously both ANARCHY and FREEDOM desperately need to find someone who will see it as his or her unique and indispensable task to push sales and find new readers.

The only consoling feature of the sales situation is that, as we all know, the minority press is much more intensively read by the people who *do* read it, than the large-circulation journals are. People who bother to seek out and subscribe to the minority press, are often people who exercise an influence in society greater than their numbers. They are often opinion-formers and activists. One of FREEDOM's great editors in the past, Tom Keell, declared that "Our propaganda is necessarily for serious people in their most serious moods. If it is merely glanced through casually and cast carelessly aside, like the ordinary daily paper, nothing is accomplished". Seen in this light, ANARCHY has a certain amount of success. Material from it has been reprinted all over the world and translated into many languages. The anarchist press throughout the world has used articles originally published in ANARCHY, and, perhaps more important from a propagandist point of view, it has also been reprinted, quoted and commented on in many non-anarchist periodicals and books.

Nor has ANARCHY hesitated to reproduce articles from elsewhere (sometimes eliciting more response for the author from his readers than in the original place of publication). This has been partly because of the policy of one-topic-one-issue, and partly because so much is published which is too good for our readers to miss just because they don't read every periodical.

The one-topic-one-issue policy which I have tried to keep to as far as possible has been intended to make the journal a monthly pamphlet to fill the gaps of contemporary anarchist literature. I am convinced that this is the most effective way to use an anarchist journal as propaganda and I am sorry that more use has not been made of it in this way by the anarchist movement.

The besetting editorial problems of any periodical of a minority movement are parochialism and sectarianism. You, as a curious outsider, pick up a magazine put out by some other minority and find that it is full of references which the uninitiated do not understand, and has a background of in-group feuding in which X is getting at Y over some historical or doctrinal difference which you can't comprehend. ANARCHY has tried, not always successfully, to avoid this: to take it for granted that anarchism is in the mainstream of modern social ideas, and to address itself to the outside world rather than to the in-group. This has involved going outside the usual circle of contributors to the anarchist press, and accepting the fact that their opinions are not always 'ideologically correct' even though the general tenor of their contributions is sympathetic. This is the policy which was followed by some of the great anarchist journals of the past – for example *La Révolte* in France and the *Revista Blanca* in Spain. It involves using the journal as a kind of anarchist shop-window, displaying to the world the quality and range of goods which the anarchist approach can offer. Looked at in this light, I think that readers will agree that an extraordinary range of anarchist insights and applications have appeared in the course of our hundred issues. The raw material for the individual propagandist is there, waiting for use.

Any editor, unless he happens to be a prolific writer himself, is at the mercy of his contributors and what they will write for him. There are very many topics which should have been discussed from an anarchist standpoint in ANARCHY, and have not been. On the other hand, several of the themes which have run through the hundred issues have taken root and blossomed elsewhere since ANARCHY began. Take the idea of workers' control of industry. When ANARCHY 2 was devoted to this topic in 1961 we called it 'an idea looking for a movement'. By the time of the Fifth National Conference on Workers' Control, eighteen months ago, Geoffrey Ostergaard, writing in ANARCHY 80 felt able to describe it as 'an idea on the wing'. Or take education. No journal has published such a budget of authoritative material on the progressive movement in education. Today we have a growing questioning of the foundations of the education system, a movement for 'pupil power' in schools, a Libertarian Teachers Association, and a groundswell of interest and concern of an essentially anarchist kind.

Take crime and punishment. No more devastating enquiry into the nature of delinquency and the penal system in our society has appeared in any journal as in ANARCHY, and a whole school of criminologists has emerged in the last few years, whose outlook is essentially anarchistic (see for example ANARCHY 98 on 'libertarian criminology' and ANARCHY 101 which will examine detention centres and approved schools).

Finally take housing. ANARCHY has continually come back to this topic, advocating a new squatting campaign. Over the last six months, it has happened. The London Squatters' Movement has not developed in the way in which we all hoped. It has not been emulated everywhere into a nation-wide campaign of direct action. But Ron Bailey and Jim Radford and the handful of people who have thrown themselves into this campaign, have provided an inspiration which is not going to be lost in the future. The battle that has been played out in suburban streets between them as *responsible* citizens, and the authorities who have destroyed houses rather than risk their being occupied by the homeless, and have hired strong-arm men to throw out squatters because they couldn't legally get the police to do it, seems to me an object lesson in the truth of

everything the anarchists have ever said about the nature of authority and the necessity of resisting it.

If ANARCHY has contributed anything to these four areas of social
concern, it will not have been a wasted effort. And there is material
in our hundred issues for many libertarian campaigns which have
not yet got off the ground. For example, in the current debates
about the future of broadcasting in this country, there is nowhere
better ammunition than in ANARCHY 93, with its advocacy of
listener-supported radio, and in the arguments about the future of
municipal housing, all the libertarian campaigning points can be
found in ANARCHY 83 on the tenant take-over.

I am convinced that the most effective way of conducting anarchist propaganda through the medium of a monthy journal is to take
the whole range of partial, fragmentary, but immediate issues in
which people *are actually likely to get involved*, and to seek out
anarchist solutions, rather than to indulge in windy rhetoric about
revolution. A goal that is infinitely remote, said Alexander Herzen,
is not a goal at all, but a deception. On the other hand, these
preoccupations lead to a neglect of a whole range of topics which
ANARCHY has ignored. Where, for example, is a thorough anarchist
evaluation of events and changes in Russia, China, in Africa and
Asia generally? It hasn't been published in ANARCHY. Or where, a
really adequate anarchist analysis of economic and industrial
changes in this country? Not in ANARCHY, I'm afraid.

One of the weaknesses of the anarchist movement throughout
the world, it seems to me, is a preoccupation with its own past. One
of its great needs is a genuinely contemporary anarchist literature in
which *all* aspects of the world we live in are examined from an
anarchist point of view. Not for its own sake, but simply to make us
effective instruments of social change.

*Freedom*                                                    *14 June 1969*

# 2.   Covering ourselves
## Rufus Segar

NOT HAVING done anything for the inside of this magazine since issue number six, I thought it was about time I wrote about what has been going on the outside of the magazine.

The way the magazine is put together is comic, awful, and for a journal of dissent, too vulnerable. The words are assembled by the editor and sent to a trade typesetters in Stepney. The proofs are made up into a dummy in Putney. The metal type made up to print the insides in Whitechapel. The picture for the cover is made in St. James's and sent to a blockmaker in Clerkenwell. The block is sent to a printer in Bishopsgate who prints the covers. The insides and the covers are collected together and taken to a binders in Fulham who folds the insides, stitches on the covers and trims the copies. The magazines are sent to Whitechapel for dispatch. Sometimes you get your magazine late.

The process is Victorian, small-scale industrial production. The typesetting, blockmaking, printing, binding and postage are paid for. The rest is not in the money economy. You get the writing, editing, drawing and distribution for free. Not that you should be grateful, consider the motives of the people involved.

I can only speak for myself. I produce most of the covers, with considerable autonomy and independence and in splendid isolation. The editor sends me the subject of the issue; sometimes with an explanation, sometimes with a clipping or a possible image, more often than not just a list of contents. From then on what you see outside is my responsibility. The covers are a by-product of the work I do, they are fitted into a varying work load and the amount of time and thought given to them is raggedly uneven. This does not relate to the quality of the covers. Some quick covers have been resounding, some laboured covers have been abysmal. The covers are the record of my response to ANARCHY a month in advance of publication without the benefit of reading the copy. With some hindsight, I am fascinated by about one in four copies, I pick at one in four, half I just can't read. This uneven reaction is like the covers produced – one in four considered, one in four uneven, and half just skimped.

The reason for doing the covers and continuing to do the covers is a combination of loyalty and passion. The loyalty is mainly to the editor and to an ill-defined group of English anarchists who are mostly impotent but full of promise. The passion is for the potency of the situation.

The editor is a posterity man, he intends that besides the copies that go out on publication there are some unbound copies put aside to be hard-back bound volumes of ANARCHY for each year since 1961. Covers will not be included. The covers are disposable.

The editor is a frontiersman. There he goes, sowing seeds of revolution, implanting pills of love and sedition into the body politic. The covers are the seed packets or the sugar on the pills.

The production of the covers has run into difficulties of copyright and censorship. It is these two subjects that made this article necessary.

Copyright is ownership and the rights of property. This has implications for an anarchist magazine (see Proudhon in No. 106). This is best illustrated by what happened about No. 89 of July 1968 about France and the May days. The cover was a newspaper photo from *The Times* which was blown up about three times and the title put on in red lettering. The image was of three posters pasted on a public building. The image was strong and dramatic and appropriate. Two others were used as fillers in the issue. All were pirated. No acknowledgements were given, no permission granted, no fees paid, they were liberated, stolen.

Whose property? The rights to the image belong to the makers and copiers. Begin with the posters, the people who made the posters and fly posted them started it all off. That was a free offer. The photographer was the first copier, he was there and snapped them into his butterfly net. He had copyright. The newspaper bought the pictures and copied them. The newspaper had copyright. Both the photographer and newspaper were ignored and the pictures were copied once again. The intention was to extend the audience of the original posters which were themselves free.

There were consequences. A year later the photographer caught up with ANARCHY 89 when she came to England. Eliane Barrault was indignant about the pictures having been used. *The Times* was the only paper in England that had used the picture (they had published a selection without naming her as photographer). On seeing the cover of ANARCHY 89 and recognising the picture as hers, she was even more annoyed at seeing a credit for the cover to someone else. The remedy was to put the record straight, and say whose pictures they were. This I have done, rather ungraciously. There was no request for payment for using the pictures because the intention of the posters, and of ANARCHY in reproducing them, both deserved support. Miss Barrault was too kind, if I had cut up and used *Paris-Match* that week I would have been off to Wormwood Scrubs.

I let sleeping dogs lie, I am dimly aware there are all sorts of copyright hounds lying about, some savage with one eye open, most of them snoozing, a dozen fleas such as ANARCHY would not disturb them. In making the cover for each issue and reproducing illustrations from a multitude of sources it is difficult to know what is in copyright or not, and if it is, who has the copyright. Knowingly I have taken quite a few pictures, whole or in part. I am not inclined to apologise for doing so.

Each issue sets the problem to find an image to assemble with words to make a cover. If there is not one to hand that I can use. I draw one. If the dogs wake up and start biting, I will draw more covers.

There are three demands to be met when infringing copyright. Money, ego, and permission to use. The money involved is not really worth bothering about, the most complex bit of piracy I can think of which means stealing the greatest amount of effort per square inch, is to completely fill the cover with an ordnance survey map. The royalty payment for this would be £7 13s. Bruised egos can be anointed with lavish credits at the time. Permission is more difficult, better not to ask than risk refusal. If there is a serious possibility of complications on this issue, assault the image, cut it, tear it, juxtapose it, alter it, add to it – anything to transform it.

The other matter is censorship. This has sometimes thrown a spanner in the works. No. 63 had on the back cover a wood engraving of a naked man on a mattress being subjected to various pressures, shown as various bandages and ropes about his body and limbs being pulled and operated by various well-dressed forearms and fists. A frontal nude with visible penis. The cover went through the pipeline until it came to the binders. There the foreman of the wire-stitchers refused the job. He couldn't have his ladies handling such a cover, they might be offended. Note that it wasn't his objection, it was the possibility of others who should be protected. With some delay and expense the issue came out.

More recently a similar thing happened to 105. The subject was Wilhelm Reich. The cover devised was too much for almost every part of the system, the blockmaker thought it was dodgy and said that the directors of the firm would not make the block. I said that if they did not want to do it please say exactly why before refusing. On consideration they went ahead and made the block. The cover printers then refused to print it. One of the contributors saw the cover proof and threatened to withdraw his article if the cover was used. I can't even reproduce it in the body of the magazine. Any one who wants a copy send a stamped addressed envelope to Freedom Press.

That's all, I will continue with the good, bad and indifferent work, and may write a progress report in No. 208. Meanwhile if there is anyone who is capable of doing a more dramatic and provocative job on one or many covers, please get in touch.

*Anarchy 107*                                                    *January 1970*

# JOURNEY THROUGH UTOPIA

*by*
*Marie Louise Berneri*

The author has set out to give a description and a critical assessment of the most important (not necessarily the most famous) Utopian writings since Plato's *Republic*. The book brings out in a striking way the close relationship between Utopian thought and social reality, and is of importance because it warns us of the doom that awaits those who are foolish enough to put their trust in an ordered and regimented world.

Lewis Mumford, himself the author of a notable work on Utopias wrote of this book: "As an old student of Utopias I have a special regard for it. It is the most comprehensive and the most perceptive study of that ideal land that I have come across in any language. As a work of scholarship it is superior both to my own study and that of Hertzler, but what gives it even more special merit is the fact that it is such a book as only a brave intelligence and an ardent spirit can produce; one who was an enemy to the forces that would degrade man into a servile automaton, and a friend to all that fosters freedom and creative expression....Altogether an admirable book."

339 pages A5 (8"x5") FREEDOM PRESS  ISBN 0 900384 21 2

# ANARCHY
# 1961-1970

● The first issue of the monthly journal *Anarchy* edited by Colin Ward and published by FREEDOM PRESS appeared in March 1961. Volume 1: 1961 consists of 10 issues. Thereafter, for the next nine years each volume consisted of 12, 32-page issues. Most of the covers were the work of Rufus Segar.

● In 1971 FREEDOM PRESS produced 100 bound sets of *Anarchy*. All that is available (1987) are bound volumes for 1968-1970.

● There are still (1987) original copies — with Rufus Segar's covers — of about 30 issues of *Anarchy*. (Examples of Rufus Segar's work have been used on the cover of this volume.)

● *Anarchy* is also available on microfilm.

We have prepared a detailed list of volumes and original issues of *Anarchy* that are currently available. Interested readers should send an s.a.e. for particulars to:

**FREEDOM PRESS**
**84b Whitechapel High Street**
**London E1 7QX**

# WHY WORK?
## *Arguments for the Leisure Society*

The title of this collection by various writers, past and present, is meant to be provocative. What this volume does not attempt to do is to solve the problems of capitalism which can only be solved by abolishing the system of production for profit and putting in its place production for needs. Here the distinction is made between work and employment, between useful work and useless toil, between pleasurable work and boring, well-paid, useless employment.

The contributors to this volume range from William Morris with his ever topical essay on *Useful Work versus Useless Toil* which was first published more than a hundred years ago, new translations of Kropotkin's *Wage System* and Camillo Berneri's *The Problem of Work*, to contemporary writers who all draw the same conclusions as Lewis Mumford in *Technics and Civilization* (now available as a FREEDOM PRESS title) when he declared more than fifty years ago:

"No working ideal for machine production can be based solely on the gospel of work; still less can it be based upon an uncritical belief in constantly raising a quantitative standard of consumption. If we are to achieve a purposive and cultivated use of the enormous energies now happily at our disposal, we must examine in detail the processes that lead up to the final state of leisure, free activity, creation."

210 pages          FREEDOM PRESS  ISBN 0900 384 25-5

# ABOUT FREEDOM PRESS

● FREEDOM PRESS are the publishers of the monthly journal *Freedom* and of the anarchist quarterly *The Raven*.

● FREEDOM PRESS are the publishers of books and pamphlets on anarchism and allied subjects. Our current list comprises more than 30 titles.

● FREEDOM PRESS BOOKSHOP (open Monday to Saturday) carries a comprehensive stock of anarchist literature from this country, the USA and Canada. We also issue lists for the benefit of our mail order customers.

● This book has been printed on the premises by ALDGATE PRESS, a successful co-operative venture which also undertakes commercial printing work.

All particulars from:

**FREEDOM PRESS in Angel Alley**
**84b Whitechapel High Street**
**London E1 7QX**